DEFYING THE ODDS

DAVID VERSUS GOLIATH

THE TRUE STORY OF ONE TEXAS ENGINEER'S QUEST
FOR JUSTICE AGAINST AN OPPRESSIVE STATE AGENCY

DAVID V DAY, P.E.

PAGE PUBLISHING, INC.
New York, NY

First originally published by Page Publishing, Inc. 2015

ISBN 978-1-68139-484-8 (pbk)
ISBN 978-1-68139-485-5 (digital)

Printed in the United States of America

Foreword

Engineering is the art and science of making practical application of the pure sciences, such as physics, chemistry, or biology. Engineers are who practice this art. They know how things work and use that knowledge to design, build, and maintain things that work. This is what they do by definition. So in all matters concerning engineering, an engineer would be the authority. A simple concept, right?

Well, not to Texas Department of Insurance (TDI) or the Texas judicial system, apparently.

I am not an engineer. My father, David V. Day, is—a civil engineer to be exact. Civil engineering is named as such to distinguish it from mechanical or electrical engineering and basically covers all other forms of engineering that deal with a designed, constructed, and maintained environment. My father knows a lot. It's his job to. I've spent many years tagging along with him on inspections, digging out soil samples, taking pictures of structural damage, learning the what, why, how of any given crack in a surface or structure. So while I may not be an expert on engineering, I believe it does give me insight and perspective. My father's lawyers, the Georges, seemed to think so. Enough so that I acted as a translator for all the technical terms and practices my father fervently tried to explain to them.

My father is an expert. This is an inescapable fact. This has been stated and proven on official record. In matters of engineering, he officially knows what he's doing and what he's talking about. This again means nothing to TDI and the Texas judicial system. From all that I've personally witnessed from the events that are recorded in this book, this notion becomes abundantly and heinously clear. My father's rights apparently mean nothing as well.

Fact—the board of engineering has sole authority to bring disciplinary action against a practicing engineer.

Fact—to the time that I am currently writing this, my father has been cleared of any misconduct by the board of engineering.

TDI had no authority to bring any kind of disciplinary or legal action against my father. But they did anyway, and the Texas judicial system allowed it. TDI tried to circumvent this blatant abuse of power by claiming the action taken against my father was not based on engineering matters but malpractice. But malpractice of what?

Here's a hint: it's engineering.

TDI tried to remove engineering from the equation altogether. My father defended his actions based on his experience as an engineer and position as an expert in related fields. TDI then tried to discredit him as an expert, and when that failed, they simply ignored it altogether. Throughout the proceedings that I sat in on, the only real evidence that TDI provided of wrongdoing was just that—that they were TDI, and they said my father was guilty of wrongdoing.

This was baffling to me. They acted as if they were infallible and unquestionable, like a pharaoh of old blessed with divine right. And this is the real core of the problem. TDI is a state government entity acting out of their own personal interests with impunity. This is evident in their treatment of all those who stood against them or even disagreed with their program. They have made a history of ignoring expert testimony, evidence, and arbitrarily auditing professionals. The last hearing I was at with my father, the judge very confidently said he understood the law and that it was very clear. He then sided with TDI without any further explanation. It was then indeed clear: TDI can decide whatever they want, and the courts of Texas will side with them.

If you live in Texas, this should scare you. If you live in America, this should concern you.

TDI is a state government entity using its facilities to carry out personal vendettas against professionals that keep our infrastructure going. We need them, and TDI is making it impossible for them to do their jobs without fear of persecution. Think it doesn't concern you as a bystander? If you live in a city, own a house, live near the ocean, or pay insurance, it absolutely concerns you. This is why my father's story needs to be known. Because it's not just his. It's anyone's who has ever been oppressed by corruption.

Something else I would implore you to put in perspective—according to TDI, one does not have to be an engineer to be a qualified inspector. They do not even have to have the same experience level. Yet as an engineer, you are subjected to far more restrictions and bureaucracy regardless of your experience or expertise. If the notion of someone less experienced than you is worthy of the same qualifications that you are with far less scrutiny irritates and confounds you, you will have begun to understand a fraction of the struggle and heartache my father has had to endure for years.

I hope you will take that understanding with you as you read his story.

Dennis N. Day

Defying the Odds

It was a warm sunny afternoon in Harlingen, Texas, with the temperature in the midseventies. Even though it was December 23 and two days into winter, the midseventies at noon was considered cool for South Texas, which was located on the same latitude as Miami, Florida. There had actually been a cold front come through the night before and dropped the overnight temperatures into the forties. I had only worked a half day that day and had headed home, where my wife, Paz, was waiting to pack up for our trip to Houston and north to Humble, where our two oldest children and five grandchildren, Noah, Devin, Joacquin, Gabriel, and Kai, were waiting for their grandparents.

It was a little after one o'clock in the afternoon, and David and Paz Day and daughter Cristina packed into our family van to begin the five-hour trip. It was a trip that we had taken hundreds of times before, either stopping in Houston or driving all the way to Baton Rouge, Louisiana, my hometown. As usual, Paz would drive the first shift because she did not like driving in big cities or after dark. Twenty minutes into the trip, we stopped at the fruit stand named Diana's because our middle daughter was named Diana, and we had always told her the fruit stand was named after her. At Diana's we purchased a bag of valley ruby red grapefruit and another bag of valley navel oranges. We packed the oranges and grapefruit in the van along with the luggage for a stay of several days and all the fixings to make homemade tamales including an ice chest with shredded pork and shredded chicken. Paz, who was a native of central Mexico, would always make traditional Mexican dishes for Christmas and holidays and was going to spend Christmas eve with her grandchildren, making homemade tamales.

It was close to two o'clock when we left Diana's and headed north up Highway 77 through the long stretch of over fifty miles through the King Ranch, the largest privately owned stretch of land in the United States. It was at this time that I received a call from my friend, David Vinson, the project manager for the valley's largest roofing company, Sechrist Hall. I was never a phone call away from my numerous clients, who relied on me to help them deal with the bureaucratic nightmare known as the windstorm certification program of Texas Department of Insurance or TDI. I was considered the local authority for South Texas in dealing with the rules and regulations, or lack thereof, with TDI's windstorm certification program.

When I got the call, Paz, who was driving, immediately turned the radio volume down so that I could talk to my client. Paz had not been getting a lot of sleep lately. Cristina, our youngest daughter, had been keeping her up at night.

Cristina was born when Paz was almost forty, and unbeknown to either parent until she was born, she had a genetic abnormality of having an extra twenty-first chromosome, medically known as trisomy 21 or, as most people know it, Down syndrome. As with many Down syndrome babies, Cristina was also born with an incompletely formed heart. In fact, she had a hole in her heart the size of a quarter. If the hole was not closed, Cristina would probably not make it past her second birthday. The pediatric heart doctor had recommended heart surgery for Cristina to repair the open valve as soon as she could gain some weight. Cristina, who was born on October 14, would have open-heart surgery at Driscoll Medical Center in Corpus Christi on December 20. Paz and I spent Christmas and New Year's at the Ronald McDonald house next to Driscoll's. The house is run by donations and caters to parents who have children in intensive care at children's hospitals.

Of the fifteen children who were in intensive care the same time as Cristina, only two survived past their second birthday. Cristina had inherited the Day legacy of surviving the odds. She would later be diagnosed as also having autism. This condition made her very routine oriented. Whenever her routine changed, Cristina became agitated, and usually this kept her up at night. This meant her mother, Paz, who was a stay-at-home mom, would get up or stay up with her until she fell asleep. Cristina was now twenty, and her school routine was changing as the special education department at her high school was transitioning her to begin the process of having a life outside of school and, if at all possible, securing a job.

Cristina was not adapting well to the change in routine and was staying up at night. Paz had spent the days before the trip getting everything ready for the trip, and with Cristina at home for the holidays, she was not able to take any afternoon naps. Paz was tired when we left for the drive, but it was early in the day, and she could nap later when I drove.

As I spoke on the phone for a call that lasted over fifteen minutes, Paz found it hard to concentrate. She usually relied on the radio or talking to me or singing along with Cristina's songs on a CD to keep her mind occupied. But now with me on a long business call, she found herself struggling to stay awake. As anyone who has ever driven on long trips knows, your eyelids become heavier and heavier until you cannot keep them open anymore. Usually survival instinct kicks in and wakes you up, and that adrenaline rush will last until you can stop or at least get some caffeine in you.

The long days and nights had finally caught up with her, and sleep overtook her. The van was coming up on a long turn immediately before an overpass in the King Ranch known as Norias Pass, an old watering hole for stock. As the road curved and the van kept going straight, it crossed onto the shoulder on the left-hand side of the road. This shoulder is only five feet wide compared to the right shoulder that is the width of a car lane.

As the van crossed on to the shoulder, the vibratory bumps built into the road shoulder for the sole purpose of alerting drivers that they have crossed onto the shoulder began to vibrate below the wheels. I was deep into my conversation when I was interrupted by the vibrations. I glanced over at Paz and saw her slumped in her seat. I immediately called her name in a loud voice, and her head popped up. Since her hands were still on the steering wheel, I thought that she still had control.

When Paz was startled out of her sleep and saw the van going off the left shoulder, she immediately turned the wheel to the right. I wanted to grab the steering wheel, but Paz had pulled the steering wheel to the right so hard that she put the van into a skid to the right at over fifty miles per hour. I was thrown back into my seat and watched hopelessly as the van careened across the road to the elevated overpass and then over the edge.

What happened next is one of those literal moments when one's life flashes before their eyes. It was comparable to when a roller coaster goes over that first peak and begins its downward descent going through turns and loops.

The van went over the shoulder down a forty-five-degree embankment approximately fifteen feet down going approximately forty-five miles per hour. Because the van went off the steep embankment going forward at about a forty-five-degree angle, the van made two complete turns as it tumbled down the embankment. The air bags on the passenger's side deployed on the first roll, but when the van hit a second time on the passenger's side, it threw me into the door handle right at the point of the seat belt connection to what I would later recall felt like being blindsided in football and getting a hip pointer. As the van approached the bottom of the hill, it spun around facing back into the road and began a third roll but did not make it over and came back down, landing upright one hundred yards from where it went off the shoulder, fifteen feet down and facing into the embankment and slightly facing south. And then it was over.

Paz was holding her head and screaming in Spanish, "Dios mio, Dios mio [Oh my god, oh my god]." I thought she was just upset for running off the road but then saw she was holding her hand over a large cut on her right forehead. Paz asked about Cristina, and I glanced over my shoulder to where Cristina was still strapped into her seat behind Paz. Cristina was alert and asking what happened.

To calm Paz, I stated Cristina was okay, and calmly as I could, I asked Paz if she had fallen asleep. Paz replied, "I think so." My heart was racing, but the instinct to protect my family was kicking in, and I surveyed the situation. The van's rollover-protection function had killed the engine, and the van was not on fire or in danger. I knew I had to call for help, but my phone, which was in my hand when we went over, was nowhere to be found. I asked Paz if she had her phone, and she was able to get her phone and hand it to me. I was unfamiliar with the phone and opened the door, which was very difficult to do and began walking up the hill to get a signal.

As I approached the top of the steep embankment, two cars, which were trailing the van and witnessed the rollover, had already pulled over, and one of the two men was already dialing 911. He had the operator on the phone and asked me if anyone was hurt. I said I didn't think there were any serious injuries, but my wife was bleeding from her head. One of the drivers then told me that I was bleeding from broken glass that had embedded in my scalp. The operator dispatched two ambulances from Raymondville, Texas, twenty miles to the south of the accident site.

The three of us then headed down the hill to survey the situation. For the first time I saw how badly my van was damaged. All side windows were broken, and the front windshield had caved in. It was the mirror on the windshield that had cut Paz's head. What caught my eye more than anything else was the ice chest, which had been sitting between the seats next to Cristina, was now lying before the rear-passenger-side tire, totally crushed. Thank God for seat belts. The three of us approached Paz's side of the van, and one of the drivers attempted to open the door, which was jammed shut, but could not get it to budge. I was still pumped with adrenaline and could have lifted the van if it was on its side, grabbed the door, and ripped it open.

One of the drivers grabbed a napkin and held it to Paz's head while I turned my attention to Cristina. Cristina was sitting with her legs folded beneath her, and I did not know if her legs were hurt in the rollover. Her window was broken out, and I reached through and unfolded her legs, examining each one to see if she had any injuries. I unbuckled her seat belt, and Cristina got up and climbed into the backseat, which is something she would do when she was upset, but this time I was glad to see she was walking and apparently unhurt.

I then noticed she had no shoes on and asked the other two men if they could find her shoes. One of them found her shoes and socks fifteen feet from the van. I then realized I could not find my phone and asked one of the men to call my number. The phone was also found fifteen feet from the van.

I retrieved my phone and immediately called my daughter Diana. Diana was living at home at this time and was working for an environmental firm in Harlingen, Ambiotec. Diana usually rode with her parents on our trips to Houston but had remained home on this trip because she wanted to work until five and was going to take her own car so she could go to Louisiana after Christmas in Houston. Diana answered her cell phone and could immediately hear the concern in her father's voice. I didn't know if she should come to the crash site, which was forty minutes away, or wait at the hospital in Harlingen, where the ambulance would take her mother. I told her to call her brother Sam in Humble and let him know that we would not be coming and then to get on the road and I would call her with further instructions.

I then looked at my phone and saw four missed calls from David Vinson and realized that David Vinson had been talking to me when we went off the road and must be wondering what happened. I called Vinson back and could hear the concern in his voice, asking what happened. Vinson had heard the whole thing as it happened, the screeching of the wheels, the thuds as the van rolled, and then just silence. He didn't know who was driving and thought that he might have caused the accident. I assured him everyone was all right and told him my wife was driving and fell asleep at the wheel.

Vinson then volunteered to take his truck and retrieve all of our belongings. I asked him to find my camera and take a lot of pictures for the insurance.

The first responders to the accident scene were the border patrol agents who were stationed at the Sinton checkpoint about twenty miles to the north. They assisted in calming Paz and getting the accident details. The ambulance arrived about twenty minutes after the accident and brought down two stretchers for Paz and Cristina. Cristina did not want to leave the backseat, and I had to lift her 140-pound body over the seat and hand her to the EMTs.

I walked with Cristina up the hill and saw a second ambulance there for me. I asked if I could ride with Paz and Cristina, but the EMTs said that for medical reasons they needed to put me on a stretcher and transport me to the hospital in case I had any internal injuries. I did notice that on my third trip up the hill, my right hip was very sore. I climbed on the stretcher and allowed the EMT to put a neck brace on and place me in the ambulance.

While riding in the ambulance, I took inventory of my injuries. I had a large goose egg on my right forehead and glass in my forehead. My right hip was very sore. The EMT gave me an ice bag to hold on my head while he checked my vital signs. I made several calls while in the ambulance, one to Diana to tell her to meet us at the hospital and accompany Cristina and a second one to David Vinson to give him directions.

The ride to the hospital was almost as eventful as the van going over the hill. The expressway was under construction, and the ambulance had to exit to the temporary shoulder lanes. A truck carrying deer corn had overturned earlier and spread deer corn all over the road. When the ambulance braked to come to a stop, it hydroplaned on the corn and almost hit the vehicle in front of it. The gurney that I was on slid to the front of the ambulance and hit the front wall. Fortunately, no one was injured.

At the hospital, X-rays and CAT scans were run to see if there were any injuries. Miraculously, Cristina only had two small bruises where the seat belt contacted her waist and chest. I had minor cuts on my forehead and the goose egg on my head. My right hip had a deep bruise but nothing torn or broken. Paz got the worst of it and had to get seven staples in her head to close the cut, but no other injuries. Her neck was very sore for what would be the equivalent of whiplash.

David Vinson was the first to arrive at the hospital and showed me the pictures he had taken. He had also collected all of the family belongings and had them with him. In the bag of belongings from the front of the van was the family crucifix that I had gotten from my mother when she passed away. Paz kept the crucifix at the front of the van between the seats in the drink tray. Paz believes that the crucifix kept the family safe, and I had no reason to doubt her.

Cristina and I were released from the hospital within three hours, and Paz remained to have her stitches installed but was released several hours later. My good friend Michael Amaral, who is a physical therapist, had arrived at the hospital shortly after we had arrived. He volunteered to walk me around to make sure my hip was okay. For the first time since the ambulance took her away, I was able to see Paz. When I leaned over to show her the bruise on my head, I felt the room spinning from the blow to my head. I immediately stood up and regained my composure. I wanted to leave the hospital and was not going to let some dizziness stop me.

By the time we were all home, all of the kids soon arrived, Sammy and Veronica from Houston and Dennis from Austin. It looked like the family would get together after all.

In the days after the accident, Sammy and Veronica agreed to take Cristina with them to Houston so that Paz and I could recover. Dennis and Diana stayed through Christmas. Our good friends Ken and Thea Stolar came to visit. Ken is an insurance adjuster for automobile accidents. When he saw the pictures of the crash site, he assured me that the van was definitely totaled. He stated that when he saw a scene like that, he typically would ask how many fatalities. It was at that time that I remembered I had the phone number of the gentleman who stopped to help when the van went off the road. He had used his cell phone to call my phone, and his number stayed registered on my phone.

Paz and I called him to thank him. He said he was just glad to hear we were okay. He had seen the whole accident and said when he saw the van disappear down the hill, all he could see was debris fly into the air each time the van rolled. He thought for sure he was going to find bodies at the bottom of the hill, and when he finally came to a stop and got out calling 911, he thought it was a miracle when he saw David Day walking up the hill.

Paz and I pondered his words and told the Good Samaritan that it was people like him who made the difference in this world.

My family and I had defied the odds. Our van had rolled at just the right angle to avoid serious injury. I knew it was time to tell my story. For the past three years I had been embroiled in a battle with TDI that had my professional engineering license and career on the line. It was a battle that no professional should have to fight. I was not just taking on city hall; I was taking on the state of Texas.

Many engineers had fought with TDI and lost due to lack of funds or lack of will. The engineering profession has bad apples just like any profession, but the abuse that good engineers were enduring at the hands of an out-of-control bureaucracy running the windstorm program for TDI bordered on criminal treatment.

I alone would fight back, and now that I had survived one more obstacle that life had thrown at me, once again I had defied the odds, and now after promising myself that my story would be told, I decided it was now time to tell the story, the story of an engineer who defied the odds, the true life story of David versus Goliath.

David Day's Story

What are the odds that I, David V. Day, PE, would be the first Windstorm appointed engineer by TDI to take my TDI case to a district court? Numerous engineers had been railroaded at the personal behest of Sam Nelson, chief engineer for Texas Department of Insurance, a man who epitomized the Peter Principle of rising to and far exceeding his level of competence. The only problem is that he was kept in his position by a bureaucracy run amok with incompetent people who didn't know, didn't investigate, or didn't care what Sam Nelson did.

I had long ago decided to take a stand, and eventually the light of truth of Nelson's incompetence and fierce retribution, which rose to the level of criminal actions against engineers, would be shown.

So what were those odds? In only four generations, I could take my family history back to 1813, when my great-grandfather was born, Dr. Richard Hance Day. Dr. Day was one of four Day brothers, who were all doctors. He married and had eight children with his first wife, who died after the birth of his eighth child. He then married the children's nanny and had five more children, and then his second wife died after the birth of their fifth child. He then married the current nanny, Susan Rentrope, who would bear him three children and outlive her husband. When R. H. Day was sixty-three, he fathered his sixteenth child, Robert Brown Day, born in 1875. Robert B. Day would become the grandfather of David V. Day.

Robert B. Day married Eudora Slaughter in 1903. It was his second marriage, his first wife having passed away. Robert Day had four children. The third child, John Wilton Day, was born in 1908.

John Day attended LSU on a track scholarship and graduated in 1929 with a BS in electrical engineering. The Depression would hit in 1929, and John Day would work odd jobs for over ten years until he settled down at the ESSO refinery in Baton Rouge and then married Catherine Lanius, ten years his junior, who had moved across the street from his home when she was ten years old.

Though not married until he was thirty-four, John Day had eleven children. Number 10, David V. Day, was born in 1957. The odds of me being the tenth child of a man who did not marry until he was thirty-four because of the Depression and the grandchild of a man who was the sixteenth child from a third wife are astronomical, but it is these kind of odds governed by fate as were many of the events in my life that brought me to the Harlingen, Texas.

I grew up in Baton Rouge and attended Catholic school until the eighth grade and one year of public school before moving to Woodville, Mississippi, and attending high school at a small private school, Wilkinson County Christian Academy (WCCA). I excelled at athletics at WCCA, but the small school curriculum was limited. I could have played college football at a smaller school, but the day after my high school graduation, I broke my ankle on my senior trip to Florida. The ankle injury ended my sports career, and once again fate sent me to the school I was always destined to go, Louisiana State University (LSU).

Both of my parents had attended LSU, and seven of the eleven children of John and Kitty had received one or more degrees at LSU. Ten of the eleven received bachelor degrees, eight received master's, one juris doctor, and one PhD. I began in the career I had always wanted, civil engineering. My weak math background from high school put me a year behind. The year I started LSU, 1976, was the largest enrollment at LSU in history, and the disciplines did not have the room for the freshman influx. Some freshman classes would have as many as 50 percent failure or dropout rates. I spent my freshman year on scholastic probation and even spent one quarter at University of Southern Mississippi to bring up my grades. When I returned to LSU, a new program, the school of construction, had started, which combined civil engineering and business management. Once again fate had intervened and guided my career. The school of construction was recruiting students and was not trying to weed them out. I began to excel in my classes while working my way through school.

The summer of 1978 I was offered a job at a large cattle plantation called Shamrock Plantation, owned by Charles Graves, who was also the president of the largest offshore pipeline company, J. Ray McDermott, which also owned the largest pressure vessel company, Babcock & Wilcox (B&W). Once again fate intervened, and it was on Charles Grave's recommendation that I got my first job with B&W. My first project with B&W was in Wheatland, Wyoming, and then to their home office in Akron, Ohio. While in Akron, B&W landed the construction of the largest coal-fired power plant in the country at Delta, Utah.

I moved to Delta, Utah, in 1983. Utah is predominantly Mormon, and there was only a small group of Catholic families, who were all transplants to Delta. In that small Catholic community, there were only two single Catholics, myself and a young widow with two small children, Maria de la Paz Reyes Trujillo.

Paz was from a small town in central Mexico, Peribán, Michoacan. Her father had died in 1964 when Paz was ten years old and is one of ten children. Her mother, with little resources to care for ten children, migrated to Los Angeles, where her cousin got her a job at a sewing factory. Her mother bought her children to Los Angeles one at a time. Paz came in 1972, when she was eighteen years old. Paz took a job at a sewing factory, where she met her future sister-in-law, who introduced her to her first husband, Samuel Trujillo.

Sam Trujillo was one of five brothers who had purchased a ranch in Delta, Utah, where a proposed power plant would greatly increase property values. While working on this ranch, Sam Trujillo was injured while corralling a bull and died soon after from a brain aneurism. He died leaving Paz eight months pregnant and with a ten-month-old child. Paz would leave one year later to Delta to help her ex-husband's family start a catering business to serve the growing community being brought by the power plant.

For three years Paz and I were placed together on a couples' bowling league, and when the job ended in 1986, Paz and I were married in San Gabriel, California. After we were married, we moved to Bay City, Texas, where I took a job at the construction of a nuclear power plant. While working at the power plant, the unit that I was working at was put on hold, and I was laid off with my wife seven months pregnant. I immediately began a job search and had job opportunities in Chattanooga, Tennessee, and in Harlingen, Texas, with a national testing laboratory, Professional Service Industries (PSI). Paz looked at the map and saw that Harlingen was on the Mexico border and decided for both of us that we were moving to Harlingen. Surprisingly, PSI had offered the position to their in house engineers, but no one wanted to move to Harlingen. What are the odds that a woman from central Mexico would meet a young engineer from South Louisiana in the center of a Mormon Utah and end up living in Texas on the Mexico border?

What are those odds? Those were the same odds that I, having been born with a rare genetic abnormality of one blue eye and one brown and green eye, had faced my whole life. And now in Harlingen, Texas, having successfully raised five children and started my own engineering practice, I would soon incur the wrath of the chief engineer of TDI, Sam Nelson.

The History of TDI
Windstorm Certification

Because of some devastating hurricanes and increased population growth on the Gulf Coast, insuring property along the coast was becoming very expensive. Building codes were strengthened to provide stouter structures to withstand the higher winds from hurricanes and tropical storms. Florida led the way by creating their hurricane code and test acceptance standards (TAS). Miami-Dade County created their own notice of acceptance (NOAs) for all components attached to a building structure.

Texas followed and, through a legislative act, created the TDI Windstorm Certification Program. This program was created to provide a formal acceptance of a structure to be placed in the already created Texas Windstorm Insurance Agency (TWIA). TWIA was created in 1972 as a semi-quasi-governmental/private insurance agency, a catastrophe pool for high-risk homes along the fourteen counties making up the Texas Gulf Coast.

When the windstorm certification program was created, the intention was to make it similar to Florida with local offices created to monitor and approve construction. Fourteen TDI offices were established from Brownsville to Beaumont. The state legislator who sponsored the legislation in 1987, Don Lee from Harlingen, retired from the legislature to personally run the program. The second manager of the program was Dick Roland, also of Harlingen. (See letters from Don Lee and Dick Roland.) Under Lee and Roland, the program worked well with very little cost to the consumers by using state inspectors in local offices to perform the certification inspections. The homes still had to be accepted by the local building official, but they generally deferred to the TDI inspectors for the framing and finishes. This arrangement was successful for the first seven years of the program. With the exception of the Angleton office, all TDI offices had over 90 percent acceptance rates for inspection and certification. The exception was Angleton, and this office was run by Welch Watt and had over a 90 percent rejection rate.

Mr. Watt had a degree in economics from Texas A&M and had worked as a construction worker during school but had never run his own company or even run jobs. Mr. Watt had a very myopic view of shingle installation and had an extremely literal interpretation of shingle installation instructions. Mr. Watt enforced an out-of-date shingle placement demonstration that had been around since the fifties. (See NRCA shingle nail placement detail.) This detail showed four conditions of nail installation:

1. Proper nail placement with nailhead firmly on top of shingle

2. Overdriven with nailhead halfway through the shingle thickness

3. Underdriven with nailhead over ⅛" above shingle surface

4. Crooked with nailhead at 45 percent angle to the shingle surface

If Mr. Watt did not find the nailheads as shown in the proper position, he would reject the shingle. Mr. Watt rejected over 90 percent of the roofs that he looked at. His rejection rate was so bad that Dick Roland, the windstorm manager at the time, would recommend the roofers and homeowners that had been rejected secure services of local engineers to certify the roofs.

The problem with Mr. Watts's interpretation of the nail diagram is that he was flat-out wrong. The majority of roof shingles are nailed with air-gun-driven nails. When a hammerhead contacts a shingle surface, it will compress the shingle surface approximately half the thickness of the granule surface. The nailhead will come to rest on this compressed surface. When a nail gun shoots a nail, it will compress the shingle surface only at the diameter of the nailhead. The nailhead will be at or slightly below the granule surface, and this is where it needs to be.

A shingle is composed of a ninety pounds per one hundred square feet (SF) saturated felt with mineral granules in an asphalt base adhered to the felt surface. The mineral granules serve as ballast to provide weight to the shingle area and also as ultraviolet (UV) ray protection. Asphalt bitumen will degrade over time when exposed to sunlight. The granules reflect the sun's rays and provide a matrix for the bitumen to cling to. Flat roofs would use a gravel ballast to protect the bitumen. A gravel-ballasted roof had a projected life of fifty years, and some have lasted one hundred years.

Gravel ballast cannot be practically put on a sloped roof, so granulated shingles were developed to cheaply and efficiently cover sloped roofs.

With the development of pneumatic guns, framing and shingle installation time was cut down by as much as 75 percent.

With Mr. Watt rejecting properly driven air-gun nails, the roofers would refuse to have Mr. Watt inspect their work. If Mr. Watt did allow air guns, he would do so only if the air pressure was throttled back and the nail would not compress the shingle surface. Though Mr. Watt would accept this condition, it was actually incorrect because the nail was not properly compressed and was in fact underdriven.

When Dick Roland left TDI in 1995, Watt was appointed as his successor. Watt immediately began to enforce his intolerant inspection methods on all of the TDI offices. Those inspectors who disagreed with him soon found themselves under severe scrutiny and subject to disciplinary action.

It became so bad that the TDI inspectors would either leave or refuse to accept any roof installation so that they would not be overruled by their supervisors. Roofers were left with no choice but to increasingly turn to engineers to get their roofs certified.

One of the TDI inspectors in the Harlingen office was Delton Lee. Delton was the son of Don Lee, the Harlingen state representative who sponsored the legislation that created TDI Windstorm Certificate Program. Delton was a navy veteran and a contractor and one of the more qualified inspectors in the program and definitely the most qualified in the TDI–Harlingen office.

Delton left the TDI program in 2000 and used his navy time to get early retirement. He left early due to the continued harassment from his TDI supervisors. Delton would start his own construction company and used me as his windstorm engineer. Delton and I would become good friends, and I received much advice and insight from Delton on TDI practices.

After Watt took over as manager of TDI Windstorm, he appointed quality control supervisors to go behind the TDI inspectors to critique their work. The TDI inspectors were having their certifications rejected because they were not calling gun-driven nails overdriven. Delton stated that the quality control inspectors would pull up shingles until they found what they would call overdriven nails. It was TDI's practice as well as industry standard to perform an initial inspection and then, when the roof was complete, to do random checks to verify consistency before certifying a roof. No inspector inspects every nail, and every nail is not going to be perfect. A bad nail can be found on any roof if one keeps looking.

Rather than reject an acceptable roof, Delton took the opportunity to leave early and went back into construction. With Delton leaving, the TDI inspectors who remained in Harlingen and in other offices would become increasingly stricter, and the majority of the roofers turned to engineers to inspect their work.

When Watt took over as manager of the windstorm division, he brought with him his bias against engineers. Mr. Watt had repeatedly had his rejections overruled when he was in the Angleton office. Mr. Watt did not have control over engineers, so he turned to his newest ally, Sam Nelson, who had recently been promoted to the position of chief engineer for TDI based solely on seniority.

Mr. Nelson had worked for TDI since 1986. He started with TDI in the sprinkler pipe division. At that time, sprinkler pipe systems had to be approved by TDI before they were installed. According to architects who were sending sprinkler designs to Austin, they constantly encountered inconsistency and obstinacy from Nelson. He never accepted a design on first submittal even if it was identical to a design that had been previously approved. Because Nelson's obstructionism was reaching epic proportions, the state legislature actually phased out design requirements and allowed the warranty manufacturer to provide the system design. Mr. Nelson's position was phased out, but unfortunately for all the residents of coastal counties in Texas, the acting chief engineer for windstorm, Randy Shackleford, left TDI to take a position with Simpson Strong-Tie, the nation's largest supplier of hurricane connectors for structural framing. According to court testimony in TDI v. TWIA, Nelson had two weeks transition with Shackleford prior to Shackleford leaving and Nelson assuming the position.

During Shackleford's tenure as chief engineer for TDI Windstorm, not one engineer was disciplined by TDI. If there was a dispute between TDI Engineering and a private engineer, TDI would not issue a certification for the property. Without the state-issued certificate WPI-8, the building was not eligible for insurance through TWIA and would have to get insurance through private insurers. Engineers were licensed and governed by the Texas Board of Professional Engineers (TBPE). Any entity or citizen could file a complaint against an engineer, and it would be handled by TBPE. This is similar to any other profession such as doctors or lawyers, and the state of Texas created laws to govern these professions in the occupations code. (This will be discussed in depth later.)

Nelson brought with him his same obstructionism and obstinacy to his new position. The state legislature had recently given TDI the authority to appoint, audit, and discipline engineers through the State Office of Admission Hearings (SOAH) courts. With this new power, Nelson immediately began to audit engineers in a way that was never intended or authorized by the legislation.

The act that created the windstorm certification program was very specific and was also in direct conflict with the occupations code (a subject that will be discussed at great length later). There are two sentences in this act that concern audits; the first sentence is that TDI may request plans, calculations, reports, and product evaluations from any engineer for any project at any time preconstruction or postconstruction. And sentence two states, TDI may perform those audits at random. It can be stated categorically, and without exception, TDI audits have never been at random. They are planned and targeted at engineers that do large volumes of work in residential construction and are performed repeatedly on these same engineers no matter how competent the engineer or whether there has ever been a problem with the engineer.

The best comparison of the TDI audit process is the recent actions of the IRS in targeting conservative groups applying for or operating under 501(c)(3) status.

Neither Nelson nor the majority of his staff had any structural design experience; in fact, Nelson's only structural experience was the two-week transition he had with his predecessor. Nelson's knowledge was limited to the prescriptive portions of the code. Even though a design may be totally appropriate and safe, if Nelson or his staff did not understand it, they would ask for substantiating calculations even though what was provided was more than substantial.

Engineers were constantly requested to provide substantiating evidence. Neither Nelson nor TDI staff would ever show by calculations or code reference that an engineer was wrong. They would simply ask for more substantiation.

More than once I submitted peer reviews of my work by full-time practicing structural engineers only to have TDI reject it.

Engineering and the design of structures is based on the strength of materials determined through testing and the laws of physics. Those laws are irrefutable and cannot be challenged no more than one plus one equals two can be challenged. Engineering design is also governed by codes, which are usually the consensus of opinion of governing bodies and usually change on a yearly basis. There have been five versions of the International Building Code (IBC) and International Residential Code (IRC) from 2000 to 2012. The laws of physics for applying forces have not changed since Sir Isaac Newton first defined them.

The act which created the TDI Windstorm Program also created its governing body; the likes of which do not exist in any other state or entity. In no other state does a state agency other than the licensing board have the authority to appoint engineers to do private work. If an engineer is not on the appointed list of TDI, he cannot do certification work for TWIA.

When the act was created, an engineer who wanted to have his work certified by the state in order for it to be eligible for insurance through TWIA would have to be appointed by TDI. The appointment at that time was based on the engineer signing an affidavit stating that he had five years of experience in inspection and design in a high-wind region.

The certification process involved submitting a form WPI-1 listing the type of work to be done, be it new construction or repair, and the physical address of the property. Once the work was completed, the engineer then had to submit a form WPI-2. (See form WPI-2.) On this form the engineer had to affix his seal and sign a statement acknowledging that he was the engineer of record (EOR) and was responsible for the design and inspection of the work. Once the WPI-2 was submitted, TDI would submit the form WPI-8 to TWIA indicating that the property was eligible for insurance. Alternatively, if a homeowner elected to have TDI inspectors such as Delton Lee or Welsh Watt inspect their home, then no engineer seal or signature was required.

The TDI certification program should have been rendered unconstitutional because a state agency with taxpayer-funded inspectors was performing the same function as engineers and not charging anything for repairs and only $100 for new construction. There is no equivalent of this program in Texas or anywhere else in the country.

The Engineering Practice Act

All states have a governing board created by state legislatures to govern professionals. These boards adopt national policies which govern professionals: doctors, lawyers, CPAs, architects, and professional engineers. The laws which govern professionals are generally codified in state legislatures in the occupations code. This code sets the minimum standards for obtaining licensure in the states in which they practice. The occupations code also sets the standards for the practice of the varying professions and outlines the standards of disciplining professionals when they violate the rules of professional conduct.

In Texas, the state legislature created the Engineering Practice Act for licensing and governing the practice of professional engineering. The act created the Texas Board of Professional Engineering (TBPE) with members appointed by the governor. There is a full-time staff with an executive director (ED).

Within the rules of the Engineering Practice Act (Section 1001.401[e]), "a license holder shall not be required to provide or hold additional certification, other than a license issued under this chapter, to seal an engineering plan, specification, plat, or report." This one sentence is in clear conflict with the Windstorm Act which allows TDI to appoint engineers to do windstorm certification.

The Texas state legislature went even further in the Windstorm Act in 2011 by requiring engineers wishing to do windstorm certification to be specially qualified by requiring TBPE to create a special qualification and screening process for engineers wishing to do windstorm certification including taking a written online exam and submitting a supplemental experience record (SER). This qualification and screening process is even more in direct conflict with 1001.401(e).

TBPE attempted to explain it away on their website under "frequently asked questions" (FAQs). The question was asked specifically why windstorm engineers had to go through a separate qualification. The answer given compared it to cities asking for statements of qualifications (SOQs) for engineers to do work for the city. With all due respect to TBPE, this answer is completely wrong. It is in fact the opposite of what is being done to Windstorm appointed engineers.

Cities asking for SOQs can only employ one engineer per contract, and the state procurement act requires selection based on qualification and work history. No engineering firm is excluded from submitting an SOQ, and no engineer is excluded from doing private work in any city or municipality.

By allowing TBPE to appoint engineers to do windstorm work and allowing TDI to pick or exclude engineers from this list, a qualification other than being licensed is definitely being placed on professional engineers.

If an engineer lives in one of those fourteen coastal counties and practices structural engineering, he will have to deal with TDI whether he likes it or not. This places a burden on engineers that live in coastal counties that is not on any engineer in the rest of the state.

Wind loads on a one-story house on South Padre Island or Galveston are no higher than wind loads on a multistory building in downtown Houston, San Antonio, Austin, or Dallas. Yet none of those high-rise structures require the design engineer to be appointed and screened by TBPE. As an example, the wall load pressure at 30' on South Padre Island is 46.6 pounds per square feet (psf). For 16 stories or 160-foot-tall structure in Austin, the headquarters for TDI, the wall pressure would be 48.7 psf. These numbers come right off a load table, 27.6-1, printed in ASCE-7 2010 edition.

An engineer who refuses to deal with TDI will not be able to get any design work in a coastal county. There are exceptions for proprietary firms such as Wal-Mart designers or very large design firms who can afford to hire smaller firms to do the inspection and certification. The catch for both of these exceptions, the design will have to be certified by an appointed engineer, and if audited, these excepted engineering firms will still have to defend their designs to engineers in Austin who have never designed a high-rise or large-scale structure.

The engineer who certifies those structures designed by other engineers will be listed as the EOR for the structure on the TDI website and, as far as TDI is concerned, is the only engineer responsible for the structure. This is an unfair burden for any engineer and is a burden that is not found anywhere else in the country or even the rest of the counties in Texas outside of the fourteen coastal counties. TDI has sold their windstorm certification program to the Texas state legislature as something that is necessary to prevent high losses during hurricanes. The truth is that homes that did not participate in the TWIA risk pool did not fare any worse than those structures in the program. Also Texas homes certified in the program did not fare any better than homes of similar age in Florida, Louisiana, Mississippi, or any other state that has been hit by a hurricane since 1988, the year that TDI was created.

The Engineering Practice Act is enacted by the state legislature to protect the public by governing the practice of engineers by providing criteria for licensing of engineers and establishes a formal process for bringing a complaint against an engineer. This process protects the public and protects engineers.

This is specifically why the act has the provision that no entity can require anything more of an engineer than his license to practice engineering. TDI certainly is a state entity, and they are certainly requiring engineers to certify a structure be appointed. The whole process of requiring engineers to be screened by TBPE and then selected by TDI is in conflict with the practice of engineering and in clear violation of the requirement listed in 1001.401(e).

There is not one engineer on the appointment list that thinks the process is fair, but as stated before, if an engineer desires to practice any form of structural engineering in one of the fourteen coastal counties, he has to deal with TDI.

The big question or the proverbial elephant in the room is, Why does TBPE or the Texas Society of Professional Engineers or American Society of Civil Engineers (ASCE) allow this to happen?

If you ask TBPE, they will simply state that the state legislature has empowered TDI to do what they do. TBPE totally ignores the legislative act that prohibits such requirements as appointing engineers.

So why is it happening?

There are currently approximately eighty-eight thousand professional engineers registered in Texas. Professional engineering includes all disciplines: civil, mechanical, electrical, chemical, petroleum, aeronautical, environmental, and structural. All of the above disciplines can only receive a professional designation of professional engineer with the exception of structural engineering. There is a separate licensing requirement and separate test to be licensed as a structural engineer. The majority of the engineers who practice structural engineering are registered as professional engineers. There are many reasons for this, and below are just a few.

Structural engineering involves providing calculations and details for static structures, buildings, bridges, retaining walls, signposts, bleachers, and so on. The ability to provide these calculations requires knowledge of all building materials including but not limited to steel, concrete, wood, masonry, aluminum, plastics, and so on. A registered structural engineer should have knowledge of the majority of these structures and building materials. The average registered structural engineer is proficient at and designs mid- to high-rise buildings of steel, concrete, and masonry.

An engineer who does other civil disciplines such as water and wastewater, surveying, streets and drainage, or environmental and also designs the structures to accompany them will not get a structural engineering license but is perfectly capable of designing small residential or commercial structures but would never attempt to design a high-rise structure, bridge, or stadium.

Also, evaluating a structure postconstruction for damage from wind, fire, or corrosion requires a working knowledge of structural engineering. Those engineers that started practicing early with a large structural firm will generally get the experience to take and pass a structural engineering exam. Those engineers who only do structural as part of their practice will not generally have the expertise to pass all phases of the structural engineering exam, and there is no need for them to. Once licensed as a professional engineer (PE), the PE can practice in any discipline that he feels competent in, and only TBPE can question that competence.

If a PE who does the majority of his work designing wood-framed homes, he will be more proficient at designing wood homes than a registered structural engineer who rarely designs wood structures.

Currently there are only approximately two hundred appointed engineers to do windstorm design and certification in the fourteen coastal counties in Texas. This is down from the over nine hundred engineers that were appointed prior to TBPE requiring that they be screened. This will be discussed at length later.

Two hundred or nine hundred professional engineers out of eighty-eight thousand are less than 1 percent of practicing engineers. And even in their local groups, they are a small minority. No professional society of engineers or even TBPE fully understands what is required of Windstorm appointed engineers. If they did, the whole process would have been scrapped long ago. If the same requirement applied to all 88,000 professional engineers, the appointment process would not have lasted more than a few months.

There is precedence for this. In 1998 the Texas Department of Health (TDH), currently Texas Commission on Environmental Quality (TCEQ), required professional engineers to attend class and be certified to classify soils for on-site sewage facility (OSSF) or septic fields. Prior to 1998, TDH required a percolation test be run on existing soils to determine their absorption rate for OSSF trench design. This test was not very accurate and often in contradiction to the soils actually in place. This test was replaced in 1988 with the soil classification test per the uniform soil classification standards to determine the percentage clay in the soil. Clay-type soils are very impermeable and are ideal for containing water, not absorbing it.

This new law requiring soil classification for septic system design affected professional engineers in every county in the state and a fairly large percentage of civil engineers. I had just begun private practice as a professional engineer in 1998 and was one of the first class to get certified to classify soil. I took the twenty-hour course at the Texas A&M–San Antonio extension campus and passed the test. The class was approximately 50 percent engineers and 50 percent level 2 OSSF installers who also had to be certified to classify soils. The course was interesting and beneficial but was contained in the soils lab that any civil engineering student would have taken during college.

The engineering profession soon rose up in unison and bombarded the TBPE with requests to stop this onerous practice. After all, why should a professional engineer be required to be certified to perform a simple test that was already part of his practice?

Within two months of the soil classification certification requirement of engineers, TDH quickly revised the program and dropped the requirement for professional engineers to be certified to classify soils. Only level 2 installers were required to take the certification course. The requirement for professional engineers to be certified to classify soils ended as fast as it began.

How does this compare to professional engineers being appointed by TDI to practice their profession in a coastal county? TDH, now TCEQ, and TDI are both state agencies. Both were the recipients of legislation empowering them to govern the practice of engineering. One was overturned immediately; the other has been in place since 1988 and allowed to continue for twenty-six-plus years. The difference is the TDH act affected engineers throughout the entire state and all counties. The TDI act only applies to engineers who practice structural engineering in 14 out of 254 counties in Texas.

The small group of appointed windstorm engineers did not have the voice or clout or political will to get the onerous appointment process stopped. An individual professional engineer defending himself or herself from TDI Engineering Department could spend a $100,000 fighting the state. This is the equivalent of David versus Goliath. In the end, David won!

The Building Process

To understand the uniqueness of the TDI windstorm certification process, one must understand the building permitting process.

At the time the program was created in 1988, TDI was operating under the Southern Building Code (SBC) 1973 edition. They are now operating under the International Building code (IBC). Both of these codes in chapter 1 give the power to enforce the code to the local building official. Any new construction, addition, or alteration in 1988 and today are required to be permitted by the local building official. The code gives very specific language on the power of the building official and who can overrule a building official.

The code since 1988 has always mandated that a board of appeals be created to give citizens recourse when they are treated unfairly by a building official. The code also mandates that the building official will not have a vote on the board of appeals. The other power to overrule the building official is the legislative body that adopted the code.

In every state, including Texas, when a citizen, corporation, public entity, or government agency wished to erect a structure, they first must apply for and obtain a permit. To obtain a permit, the requestor must provide plans, specifications, and sufficient data that describe the structure to be built. The building official will then take the data, and if it complies with the intent of the code, it will issue a permit for the construction of the structure.

The building official's responsibility does not end there. The building official is tasked with enforcing the code during construction and, where required, issuing a certificate of compliance or condition of occupancy (CO). The building official has the power of law to stop construction if a structure is not being erected per local adopted codes and ordinances.

The amount of oversight varies from state to state and more so from city to city. Only in Texas does a state agency have the power to ignore the building official and usurp the power of the building official but not be subject to the board of appeals. The state of Texas through the Windstorm Act created the certification process. Through this act TDI mandates that the wind provisions of the code be enforced and have tasked private appointed engineers with the responsibility of ensuring that the code wind provisions are enforced.

A homeowner or contractor can hire an appointed engineer to design his home, take the plans to the building official, and obtain a permit then, during construction, have both the building official and design engineer inspect and approve the construction of the home and receive a CO from the building official and a windstorm certificate from the design engineer.

TDI can come in at any time during construction and even years after construction and audit the structure. If the TDI Engineering Department determines that the structure does not meet their standards, they can either withhold the certification or cancel the certificate. This action will prevent the home or structure from obtaining windstorm insurance through TWIA. The homeowner will have to obtain more expensive insurance through private carriers, and the resale value of his home may be greatly affected.

The homeowner did everything he was supposed to do but still can be overruled by TDI. What is the homeowner's recourse? The building official is a government employee and exempt from prosecution. If the engineer was indeed negligent, then the homeowner can sue for damages.

Proving the engineer was negligent is difficult. TDI rejecting the work does not mean it is wrong, and in fact, in the last legislation that created the engineer being approved by the board, TDI got inserted into the act, "If TBPE determines the engineer did not do anything wrong, TDI can still refuse to issue a certification."

There is no board-of-appeals process for the homeowner to follow to undo a wrong TDI decision. It is not uncommon for engineers and building officials to disagree. In Florida and California and several other states, the design plans may be rejected and returned to the engineer for revision. The engineer will then make the revisions and resubmit. But once the plans are accepted by the building official, they cannot then be rejected by the building official even if the plans had omissions. Field inspections may reveal areas that need to be revised, and the engineer will make the revisions. All of this is done while the home or structure is being constructed so that when the structure is complete and the CO is issued, the home is safe to occupy and has to be insured by the insurance industry. Only in Texas in the fourteen coastal counties is this process different.

Does TDI rejecting a structure mean the structure is substandard or even in any way defective? Not likely! The same homes rejected by TDI are routinely accepted in Florida, California, and throughout the country. What is the requirement to become an employee of the TDI Windstorm Department? Not much! Currently a TDI state employee who is a building inspector has to obtain an ICC code inspector certificate within six months of being hired. This certificate requires that the inspector take an open-book exam. I had one of my engineering graduates take the test, and he easily passed it. It does not require any special knowledge or experience and certainly would not give the inspector the knowledge or experience to question an engineer with over thirty years of experience, which is frequently the case with TDI inspectors.

TDI currently has five engineers in the windstorm program. Only one practiced as a structural engineer. The manager, Sam Nelson, has no design experience, and according to his own testimony in TDI v. TWIA, he only had a two-week transition with his predecessor, Randy Shackleford, who was a good structural engineer and now works for Simpson Strong-Tie.

It would be assumed that someone who is going to be auditing structural engineers would have at least a master's in structural engineering and at least five years structural design experience. This is not the case with the TDI Engineering Department. The engineers in this department have no special expertise in structural engineering and have frequently misinterpreted the code to the detriment of the appointed engineer and the building owner. In any other state or in any county outside the fourteen coastal counties, these incorrect interpretations by TDI could be overturned by a board of appeals.

TDI engineers are not infallible, but the Texas state legislature through the laws of unintended consequences have created this monster where any decision no matter how wrong or how costly that is made by TDI is deemed to have the power of law behind it.

This does not have to be and, in fact, shouldn't be. There are numerous laws that have been on the books for years that should supersede the Windstorm Act or at least confine it to the original intent outlined in the letter by Don Lee. It is way past time that the TDI Windstorm Program is made to fall in line with the rest of the country.

David V. Day's History with TDI

What are the odds that a man born and raised in Louisiana, met his spouse in Utah, migrated to Texas by random chance, and began his private practice in Harlingen, Texas, would be the man who would finally expose the corruption in the TDI program? My story is not unique among Windstorm appointed engineers. There have been numerous appointed engineers who have been persecuted by TDI, but only one case had finally made it to district court, and the odds are that the TDI reign of terror may finally be exposed.

My history with TDI began in 2000. I was working as a private engineering consultant out of my home in my own company, Day Consulting. With my construction and inspection background, I was mainly working as a third-party inspector on government grant jobs and also doing forensic damage assessments for building foundations. During this time, I received numerous inquiries about windstorm certification.

At that time I had not heard of the program and consulted with a local structural engineer about the program. He told me about the program and described it as mostly being a prescriptive program that applied to residences. He only participated in the program to certify the large structural jobs that he was involved with. He did not do private work. He then referred me to an older engineer, Charles Durivage, as someone to refer work to.

I contacted Durivage to find out more about the program and inquire if Durivage was interested in taking referrals from me on all the requests that I had been getting. Durivage had recently been put under the microscope by TDI for certifying work that had previously been certified by TDI-appointed inspectors and found acceptable.

TDI had audited several homes in the same subdivision in Port Isabel that Durivage had inspected. TDI inspectors had accepted and certified numerous homes of similar construction. These homes were on an island in the bay at Port Isabel, and the ground elevation was below flood elevation. The structures were elevated approximately four feet on timber posts that sat directly on a poured-in-place slab that was previously used as a trailer pad. Durivage did what most prudent engineers would do; he accepted the precedent that had already been established by TDI.

One of the structures was investigated during a random audit by TDI Engineering Department. When TDI analyzed the tie-down method, they concluded that it was not sufficient to prevent lateral racking. This was a correct conclusion, but TDI Engineering only went back and looked at those structures that had been certified by engineers, which included Durivage and several others. They did nothing to the numerous homes that had been accepted by TDI employees. They actually brought charges against the engineers in a state office of administrative hearings (SOAH) court and levied fines against the engineers. It was later determined by TBPE that TDI could not be fining engineers; only TBPE could fine an engineer. It is ironic that TBPE had a problem with TDI fining engineers but had no problem with TDI bringing charges in an SOAH court against an engineer. Appointed engineers were actually better off when they could be fined by TDI because when the practice of fining was discontinued, TDI went after complete removal from the appointment list as their way of punishing engineers, and TBPE had no problem with this. This will be discussed at length later.

The windstorm certification process is a three-step process:

1. When the property is ready for construction or when a permit is applied for, a form, WPI-1, is sent to TDI with all of the construction information on it. The property will then get entered into TDI's database.

2. When the construction is completed, the engineer of record will submit a WPI-2, a form that states the construction meets the wind provision of the applicable code. The engineer of record must sign and seal this form.

3. When TDI receives the WPI-2, they will issue the WPI-8, which states that the property construction is certified.

When charges of improperly sealing a WPI-2 were brought against Durivage, he defended himself by rightly pointing out that he was following precedence established by TDI inspectors. TDI replied that the inspectors were not engineers and that Durivage should have known better. There are two major problems with this defense by TDI:

1. TDI took no action against the homeowners that had properties inspected by TDI, and

2. TDI had a written prescriptive code that in no way met the wind provisions of the code in numerous instances. Wall bracing that TDI was concerned about for these above ground structures also was not enforced on any structure west of Highway 77, the midpoint of Cameron County. If TDI was not enforcing braced-wall requirements west of 77, Durivage was only following their lead in accepting elevated structures in Port Isabel.

The homeowners that had homes certified by engineers either never received a WPI-8 or had their WPI-8 pulled. The homes that were inspected by TDI inspectors were left alone. This is an unfair if not illegal practice by TDI. What TDI should have done is required that all of the homes they found to have interior-foundation bracing be properly braced to maintain their insurance and given them time to comply. It is not uncommon for TWIA to require additional work be done to a structure, especially roof repairs, before renewing a policy.

Prior to adoptions for the IBC and IRC codes, TDI had prescriptive guides for residential construction. If the construction complied with the guide, then the work was accepted by TDI inspectors, and if an engineer was audited and the structure complied with the guide, then the structure was accepted by TDI and granted a WPI-8. The trouble is that the guide did not comply with the Southern Building Code (SBC) for bracing. The WPI-2 only had one choice for structures in the western half of first-tier counties, which was designated by TDI as Inland II, and that was to comply with the wind provisions of the SBC. There was only one box to check (refer to WPI-2 in attachments). The WPI-2 made no mention of the prescriptive guide. There was no box to check that referenced the TDI prescriptive guide. TDI was routinely accepting work that would not meet the SBC code, but they gave the engineer no alternative but to check the box that the structure complied with the SBC. This was one of the numerous contradictions within TDI that engineers had to put up with without having a board of appeals to hear the case.

Durivage was referred to TBPE by TDI, and the board took no action against Durivage. Nevertheless, Durivage paid a fine and was put on a one-year probation period by TDI. All of this had just occurred when I first called Durivage.

Durivage was rightly concerned that he may lose his appointment and not be able to certify structures. Durivage had at the time several large-tract home builders and subdivision developers who used him exclusively. When Durivage met me, he saw the opportunity to partner up with another engineer who could support himself but get on the appointment list and certify properties if necessary.

Durivage was nearing retirement age, and I had seen several successful mergers where an established engineer partnered with a younger engineer and then retired. I entered into a joint-venture expense-sharing agreement with Durivage. The partnership retained the name of the company that Durivage already had, Control Engineering Associates (CEA). The partnership was set up so that each engineer earned his own funds but shared office expenses and common labor expense. Each engineer had their own DBA (doing business as) CEA. The joint venture or CEA joint venture was not supposed to earn any money according to the articles of incorporation that governed the joint venture. Each partner was supposed to contribute enough funds to pay common expenses: rent, utilities, secretary, labor, and office supplies.

The joint venture soon evolved into a billing entity that billed clients directly, and the funds were deposited into the joint venture. Though this was a violation of the joint-venture agreement, each partner found it more convenient for the joint venture to self-fund rather than make contributions. Because I had very little cash flow when the joint venture was formed; Durivage loaned the joint venture the first funds to get it started. Also, the original clients were all Durivage's clients.

The joint venture was not formed until I got on the TDI appointed engineers list. At that time in 2001, an engineer was only required to sign an affidavit that stated that he had five years of design and inspection experience. Once I was on the list, I soon started receiving direct requests. Though Durivage had been in the program for many years, he was not as well-known as me. I had dealt with the majority of the contractors in the Rio Grande Valley while managing Professional Service Industries (PSI), a geo-technical and material-testing lab that I had moved to the valley to manage. After the joint venture was formed, the majority of the work that came into the joint venture was sealed by me. Around 80 to 90 percent of the designs that were done by the joint venture were sealed by me.

When the joint venture was formed, the majority of projects done by CEA were residential structures that were designed in accordance with a prescriptive guide that was created by TDI. For residences that were constructed on South Padre Island or Seaward and those that were constructed east of Highway 77 or Inland I, there were tables for shear-wall (lateral racking resistance) requirements and prescriptive guides for framing. For structures erected west of Highway 77 or in cities bordering Highway 77, there were no design requirements, only prescriptive framing requirements.

My first run-in with TDI was on a residence located on the outskirts of San Benito, a city that was located on Highway 77 and considered Inland II. The homes construction was similar to numerous structures that I had already designed in Inland I area. The residence had a San Benito address, and I turned in the WPI-1 listing it as Inland II. The home was in the San Benito Extraterritorial Jurisdiction (ETJ) but not within the city limits. TDI put this home under audit and asked for all design information. The home was totally within the prescriptive requirements except for a gable end wall. A design was turned into TDI for the wall and rejected by TDI for no legitimate reason other than it was something they had not seen done before. I turned in two more designs for this wall that were verified by two separate structural engineers, but TDI refused to accept them. TDI was wrong to question the design and produced no evidence that anything I submitted was wrong. They simply gave their universal response when something is submitted that they do not understand: "You have not substantiated your calculations," which translates to, "We do not understand what you did and are not going to accept it." The home was never accepted by TDI, and the homeowner was forced to get insurance through the private market. This home was similar to numerous homes that had been certified by other engineers, and had it been one mile farther to the west, it would have had to be accepted by TDI. This home was doomed because it was audited and rejected by TDI. There is no appeals process for this homeowner.

From this experience I quickly learned what TDI would accept. What TDI would accept though would change when TDI adopted the international codes in late 2003. The new codes required design for any structure erected within historical one-hundred-year Category 3 hurricane occurrences. In Texas this was designated on the American Society of Civil Engineers (ASCE) design standards, ASCE-7, as 130 mph for the barrier island, 120 mph for the seaward half of the coastal counties, and 110 mph for the inland half of the coastal counties. These three areas were designated Seaward, Inland I, and Inland II by TDI.

TDI now required structural design for all framing to resist the wind pressures for the abovementioned wind speeds. There was no precedence for this. Structural designs in a high-wind area are not new, and all commercial structures had always required design.

Residential design was new for Texas, but there was plenty of precedence for Florida, and California had been requiring structural design for residences for some time. The difference is that in all states but Texas, the design is controlled by the local building official and, in the fourteen coastal counties of Texas, is controlled by TDI from the state capital in Austin.

With the adoption of the international codes, the WPI-2 that the engineer signed for Inland II cities changed for the first time from having to meet the 1973 SBC code. The wind pressures per International Building Code (IBC) were actually much lower than those required by the 1973 code. The 1973 code listed the same pressure from the coast to 125 mph inland. Any engineer who interpreted this requirement in 1973 as applying to the coast only and interpolated as the hurricane moved over land to a lower pressure inland would have been correct. Only an unknowledgeable engineer working in TDI in Austin would enforce the same wind-derived pressures for the coastline to 125 miles inland, but that is what TDI required.

The guide that TDI developed in-house for engineers to follow was supposed to be based on the 1973 wind pressures but in no way met them. The WPI-2 form made no mention of the prescriptive guide that TDI used to certify structures. An engineer certifying a structure in Inland II only had one box to check, and that was the one that stated that the structure met the wind provisions of the 1973 SBC. This was essentially an incorrect statement, but TDI required it, and the TBPE enforced it, so engineers signed it.

At least with the adoption of the I codes, TDI changed the WPI-2 form to correctly reflect the appropriate wind speed for the three design areas: 130 mph for Seaward, 120 mph for Inland I, and 110 mph for Inland II.

Engineers now had clear guidance on what pressures to apply for designing the lateral, uplift, and overturning resisting systems. The major obstacles that engineers now faced are that no one in TDI Engineering Department had ever designed a structure to the international codes. Engineers were now subject to the whims of the TDI engineering audits. Because TDI Engineering had no practical experience, they relied purely on prescriptive methods that they had developed in their previous guides.

Anytime an engineer applied a principle that was not in TDI Engineering's prescriptive knowledge, it was usually very difficult to prove it in a TDI audit.

A New Beginning

In 2005, I left Durivage and Control Engineering Associates and started my own company, Civil and Structural Associates, CASA Engineering LLC. I did it with a $25,000 credit card loan. Much of the work followed me, and I earned exactly the same fees in my first month with CASA as I had in his last month with CEA joint venture.

In 2005 Hurricane Katrina hit Louisiana and Mississippi, and then in 2005 Hurricane Rita hit East Texas. This was after 2004, when four hurricanes hit Florida. Insurance companies were taking great hits to their funds on hand. The insurance companies in Texas were looking to dump high-risk properties, so the major insurance companies started dropping coverage in Texas, and more residents were being forced into the catastrophe pool TWIA.

This presented a big problem for TDI and TWIA. Many of the homes that were trying to get into TWIA did not have a windstorm certification or WPI-8. The windstorm program had always been voluntary from the time of its conception in 1988. A residence in a coastal county could get insurance from the private market or through TWIA. All of the insurance companies rightly assumed if the homes were inspected and given a certificate of occupancy by the building official, then they should be eligible for TWIA. All of the engineers in the program soon found out that this would not be the case.

As the private insurance companies pulled out of coastal areas and stopped offering coverage, the homeowners and their insurance companies increasingly requested a policy from TWIA. The only way to get a policy from TWIA is to get a windstorm certification form WPI-8. TDI in Austin will not inspect a home after it is constructed. There is no written policy or law to prevent them from doing post-construction inspections; they just refused to do it. So the home-owner or insurer had no choice but to hire an engineer to certify a structure.

A TDI appointed engineer cannot issue a WPI-8; only TDI can do that. TDI relies on their in-house inspectors or appointed engi-neers to issue a WPI-2. When this form is received, TDI will issue a WPI-8, and then TWIA will then issue a windstorm insurance policy.

At the time, there were several engineers who relied on ex-TDI in-house inspectors to inspect structures, and then they would cer-tify them for a minimal fee. When those engineers were audited, they could not defend their designs or even produce a design because they had done none. It did not mean the home was improperly con-structed, it just meant the engineer could not produce the calcula-tions to prove that the framing would withstand the wind pressures.

It was during this time in 2006 that I picked up many clients by taking on homes that had been constructed but never certified. I had a very simple approach. The city or county inspectors were enforcing all uplift anchors at sole plate to stud, stud to top plate, and top plate to rafter, and usually these clips could easily be verified. I would use a very conservative approach on the shear walls by assuming mini-mal nailing patterns and minimal shear-resistance values. Shear walls are the walls with sheathing that resist lateral wind loads or racking. Steel- or concrete-framed structures are ridged structures. A wood-framed structure is considered a flexible structure. The sheathing, be it plywood or even Sheetrock, provides the rigidity to resist lateral wind loads. My analysis worked for most walls, and where there were not enough shear walls, then sheathing could be added at the inte-rior walls to sufficiently brace the homes. At walls where there was minimal bracing, steel columns and beams could be added inside the walls and over the headers to stiffen the walls. I had developed tables that would give me shear capacities for various walls depending on their lengths.

My designs were put to the test when I took on several homes that were already under audit. This was something I would later find out was not being done by any other engineers in the program.

In the small coastal town of Laguna Vista, Texas, there was an engineer, Sylvester J. Crooks, who was doing the majority of wind-storm certification in this town. Crooks was a retired engineer from the US Army Corps of Engineers. He did not do any comprehensive designs and relied solely on his inspector, Charlie Watkins. Watkins had worked for TDI as an appointed inspector. Watkins's previous profession before joining TDI when it was founded in 1988 was as a beer-truck driver. Watkins knew the prescriptive code but was not capable of designing shear walls, particularly on the majority of the designs in this retirement community, where the houses faced the golf course and had numerous openings and very few shear-wall segments. When TDI audited Crooks and found he had no designs, they put all of the homes he was working on under audit and refused to accept any of the homes that had already been turned in with a WPI-1 listing Crooks as EOR. The owners of these homes and the contractors who constructed them were being penalized for the engineer that they chose. As one of the builders would later tell me, he was duped. Watkins had told them all that he was an ex-TDI employee and knew what he was doing. Watkins secured the work, did all the inspections, kept all the paperwork, and then hired Crooks to certify them sight unseen.

Crooks was on the appointment list. Watkins had previously worked for TDI, so why would a homeowner or contractor have any reason to believe that they could not produce designs? After all, a plan had been turned into the building official and accepted, and the building official had inspected and accepted the construction and issued a CO. All of the above entities, the contractor, the engineer, and the inspector, had been working with the TDI prescriptive codes for years, and in fact, most of these homes would have met the requirement of the TDI Windstorm Program when it was founded in 1988.

Who was to blame here? When rules are set in Austin governing local building for insurance purposes where engineers have to turn in plans to the local building official but be subject to audit by TDI in Austin, conflicts will arise. Whatever the intentions were in 1988 when the windstorm program was created, it had now morphed into something it was never intended to be, a centralized bureaucratic entity with the ability to make rules and interpret code without any seeming accountability. I would later prophetically compare them to the IRS, who has the power to audit and harass and impede progress without any seeming accountability.

Bureaucracy and
Strong-Arm Audits

There were several titles that would have been appropriate for this chapter: the name of an individual because there were several who epitomized the incompetence and bureaucratic stronghold of TDI, "Bureaucracy" because TDI Windstorm Program was the epitome of an unaccountable bureaucracy, or "Audit" because it was through this process where incompetent individuals as engineers and inspectors and managers exercised their most heinous power.

When I first took on Crooks's ex-clients in Laguna Vista, Texas, I naively thought that if I was upfront and volunteered information, I would receive an equal response from TDI. Boy, was I ever wrong! I would soon find out that TDI was not going to be cooperative. They would throw out every roadblock they could conceive of to keep an engineer from taking on an audited property. Somewhere from the commissioner on down, TDI had made the decision that they wanted to limit the number of homes that would be put into the risk pool. They did this by not requiring the older homes to be brought up to standards, as was being done in California for homes in earthquake-prone areas. TDI made the decision that large custom homes presented a threat to the insurance rates, and TDI was going to minimize that risk.

There was no research to support this, and there is certainly no economic principle that supports it. If anything, the four hurricanes in Florida in 2004 and Katrina and Rita in 2005 proved that the new homes with uplift strapping and wood sheathing faired very well in the hurricanes. It was the older, substandard, or worn-out roofs that suffered the most damage and contributed to the greatest insurance costs. And Economics 101 will tell you that the more homes in the program sharing the costs, the more solvent the insurance program will be.

TDI ideology seemed to be driven by the foolish ranting of the current windstorm director, Welch Watt, who repeatedly said in a public forum that 66 percent of all new roofs were being put on incorrectly. This is actually a step down for Watt, who, when he was manager of the Angleton office, rejected 90 percent of all new roofs. There are actually television and newspaper snippets of the TDI commissioner stating that 66 percent of all roofs are being put on incorrectly.

I stepped into this hornets' nest when I agreed to take on six homes that had belonged to Crooks and one home that had belonged to Bob Burkhart. Burkhart will be discussed at length in a later chapter.

I agreed to take on all the homes under audit because I was going to pick up five new clients building large custom homes. The homes were in varying stages of completion, from being in the framing state of completion with all framing members exposed to being completely finished and occupied. All of the homes were under audit by the same engineer in Austin, Stephen Harp, an engineer whose name will be repeated numerous times for the rest of this book.

Harp was a recent addition to TDI and began when TDI adopted the I codes and all engineering went from prescriptive to design. Harp had worked briefly for a home designer in Corpus Christi, Ronald Voss. His experience there was related solely to prescriptive design of residential homes. Harp spoke very slowly and was slow to respond. Harp was prone to outlandish, insulting criticisms and would repeatedly state that you were wrong and that he was not going to accept it. If an engineering principle was new to Harp or did not fit into his prescriptive realm of knowledge, he simply would not accept it. At TDI, once a decision is made, no matter how wrong, they stand behind it all the way to the top.

Harp would typically take a submittal and start looking for something wrong. Many times engineers use simplified pressures that are more conservative for expediency, and Harp would send back a letter stating that the pressure that was used did not match the pressure in the ASCE-7 design table. He would make the engineer write a letter back stating that the pressures used were higher than what was needed and therefore okay before he would proceed with the rest of the audit. Typically Harp would produce a letter with ten to twenty items that he stated were wrong or needed substantiation. The engineer would send back a reply showing why everything in the original submittal was correct and would give some more detail as substantiation. After four or five letters from Harp and months of needless hassle, the engineer would get a letter from Harp stating that a WPI-2 could now be turned in, and the home would be granted a WPI-8 by TDI.

I managed to get all six of my audits passed at an average time of six months, the longest being eighteen months and the shortest being three months. In all six cases, the home was accepted as constructed without any changes to the design. In no case did Harp provide any evidence or supporting calculation that anything turned into him was wrong; he just kept requiring additional information. Often he would ask for information that was not included in his initial letter, in letters written three and four months later.

The contractors and homeowners in all six audits never criticized me for the delays. They all read the correspondence and the replies and marveled at my patience for putting up with such bureaucratic incompetence. If a homeowner had the audacity to call TDI and ask why their home was not being certified, they would simply state that the engineer had not provided all documentation requested. In all six audits in Laguna Vista on me, all information was sent in initial audit request. I would have to spend three to eighteen months explaining where the information was contained in my submittal. Many times the same information was resubmitted two or three times before it was accepted.

Harps incompetence was easily recognizable by the homeowners and contractors who had to deal with him. The best example one homeowner related to me is the time he called Harp to ask a specific question about an audit reply. Harp was apparently much disorganized and asked to call the homeowner back when he found the letter I had written. The homeowner insisted that Harp get the reply and give him an answer. Harp told him to wait just a moment and put the phone down while he began to shuffle papers on his desk. The homeowner patiently waited over five minutes and then started yelling into the phone to get Harp's attention. When Harp finally picked up the phone five minutes later, he had forgotten who he was talking to and what was wanted.

That homeowner told me that it was at that moment he realized what he and I were dealing with, and he provided me support and help to get the audit complete.

If Harp had worked for the city of Laguna Vista and had provided the same service, he would have been brought up in a commissioner's meeting and either disciplined or fired, but because he worked for the state in a voluntary program, there was not much a homeowner or contractor or engineer could do to stop the nonsense.

The city manager of Laguna Vista, who had asked TDI to get involved when she could not get structural plans from Crooks, stated to me that it was one of the biggest regrets of her career. Even her own home was put into jeopardy. She had bought a home that didn't have a windstorm certification. The home was well built and had plenty of walls that would count as shear walls, but proving it to TDI would probably entail needlessly removing Sheetrock and stucco to verify nail patterns. The IBC gives a value for unblocked minimally nailed wood sheathed walls as 180 psf. This would be a valid assumption that any building official in any area in the country would accept without proof, but not TDI. I gave her one price for certifying the home with normal engineering evaluation and another price if TDI audited it, which was four times as much. Luckily the home was not audited and got approved.

At the Laguna Vista city manager's request, TDI did a random walkthrough of some of the newer homes and flagged several for audit. This automatically put these homeowners in jeopardy. The prudent thing for TDI to have done would have been to request plans from the city hall that had not yet been issued a permit and asked for substantiating calculations. This is the way it is done in the rest of the state of Texas and the rest of the country. If TDI had a problem with the design, it could be addressed before the permit was issued, and the owner could have some input by making decisions to eliminate a window or choose a different door to help beef up some walls. In this way, the design is guaranteed, and no changes would have to be made during construction.

With TDI's policy of auditing a home at any time during construction, it puts the homeowner, the contractor, and the engineer in jeopardy. Minor errors can be made during design. There may be some framing conflicts that shorten a shear wall that have to be picked up at other locations. These are problems that occur on every project, big and small, and are dealt with by architects and engineers on a daily basis.

Minor errors in calculations are generally waived if the calculated loads are within 10 percent of the design loads. That is what safety factors are for. TDI's zero-tolerance policy does not permit errors. Numerous designs are rejected for a math error even when the math error might result in a higher value.

There have been many engineers who properly designed structures but could not prove the design in an audit. TDI does not prove the design is deficient; they just repeat their standard mantra, "Design does not substantiate." Many of the engineers throw in the towel and resign from the program. In all the audits I reviewed in my dealings with TDI, which numbered in the hundreds, the majority were at best a difference in opinion between the engineer and TDI, or TDI was flat-out wrong to reject the design or product installation.

After I passed the six audits, TDI left me alone for a year until 2008. That is the year Hurricane Dolly hit.

The Trouble Begins

Hurricane Dolly hit July 23, 2008. It originated in the Caribbean and hit directly on South Padre Island with maximum winds of 110 mph and headed almost directly west up Highway 83. The storm stalled over the Harlingen area and McAllen and lasted over ten hours before moving on. There was significant flooding, and thousands of roofs were damaged.

CASA was inundated with requests for reroof certifications and for remodeling homes and commercial structures that had water damage.

TDI had taken their office out of Harlingen when the prescriptive codes went away in 2003. In 2008, after Hurricane Dolly, because of the amount of storm damage, TDI established a temporary office in Harlingen to handle requests for repairs and re-roof certifications. During this time there was more work than the local roofers could handle, and numerous roofing companies descended on the valley from all over the state. These were big roofing companies from San Antonio, Austin, Laredo, Dallas, and other areas. There were literally hundreds of years of roofing experience, but no amount of experience would prepare a company to deal with TDI.

These roofing companies applied shingles the same way they do everywhere else in the country. It must be noted that the shingle application for the fourteen coastal counties in Texas is the same as anywhere else in the country. All shingles anywhere have a four-nail application, and this application is good for TWIA. There is a six-nail application recommended for high-wind areas, but the four-nail application meets the 130 mph maximum winds for the barrier islands. And practically 100 percent of all large roofing companies apply the nails with a pneumatic gun.

These roofers soon found out that TDI inspectors were not going to accept the gun-driven nails because, as discussed earlier, all TDI inspectors enforced the Welch Watt interpretations of nail placement and reject the shingles anytime the nailhead is below the granule surface, which occurs anytime the nails are properly driven with a pneumatic gun.

Why would a roofer use inspectors that were so strict? The new roofers did not know any better, but even the regular roofers would occasionally have to work with them. The answer is that the TDI inspections were free. There is no charge for a TDI inspector to perform windstorm inspections on roofs, windows, doors, sidings, and vents. And when TDI was doing prescriptive certification of complete homes, the fee was only $100. TWIA and TDI distributed flyers to all insurance offices and owners, and new roofers would think they were getting a bargain by hiring the TDI inspectors. This generally turned out to be a very costly mistake.

TDI inspectors will not let shingle applications start unless they are present. This may hold a roof job up to two to three days before the TDI inspector could get to the roof. If a nail gun was used, the shingles were rarely accepted, and the roofer was forced to tear them off and renail new shingles with hand hammers. Applying shingles with hammers takes over twice as long as with an air gun. The roofer and owner would soon find out that using TDI for free would cost them almost double for the roof job. The new roofers learned very quickly not to use TDI free inspectors and would gladly pay the $250 to $300 fee for doing reroof certifications with an appointed engineer.

Hurricane Dolly hit in July of 2008 directly on South Padre Island. In September of that same year Hurricane Ike hit directly on Galveston Island and proceeded up Interstate 45 toward Houston. Like Dolly, Ike was not a Category 3 storm and had maximum winds of 110 mph. But Galveston Island has ten times the populations of South Padre Island, and the surrounding cities are much more populated than Cameron County, where Dolly hit.

After Ike hit Galveston, TDI closed their office in Harlingen and moved all inspectors to the Galveston-Houston area. Those roofers and homeowners who had started working with TDI were basically out of service, and because it may have been days or weeks before a TDI inspector could look at their roof, almost all of those roofers and owners turned to the private appointed engineers to get their work finished.

Generally a private engineer would not touch a property once TDI inspectors had looked at them because they risked being put under audit if the roof was anything less than perfect. The TDI inspection process is to have the roofer apply one or two bundles of shingles and then hold for the inspector. If the inspector finds any overdriven or crooked nails, they will ask the roofer to make corrections. TDI will never write on their field form that the roof needs to be redone. They just state that corrections are needed. If the roofer complains, TDI will offer for the roofer to get a private engineer to finish the inspection process. This is where TDI is at their most insidious behavior.

Offering for the roofer or owner to get an engineer to finish the inspections is nothing less than fraud and entrapment. TDI inspectors will not tell the roofer or owner that the roof is rejected and will not be accepted unless the shingles are taken off and new shingles applied. They do not tell the owner or roofer that if they get an appointed engineer to finish the inspection process and that engineer accepts the roof that TDI will still reject the engineer's certification and require the roof cover to be taken off and redone. Then if the engineer cannot get the roof replaced, TDI will take enforcement action against the engineer in a state office of administrative hearings (SOAH) court.

I would soon find out how this process worked when I accepted four roofs that had previously been inspected by TDI and found deficient. This does not mean that the roofs were deficient; it just means that TDI applied their incorrect air-gun-driven-nail criteria established by Watt and rejected the roof. In only one of the instances did I or my employees even know that TDI had already looked at the roofs.

As a rule CASA would look up any new address on the TDI website to see if it was active. TDI had a status tool on their website where the public could check the status of any job that had been started and see if it was active, certified, or flagged—meaning held for review by TDI Engineering. Once TDI accepts a job, they list the property on their website as active until the property is certified or the file is closed. The trouble with this system during Dolly and Ike is that the input operators were not keeping up with the field activity. The job may have already been finished days before it showed up on the website. On only one of the four roofs that I accepted was there any evidence that TDI had looked at the roof. At Shadowbrook in Harlingen, the roofer had given the CASA inspector, Chris Hamby, the TDI field form showing insufficient work. On this job the roofer was an installer for Lowe's, and he showed Hamby where he had made corrections. Hamby verified the corrections were made and then randomly inspected six or seven other areas and then turned in the paperwork to CASA, listing the work as acceptable.

At this time CASA had ten employees, and all inspectors were college graduates. Manny Ramirez Jr. had been with me since 2001 and had a BS in mechanical engineering from UTPA. Juan Salinas had been with me since 2003 and had an associate's in drafting design and technology and was pursuing a degree in civil engineering from TAMUK. Andrew Torres had an associate's in drafting design and technology from TSTC and was pursuing a civil engineering degree from TAMUK. Bryant de la Cruz had a BS and MS in mechanical engineering from UTPA and was pursuing a master's in structural engineering. Chris Hamby had a BS in civil engineering from UTSA and had his own construction company. Hamby had built custom homes for several years and had them windstorm certified. This was the caliber of inspectors working for CASA and all with over five years of construction experience when they worked for CASA in 2008.

By contrast, none of the TDI inspectors had engineering backgrounds. Welch Watt, the current head of the TDI inspection program in 2008, had a degree in economics from Texas A&M, but no background in engineering. Those inspectors who remained in the TDI program after 2003 when TDI adopted the I codes and went to design versus prescriptive were the ones who were willing to do Watts's bidding. If any one of them challenged or stood up to Watt, they soon found themselves on probation or hounded until they left the program.

I would find out about the conflicts with the four reroofs when I got the first of numerous letters from Sam Nelson, chief engineer for TDI, stating that I had accepted a roof with "known deficiencies" and that I must provide evidence that the deficiencies were corrected. All of the letters ended with the same sentence, "Pursuant to 38.0001 of the Texas Insurance Code, please provide us with a complete response in writing no later than ten days after the date of receipt."

This is the same kind of statement that one would find on a traffic ticket or parking fine. The consequences of ignoring it on a traffic ticket or parking fine means that the recipient gives up the right to contest the fine, or a penalty fine will be accrued until paid. With TDI, not complying with the ten-day request could have the engineer guilty of being nonresponsive and subject to being removed from the appointment list. This will be discussed in great detail in future chapters.

At the time I got the first letters from Nelson, I was in the middle of the busiest time of my life. My workload had been increased threefold, and the amount of correspondence and reports I reviewed were in the hundreds per month. On top of that I was flying to Houston and doing inspection work in the Galveston area on two of the largest projects that I had picked up from the restoration companies that were impressed with my knowledge and work. I was also inspecting a large new construction condominium project I had picked up from a contractor, GT Leach, who had erected the largest condominium in

South Padre Island in 2008 with CASA as the inspector and wanted to use the same team in Galveston.

The ten-day rule did not state calendar days or workdays, and many times the information needed to respond to the letters was not readily available. TDI would not supply a list of the known deficiencies, and the engineer has to go through Freedom of Information request format to obtain the information on the residence in question. I missed several of the ten-day deadlines, never deliberately, and in several instances my receptionist had put the letter on my desk with several other letters, and I never saw them. Once the secretary signed for the certified receipt letter, the time clock began even though I might not have read the letter for several days if I was out of town when the letter came. The section 38.001 is taken from the administrative code and is outside the scope of the act that created the windstorm certification program. Section 38.001, the section that is written at the end of each TDI letter of inquiry, reads as follows:

> Sec. 38.001. INQUIRIES. (a) In this section, "authorization" means a permit, certificate of registration, or other authorization issued or existing under this code.
> (b) The department may address a reasonable inquiry to any insurance company, including a Lloyd's plan or reciprocal or interinsurance exchange, or an agent or other holder of an authorization relating to:
> (1) the person's business condition; or
> (2) any matter connected with the person's transactions that the department considers necessary for the public good or for the proper discharge of the department's duties.
> (c) A person receiving an inquiry under Subsection (b) shall respond to the inquiry in writing not later than the 15th day after the date the inquiry is received.

The intention is for insurance agents who have a complaint filed against them to respond to the complaint in a timely manner or lose the right to appeal the complaint and allow the complainant to get the insurance adjustment denied. For example, if a homeowner disagreed with an insurance settlement and protested it, the insurance agent would have ten days to address the protest. This is similar to the previous example of a recipient of a traffic citation having ten days to respond or pay the fine.

TDI interprets the use of the term "agent" in 38.001 to include appointed engineers. They treat appointed engineers as their agents despite the fact that all engineers are governed by the legislatively created occupations code under the Texas Board of Professional Engineers. TDI can no more place a ten-day demand on engineers any more than they could place the same demand on an attorney or even a plumber who TDI has a problem with because he did a poor job unplugging their toilets. Just because the plumber worked on TDI's commodes does not make him an agent of TDI. This is not my sole opinion; all three attorneys who worked on my case with TDI had the same opinion. George Powell would later write about it at length in his response to TDI rulings.

It is easier to appeal an IRS ruling than to appeal a TDI decision. At least in most IRS cases, they will follow the law. TDI was inhabited by bureaucratic individuals who epitomized the Peter Principle of having way surpassed their level of competence.

When I received the TDI letters alleging known defects, I would request through Freedom of Information Act and receive the TDI field reports one or two days later. The field forms were not accompanied by any pictures and most simply stated that all slopes had overdriven or crooked nails. The form would never state the roof had to be replaced even if the inspection was done at reroof completion. The TDI field inspections typically stated that corrections were needed, implying that any deficiencies could be corrected without removing the whole roof.

To all TDI letters, I issued the basis of my certification and provided the reports and photos of all the areas that had been inspected. These reports and photos taken by CASA inspectors did not reveal any overdriven or crooked nails, and there was no reason to do further investigation or not accept the roof. The following two homes are given to illustrate the process.

PLUMOSA, HARLINGEN, TEXAS

At this home CASA received a request from a roofer to inspect a home that was already completed. The roofer stated that he was unable to get TDI inspectors because they were all in the Galveston area after Ike. There was no listing for this address on the TDI website, so the roof was inspected by CASA employee Juan Salinas and accepted.

After WPI-2 was turned in, TDI sent their first letter to CASA stating that CASA had accepted a roof with known deficiencies, implying that CASA was aware of TDI previous reports and chose to ignore them. The letter then stated that CASA needed to provide evidence that corrections had been made.

CASA responded that no deficient nails were observed in their inspections and provided the reports and product approval as requested by TDI.

TDI then responded that CASA's reply was not sufficient, that CASA needed to provide evidence that roof deficiencies had been corrected. CASA's reply was they found no deficiencies, and TDI would have to show them what it was calling overdriven and crooked nails.

I, in the meantime, went and personally inspected this roof with Juan Salinas and found no defects and submitted those photos to TDI as well.

TDI then sent field inspector Dough Klopfenstein, who is not an engineer, to meet with CASA employees Manny Ramirez and Juan Salinas in November of 2009. Doug Klopfenstein first observed the areas that CASA had inspected and found no deficiencies; he then proceeded to lift over fifty shingles until he found evidence of what he called overdriven nails. These nails had been put on with an air gun, and the nailhead had compressed the surface. Doug Klopfenstein was incorrectly calling this overdriven.

TDI then sent me a letter reiterating that deficiencies existed and requested a plan of action from CASA to have them corrected because I had accepted this roof with those deficiencies. This made no sense at all. The letter should have been directed to the home-owner or the roofer, the only two entities that could correct any deficiencies on this roof, but they sent the letter to me because they considered me, the engineer, to be their agent.

I responded that I did not agree with Doug Klopfenstein's findings but would notify the owner that their roof was not going to be accepted by TDI unless the roof was replaced. I then sent a letter to TDI asking that his WPI-2 be rescinded because TDI was not going to accept it, and the WPI-2 was based on the correct information that I had at the time that the roof was okay. I had previously sent in requests to have certifications withdrawn when I discovered either incorrect addresses or deficiencies were uncovered in future inspections that were not verifiable before. A most notable instance was when a homeowner elected to do a nail over to the existing shingles. A nail over is allowed by code and TDI. The existing shingles remain in place, and the new shingles are placed on top. There is no verifying of felt or substructure when a nail over is done.

On the one instance in question, CASA had certified the nail over shingles based on proper nail placement and adherence. When I later did an inspection on the home for a real estate transaction, I noted in the attic that the shingles were placed over spaced battens and not solid decking. Over half the nails were not into wood sheathing but only into the existing wood shingles. I notified Welch Watt and asked for the windstorm certification to be rescinded, and Watt complied. So asking for a WPI-2 to be withdrawn is not unheard of or without precedence.

But in times when an engineer is being unduly scrutinized, TDI gets amnesia. They tend to forget all their past practices where similar occurrences had been accepted. When confronted with the previous evidence, TDI will just play dumb and pretend it never happened.

TDI denied my request to withdraw the WPI-2 and once again asked for a plan of action from me to get the roof at Plumosa corrected. I forwarded TDI's letter in a certified letter to the homeowner and roofer and advised them that TDI was not going to accept their roof and issue a windstorm certification. I replied to TDI and sent copies of the certified letter to Sam Nelson with TDI.

Nelson responded that I was responsible for the roof because I had accepted it and that I must work with the current roofer or a new roofer to get the roof cover replaced. In other words, they were ordering me to get the roof fixed—this despite the fact that I did not get involved in the roof until it was replaced.

At this point, I consulted an attorney, Jerry Arriaga. Arriaga was not only an attorney, he was also a professional engineer and was on the windstorm appointment list. Mr. Arriaga sent a letter to TDI requesting by what authority they could force me to enter into a contract with a roofer or homeowner. TDI responded in typical fashion. They did not answer Mr. Arriaga's question; they just demanded I give all information on all jobs that I had been audited on. Arriaga supplied this information and asked again by what authority or code reference they could force me to enter into a contract.

To this date, TDI has never responded to that letter. Even by their own law, they had ten days to do so. When I reiterated that I could not legally do anything to a roof I did not own, TDI sent a letter referring me to enforcement for accepting a roof with known defects even though they had no evidence that I knew of any defects nor had one of the TDI engineers visited the site and verified deficient nails.

I had met several times with the homeowner of Plumosa, and the homeowner did not hold me responsible for the work. On my last visit to the site, the homeowner pointed out that all of the shingles that were lifted by TDI's Doug Klopfenstein did not reseal and had curled up in the cold weather. It is normal for unsealed shingles to curl in cold weather, but this would not have happened if Doug Klopfenstein had not broken the seal of the shingles and then not resealed them with roof cement. The only people who caused harm to this roof were the TDI inspectors lifting shingles and not resealing them.

After several months the homeowner reached an agreement with the roofer, and the roofer agreed to a new roof cover. The new roof cover was inspected by CASA, and a WPI-2 was issued, and the roof was certified. This should have been the end, but TDI's enforcement complaint against me for this roof remained in force.

SHADOWBROOK, HARLINGEN, TEXAS

This reroof was done by the Lowe's contractor representative. Lowe's will guarantee the shingles if their contractor installs them. This residence had new shingles replaced after Dolly. The roof was inspected by TDI, who gave their field form to the contractor. The TDI inspection found deficiencies at the perimeters and edges. The contractor corrected the deficiencies, and because the TDI representatives were in Galveston and no longer available, the contractor called CASA to finish the inspection.

Chris Hamby of CASA met with the contractor and reviewed the corrections and verified that they had been made. He then looked at six or seven more locations and found the shingles and nails to be proficient. He then turned in his field reports to me, and I accepted the reports and signed the WPI-2.

Soon after, I received my first letter from TDI similar to Plumosa, informing me that I had accepted a roof with known deficiencies and that I needed to provide evidence that the deficiencies had been corrected.

I responded with the CASA field report from Hamby showing that corrections had been made. TDI then responded with another letter that the roof vents had been installed incorrectly. I researched the roof vents and met the roofer at the jobsite. The roofer had the manufacturer's information on the vents, which recommend 1¼" nails. The TDI product evaluation for this vent recommended 1½" nails even though other models from the same manufacturer listed 1¼" nails for securing the vent. For the vents on this roof, the nails were penetrating the roof almost ½". Adding another ¼" to the length of the nail would not accomplish anything once the nail completely penetrated the decking. Any length over that does not add to the value of the withdrawal capacity of the nail. The way tests are run in the lab depends on manufacturer's preference. If a nail length is not specified by a manufacturer, the testing lab will use whatever length nail they have on hand to run the test. The big problem here is that once the test data is recorded, TDI will record the product evaluation as having to have that length of nail. The product evaluation should read, "Use 8d nails with length sufficient to penetrate roof-deck ¼"." Any responsible engineer would interpret the data this way, but the bureaucrats at TDI will interpret it that if you use anything other than what was used in the test, then it is not allowed, even if it is a bigger or stronger fastener.

Once I presented photos of the nails at the vents penetrating the roof-deck over ¼", TDI accepted the vents.

While I was meeting with the roofer, I was presented a copy of the shipping order that the roofer had for the shingles he used to replace the edge shingles. Because it was his only copy and we were at the jobsite, I took a photo of the shipping order and sent it to TDI as part of the evidence of corrections that had been made. The roofer also described the TDI inspection that was originally done on the roof. He stated that because it was a steep roof, the TDI inspector only inspected the edges of the roof. So the roofer and I looked at several of the shingles at the center of the roof, and they were all okay. At this time the majority of the shingles had sealed, and the roofer and I only inspected the shingles that could be lifted without damaging the shingles.

I sent all of this documentation to TDI, and TDI requested an additional inspection. The roofer and I met TDI at the residence. I showed the TDI representative, Daniel Cantu, where all the corrections had been made, and Cantu agreed with the findings and that corrections had been made. Cantu then went straight to one area of the roof where the shingles were all well sealed and asked the roofer to lift the shingles at this area. The roofer had to use a spatula and a hammer to break the shingle seals to examine the roof. All of the shingles in this area had nails in a high position that was not approved by this shingle manufacturer even though this nail location had been approved by several other manufacturers. Cantu stated that this was not an acceptable application, and he could not accept these shingles.

While Cantu was writing his report, I discussed with the roofer his options. He could make isolated repairs or do a nail over on the entire roof. The roofer stated that Lowe's would not accept a nail over, so he was just going to replace the entire roof. I informed Cantu before he left the site, and I then sent a final letter to TDI stating that the roofer had agreed to reroof the roof. The roofer also wanted TDI to inspect the reroof so that there was no chance the roof would have to be done again if TDI and CASA disagreed on the nail installation.

Welch Watt with TDI contacted me and instructed me to submit a letter removing my name as engineer of record so that TDI could take over the inspections on the new roof to be installed. I complied even though the request was unreasonable and not needed. TDI previously told me in the Plumosa correspondence that I could not request to be removed as engineer of record for Plumosa.

The roof was replaced, and TDI inspected and certified it, and that should have been the end of it, but the enforcement action remained in place against me.

During this in time in 2011, I attended a legal seminar in Austin that was specifically for engineering legal issues. The subject of the windstorm appointment process and the WPI-2 came up frequently. All of the presenters, who were all attorneys, agreed that the process was unfair, and they all recommended not signing the WPI-2. One attorney even recommended having an older engineer who was ready to retire sign the form. This was ridiculous advice, but it belied the entire problem with the program. The WPI-2 is an absolute document where the engineer of record is certifying all portions of the wind provisions of the code, literally every nail. The problem is there are no absolutes in construction, and no "qualified inspector" can truly be responsible for every nail. Windstorm appointed engineers are given an impossible task of signing a document that can be used against them if one bad nail is later found. I would soon find out how onerous this document can be, and how abusive TDI can be.

EMERALD BY THE SEA, GALVESTON, TEXAS, AND SUNTIDE III, SOUTH PADRE ISLAND, TEXAS

These two projects forever changed my relationship with TDI and ultimately were the catalyst for the writing of this book. On these two projects, I experienced the unbridled abuse of power by a state agency that can best be compared to the recent 2012 IRS scandal where Tea Party and Conservative groups were targeted and harassed by the IRS, leading to the chief officer, Lois Lerner, pleading the Fifth in a senate hearing.

I was already on shaky ground with TDI after the enforcement referrals with Plumosa and Shadowbrook. Many of the engineers in the appointment list had similar experiences after Dolly and Ike and many were forced to pay for reroofs out of their own pockets to avoid enforcement action by TDI. If I had paid for the reroofs at Plumosa and Shadowbrook out of my pocket, I would not have had enforcement action taken against me. This will be expounded on later.

Emerald by the Sea, Galveston, Texas

Because of my reputation and experience, I was referred to a large general contractor who was building the largest condominium on the Texas Gulf Coast, Sapphire Condominiums on South Padre Island. This condominium is thirty-two stories with twin towers. The contractor, GT Leach, contracted with CASA to do the windstorm inspection and certification. The building had been structurally designed by SCA engineers from Houston, one of the premier structural engineering firms in the country. The building was cast-in-place concrete with slip-form construction where one floor gets poured and the forms are slipped up to the next floor.

This project began in 2007 and was completed in 2008. At the same time GT Leach started another high-rise condominium in Galveston, Diamond Beach. Leach had a good working relationship with CASA and contracted with CASA to do the inspections. At that time CASA had picked up restoration work from the contractors who had come to South Padre Island after Hurricane Dolly. The restoration work was for all the damage from Hurricane Ike.

In 2009, I traveled to Houston every other week and sometimes more to survey and inspect the projects CASA had in the area. In addition, CASA had other inspectors traveling to Houston frequently during 2009.

When Diamond was finishing in late 2009, I was asked by Leach to represent them in a dispute with the homeowners association and lending institution for another high-rise condominium in Galveston, Emerald by the Sea.

Emerald had begun in 2007 with Leach as the contractor. The same developer had developed Sapphire, Diamond Beach, and Emerald and apparently had an affinity for precious stones. The Emerald contract specified that the owner would provide the windstorm inspection and certification services. This is typically how engineering services are handled, through the owner, and typically the design engineer will do his own inspections. The structural engineer for Emerald was also SCA. SCA as a company had chosen not to join the appointment list for TDI. They correctly reasoned that the TDI form WPI-2 required standards that were typically specialty items such as windows and roofs, and they did not want the liability for inspecting and certifying components and cladding that they did not design.

The homeowners had begun the project with a firm in League City, Norex Engineering, with Michael Scanlon as the engineer of record. After the project was started, Scanlon backed out and withdrew his WPI-1. The project continued until completion without an engineer. The project finished the month before Ike hit, and when Ike hit, there was only minor leakage, and the homeowners association filed an insurance claim against TWIA.

When the claim was filed, the homeowners association realized that they did not have a WPI-8 windstorm certification. The homeowners associated appealed to Scanlon to take back the job as engineer of record. At that time the lending institution, IBC Bank, had taken over as majority owner for the homeowners association from the developer. IBC could not get the units sold without a WPI-8 because the condominium owners could not get contents insurance without the building having a windstorm certification.

IBC contracted Scanlon to obtain all the information needed to certify the buildings. After gathering information from the home-owners association and making several site inspections, Scanlon determined that there were several areas of leaking at the windows and that the stucco cladding had not been tested for the pressures of a 160-foot-tall building in a 130 mph zone. Within TDI, there were very few product evaluations for stucco cladding, and those that were available were for residential use for structures less than 30 feet high.

Having no TDI-approved product to match the stucco applica-tion, Scanlon had a local testing lab in Houston, Force Engineering, conduct a pressure test on a full-height sample twenty feet high, which matched the tallest section in the building at the penthouse. These tests did not achieve the design pressures for the maximum pressures on the building.

GT Leach had their tests conducted by Hurricane Test Lab (HTL) from Lubbock. The HTL tests passed maximum pressures with minimal deflection. Scanlon dismissed the HTL tests and took the position that the stucco cladding would have to be removed and replaced, a task that would cost millions of dollars.

It was at this point that Leach got me involved. Leach forwarded all the correspondence to me and asked me to evaluate the test data.

I evaluated both sets of test data and interviewed both test labs. Force Engineering had run a full-height sample which would exceed the design capacity of the metal studs. When structures are designed, the main frame wind-resistant system is designed based on strength of materials and maximum spans. Steel, concrete, and wood all have design strengths which are conservative and repeatable. For instance, structural steel design strength has always been 0.6 times the yield force. All steel is tested in batches at the steel mill to assure the yield strength is in the desired strength range. Therefore, safety factors are approximately 1.5. The materials that attach to the main frame wind-resistant system, the components, and cladding have a lot more variable, such as fasteners into different substrates. Anytime a fas-tener is field applied, it is subject to operator error such as overdrill-ing or overspacing, and therefore fasteners are always rated by their ultimate strength divided by factor of safety of 3. For instance, if a nail into wood is tested at withdrawal capacity of 300 lb, the result would be divided by factor of safety of 3, and the design capacity for nail would be 100 lb.

If a component such as a door or window is to be tested on steel studs, the fasteners used would already have a factor of safety of 3, and then the entire assembly would then have a factor of safety of 1.5 for the wall substrate. A typical test for a window would have the window attached to requested substrate, steel, wood, or concrete, the window would then be subjected to increasing load until failure, and then the load would be divided by the factor of safety of 1.5, and that would be the rating given to the window.

The above is a very lengthy explanation for testing but will serve to illustrate why there were significant differences in the tests conducted by HTL and Force Engineering. The tests conducted by Force were on full-height studs as directed by Scanlon, and the limiting factor in test would be the deflection in the studs. The stucco cracked in the test when the full-height studs began to deflect.

The test conducted by HTL followed American Society of Testing Materials (ASTM) protocol for testing stucco using a 4' × 8' section of wall to test the stucco. This eliminated the studs as a factor so that only the stucco is being tested.

After I interviewed both testing labs and reviewed both sets of conflicting data, I logically concluded that the HTL tests were more indicative of the properties of the stucco and a third set of tests by a different lab be performed to verify this conclusion. I wrote a letter to IBC, and a meeting was set up at the Emerald with IBC, Scanlon, CASA, and GT Leach.

Prior to the meeting, I was contacted by Scanlon and was told by Scanlon that the building was okay except for the stucco. Scanlon stated that everything else had already been approved but that the stucco would never be approved.

The meeting was held in October of 2009, and I met all of the parties including the vice president of construction for IBC, Jennifer Hoff, Mike Scanlon, and Vicki Huckaby of Norex Engineering. The meeting ended with an agreement to do new tests. IBC agreed to have the tests done by HTL of Miami, Florida, because they had a lot of experience testing components and cladding for high-rises in the Miami area.

It took months to just adopt a test protocol, and a meeting was held at TDI in Austin with all parties to discuss the steps needed to get Emerald certified. The meeting was conducted by Scanlon, who insisted that the building would need new stucco.

After the meeting, I had a one-on-one with Hoff and her attorney and assured them that based on the previous HTL tests that the stucco tests would pass. There were already tests performed by the stucco supplier that met the pressures.

The tests were finally run in May of 2010, and as predicted, they passed with minimal deflection for 16-gauge studs at 16 inches OC and 12-gauge studs at 12 inches OC. Instead of accepting that data and certifying the building, Scanlon refused and questioned the validity of the test. It was at this point that Jennifer Hoff contacted me and asked if I would take over as engineer of record.

I did not want the job because TDI was already involved in the project. I visited the site and found it to be in sound condition. I interviewed the project manager for GT Leach and was assured that all records were available. Above all, I did not want to go through an audit with TDI on a project this size. I decided to take the job when I was told by Jennifer Hoff that she was assured by Sam Nelson that whoever certified the building, Scanlon or Day, that the building would be certified. Another deciding factor was that Vicki Huckaby, who had worked on Emerald with Scanlon, had left Norex Engineering and contacted me and said that she would help with the certification records.

I received a signed contract with IBC and turned in a WPI-1 for Emerald. I then arranged to meet with GT Leach at their office in Houston and obtained all the records for the construction of Emerald. I was given two file boxes of records to review. The boxes contained records for the structure and components and cladding, and also there were full sets of construction drawings for architectural and structural. SCA was the structural engineer. While discussing the project with Leach, I was surprised to learn that Scanlon had never visited Leach's office during his investigation of Emerald nor had he requested the construction records. Whatever Scanlon had would not have been near enough to make an informed decision to certify Emerald.

I made two more trips to Emerald and spent a total of four days touring the site. There had been a water leak at the thirteenth floor, and the Sheetrock had been taken off the wall. I was able to verify the fastener patterns for the stucco, the metal studs, and the windows where the Sheetrock was removed. The roof was fully adhered, and there were numerous construction photographs from the contractor and the architect detailing the placement of the roofing material.

At this point I was confident that I had enough records and evidence to certify the building and even pass muster with TDI if needed. I turned in the WPI-2 and two days later was notified by TDI that a complaint had been turned in by Scanlon. The WPI-2 has two boxes that can be checked. The first box is a statement that the building was designed and constructed to meet the wind provisions of the code. The second box states that the structure does not meet the provisions. This box is accompanied by a footnote that requires supporting documentation if the second box is checked. Scanlon checked the second box, signed and sealed the document, and turned it into TDI without any supporting documentation or explanation.

Upon receiving the document from Scanlon, Sam Nelson notified me that Emerald would be put under full audit. Neither Nelson nor Watt demanded that Scanlon supply an explanation. Nelson should be made to answer why Scanlon was never requested to support his WPI-2 condemning the Emerald.

I supplied all records to TDI and a letter that Scanlon had written that stated that the only problems he had found with the building were the stucco coating and the leaks around the windows. The leaks were maintenance issues that were under warranty by GT Leach; the stucco siding had already been tested and passed with minimal deflection. TDI should have accepted all of the data on face value, but instead they demanded the backup tests for all the windows which had Miami-Dade NOAs. They also wanted the stucco which had been tested on 16-gauge studs at 16 inches OC and 12-gauge studs at 12 inches OC to be tested on 16-gauge studs at 8 inches OC. TDI's rationale for testing the stucco on 16-gauge studs at 8 inches OC is that the code stated that material tests be conducted on the least material properties to be used in the assembly. The TDI assertion was that the fastener attachment to the metal stud was the determining factor in the stucco pressure tests, despite the fact that there are numerous tests on fasteners into 16-gauge metal that far exceeded the corner zone capacities for the metal studs. Because corner pressures are higher at the corner than at the interior portion of a building for floors up to 10 feet in height, the 16-gauge studs were spaced 8 inches OC at the corner zone and 16 inches OC for the rest of the building wall. For floors over 10 feet in height, 12-gauge studs at 12 inches OC were used. For convenience, 12-gauge studs were used in both corner and interior sections of building walls. The deflection of the stucco between the studs is the only thing that should have been of concern to TDI in the tests. If the stucco did not deflect at 12 inches OC, there was no chance that it would deflect at 8 inches OC. This is a test that would be guaranteed to pass, but nonetheless TDI wanted it to be run.

It is my opinion that TDI exercised this unreasonable unbridled power in an effort to break the engineer and end the audit process because most owners will not pay for expensive tests, approximately $20,000 per test to verify a product. But in the situation with Emerald, a bank, IBC, needed the building certified to sell the units. IBC and Jennifer Hoff were willing to pay for all the extra tests that TDI requested.

When it became obvious that TDI was requesting needless tests because the tests kept passing without even being close, Alexis Dick, the director of Windstorm Inspections, finally overruled Nelson and his henchmen and stopped the request for tests. Dick did, however, demand that all the leaks be fixed prior to issuing the WPI-8. It is not within TDI's jurisdiction to make such a claim. The WPI-8 is for the windstorm provisions of the code only. Sealants, flashing, and caulking are not structural windstorm issues and should not be under the purview of TDI.

It took another six months for Emerald to have all the windows rehabbed. So from the time that I got involved in the Emerald in October of 2009 to the time it was certified was approximately one and a half years and a cost of hundreds of thousands of dollars to Emerald and IBC. Not one structural item on the building changed.

Not one component varied from the tests that I had turned in. No commercial building in Texas has been put under the scrutiny that Emerald was put under and for no reason other than Mike Scanlon out of pure spite turned in a bogus WPI-2 stating that the building did not comply with the wind provisions of the code, and he was not made to answer why.

Suntide III, South Padre Island, Texas

Suntide III is a twelve-story condominium that was built in the early 1980s. The type of construction typical for South Padre Island is load-bearing concrete masonry unit (CMU) walls with prestressed hollow core planks (HCPs) for the floors and roof-deck. The HCPs for balconies and walkways are exposed to the salt air environment. The salt content in the air is second only to Bahrain in the Middle East and is highest in the United States. The reason for high salt contents is the shallowness of the gulf at South Padre Island and the warm temperature of the water.

CASA had been involved with Suntide III since 2007, when they were asked to evaluate the concrete spalling at the balcony HCPs. Prevalent at this time on South Padre Island, all of the construction from the early eighties, when there was a building boom at South Padre Island, was experiencing salt-induced corrosion on the reinforcement steel in HCPs. The prestressed tendons when corroding gain volume due to the increase in oxygen in the steel. As the tendons gain volume, they create a tensile force on the concrete cover which causes it to debond or spall.

When Hurricane Dolly hit in 2008, the building received extensive damage including loss of roof cover. The roof cover was a 60-mil single-ply TPO (thermoplastic polyolefin) membrane that was fully adhered and had been installed several years prior. Neither CASA nor I had been involved in the roof membrane that had blown off. Since I was already familiar with the building and knew how much damage was preexisting, the restoration contractor, Paramount, chose to work with me to certify the windstorm portions of the damage—for example, windows, doors, roofing, and siding. Numerous windows and doors had to be replaced, and a complete reroof had to be done as well.

Because insurance only pays for like, kind, and quality, the owners and Paramount chose CentiMark Roofing to put on a new 60-mil TPO roof membrane. This work was done in late 2008. The roof was inspected by Hamby and me of CASA.

The new roof covering consisted of removing all of existing roof cover to original concrete substrate. The parapet walls had an original aluminum-oxide-coated fabric fully adhered to the CMU parapet wall. The membrane was fully adhered and would not come off without a grinder. Once the damaged roofing was removed, a tapered insulation system of polyicynene (IsoBoard) foam was fully adhered with glue to the concrete floor. The IsoBoard was then covered with half-inch-thick cement-treated Sheetrock known as DensGlass. The IsoBoard comes in 4' × 4' sheets, and the DensGlass comes in 4' × 8' sheets. The DensGlass provides a more uniform surface to adhere the TPO membrane. After the IsoBoard and DensGlass were fully adhered with glue, the TPO membrane is then fully adhered with glue in 5' to 10' wide sheets that are heat fused at the seams to provide a 100 percent waterproof membrane. At the parapet wall a termination bar was placed to hold the horizontal sheet and the vertical sheet at the parapet wall, and the membrane was heat fused to the bottom sheet and fully adhered with glue to the parapet wall.

The company that put the roof on, CentiMark, is headquartered in Pittsburgh, Pennsylvania, and is a nationwide company. The crew that put the roof down was from Pittsburgh and had installed this similar roof system in Florida and throughout the United States. The roof was put down in late 2008. I remembered speaking to the

CentiMark foreman who was from Pittsburgh. He was not used to ninety-degree weather in November and had developed kidney stones from becoming dehydrated. The roof performed well, and after Hurricane Alex in June of 2010, which landed in Mexico, sixty miles south of South Padre Island, I was asked to inspect the roof after Alex.

Hurricane Alex produced 60 mph winds at South Padre Island and a lot of rain. A small leak had developed at the twelfth-floor condominiums below the roof. I determined the leak was from a small breach in the TPO cover at the east parapet wall from the cables used to lower the swing stage scaffold used to do routine maintenance on the walls and balconies. The breach was less than two square inches. I examined the rest of the roof and determined that it had not been affected. There were no air voids below the TPO surface, and all seams were 100 percent sealed. There had been some localized high-shear winds from Alex because numerous homes in the vicinity of Suntide III had shingles blown off.

On September 28, 2010, Tropical Storm Hermine formed in the southern gulf and headed straight for South Padre Island. It landed in the early morning of September, 29, 2010, one day after it had formed. The storm was small, producing maximum winds of 60 mph and passed through rather quickly.

Around noon on the twenty-ninth, I got a call from the restoration company asking to check the roof at Suntide III because the homeowners association had called and said the roof cover had blown off. I arrived at South Padre Island (SPI) around 2:00 p.m., and as I approached Suntide III, I saw the TPO membrane hanging over the front or west side of the building like a curtain. I met with an insurance adjuster from TWIA, and we walked the roof together.

The TPO membrane had come completely off from the east wall, where it tore cleanly from the termination bar at the top of the parapet wall and blown over the west wall almost completely intact. The majority of the DensGlass deck and the insulation layer remained intact and undisturbed. The DensGlass comes from the factory with a green fiberglass cover membrane approximately 1/32-inch thick. This membrane is what the TPO membrane gets adhered to. This membrane came off with the TPO membrane almost entirely. This indicated that the TPO was well adhered to the DensGlass, and the roof cover failed at the interface between the DensGlass fiberglass membrane and the cement-treated gypsum board. There was no indication that any portion of the roof that had been adhered in the field had failed.

The foam IsoBoard remained fastened to the concrete deck. The DensGlass cover board remained adhered to the IsoBoard. The TPO membrane remained adhered to the green fiberglass cover membrane. There was no indication that the adhesive applied in the field was improperly applied or had failed.

Still attached to the roof membrane and laying approximately fifty feet away was the aluminum roof-hatch frame. The aluminum frame was attached to two-by-four lumber which had been attached to the concrete deck. The fasteners which attached the two-by-four to the concrete deck were one-fourth-inch concrete screws at approximately eight inches OC. The screws were severely corroded, and only three had any concrete mortar attached to them. All three were at the same corner. It was obvious that the roof hatch had blown loose where only the three fasteners remained and then had enough force to break the bond between the green DensGlass fiberglass cover membrane and the gypsum base.

The roof hatch was the original hatch and had gone through Hurricane Dolly and Alex without failure. It is not common to replace hatches or AC curbs when replacing a roof. There was no indication that the hatch was defective. The aluminum structure was sound with no corrosion. The two-by-four lumber showed no signs of wood rot. The roof fasteners were concealed, and there was no visible evidence of corrosion.

What apparently happened to the roof cover during Hermine is that the hatch came loose and allowed air beneath the membrane. The pressures were sufficient to break the bond with the DensGlass and caused the entire roof cover to come off. The roof hatch had dimensions of 3' × 3' 6" with an approximate area of 10 square feet. The 60 mph winds from Hermine created approximately 20 psf pressure on the roof. The hatch is located over an open balcony and would receive both positive pressure from below and negative suction pressures from above. The hatch has a 3-inch lip all around. This lip would increase the bearing area of the hatch to approximately 15 square feet. So with only 60 mph winds, the roof hatch unsecured would be subject to 15 sf × 20 psf or 300 pounds of pressure. This pressure was enough to overcome the tested pressure of the membrane, which is 140 psf with a factor of safety of 2 or 280 lb ultimate force.

TWIA hired EFI Global to investigate the roof failure to determine if it was an insurable claim. Their engineer concluded that the membrane came off from wind and supplied a report that listed several findings including the roof hatch fasteners being corroded. He listed several other failure mechanisms but neglected to mention anything about the green fiberglass cover of the DensGlass being completely gone.

A temporary roof cover was placed on the roof by CentiMark, and the homeowners association needed a new roof put on as soon as possible. I submitted to TDI the new roof design. Because this roof cover had failed twice in previous storms, TDI put the new roof submittal under audit.

What should have been a routine submittal was rejected by TDI, and backup tests were requested by TDI on the Miami-Dade NOA that I submitted. I was supplying everything that TDI asked for when the homeowners association asked who they could complain to about the delays. I warned the owner that any attempt to get TDI to expedite the process would be met with more delays. The homeowners called TDI the next day and complained to Alexis Dick. Dick informed the owner that it was the fault of David Day for not submitting an approved product for use on the roof. The product was approved for 130 mph pressures for a twelve-story building. TDI was deliberately stalling because they did not want to put another single-ply roof on this building, but instead of stating that, they blamed me.

TWIA was only willing to pay for like, kind, and quality, and since a TPO roof cover had blown off, that is what they were obliged to pay to replace. I had already recommended asphaltic modified-bitumen built-up roof (BUR) be placed because it is a heavier roof and would not have lifted like a balloon the way the 60-mil TPO had.

The day after the owner called TDI complaining about the roof delays, Sam Nelson called the restoration contractor, Robert Ward, and told him that the roof would not get approved if they kept David Day as their engineer. He told Ward that he needed to get another engineer to certify the roof. Nelson then gave Ward the names of three engineers that he had already talked to about the Suntide III roof. The next day, October 29, 2010, Nelson called me and told me that because of "issues" with my certifications that I was going to be put under audit on all work that I did. Nelson had Welch Watt with him in his office and acknowledged him. Watt spoke up and said that I would be treated fairly in the audits and my clients would not be delayed. I specifically asked about work that had already been turned in, and Nelson, in the presence of Watt, stated that only work turned in after October, 29, 2010, would be audited.

There is nothing that legislatively empowers TDI to audit an engineer on every job he turns in. There are many things that Nelson did that he did not have legal standing to do. Nelson had grown increasingly stronger in his position as chief engineer for TDI. Nelson personally oversaw the harassment or elimination of many engineers on the appointment list. Very few engineers had the will or the funds to fight back. Nelson had an incompetent supervisor in Alexis Dick and a legal department that backed him up on every charge he brought against an engineer no matter how baseless. With each complaint Nelson successfully lodged against an engineer, he gained power in his own mind, which fed his enormous ego to the point that he actually had more power than TBPE. He saw no problem with ordering an engineer to pay for a roof even though this was totally illegal and a violation of civil law and the Engineering Practice Act. It was this continuous abuse of power that led Nelson to take me on and put me under audit on every job so he could achieve his ultimate goal of eliminating me from the appointment list because I had the unmitigated gall to challenge his authority to do illegal acts.

To assist Suntide III in getting their own roof covered, I called the three engineers that Nelson had spoken to. Nelson had not told them that this job was already under an engineer or that it was under audit. Nelson had actively sought engineers to replace me at Suntide III. This was something that totally violated the Engineering Practice

Act and was way beyond his authority at TDI. In a legitimate organization, Nelson would have been reprimanded or fired for such an abuse of power.

Because of Nelson's interference, I had to implore one of the three engineers to take on the job. David Franklin from Galveston, who had never done a twelve-story roof and had less experience than me, agreed to take on the job. I assisted him with the product submittal and the product that Franklin submitted; a BUR with modified bitumen fully adhered was selected. TDI did not request the same backup tests they had with me and did not require that the roof meet 140 mph winds. SPI had their own code and had adopted 140 mph as the design wind speed for South Padre Island. TDI only certified for 130 mph, but when I turned in a design submittal for Suntide III listing 130 mph as the design wind speed, which is all I was required to do by TDI, someone in TDI personally intervened and contacted SPI permit office and informed them that an engineer was designing a roof membrane for only 130 mph. SPI permit officers promptly contacted Suntide III and shut the job down until a design with 140 mph was submitted. SPI permit officer Jay Mitchum, who was an ex-TDI field inspector, took this action against me but did not take it against any other engineer that submitted plans to SPI. I had seen some designs submitted to SPI that didn't even have a listed wind speed or code reference accepted by Jay Mitchum. Mitchum also allowed shingles only approved for 110 mph to be used on the island because TDI accepted them. The selective enforcement by Jay Mitchum seemed to only coincide with TDI personal requests.

The Suntide III homeowners association (HOA) never blamed me for the roof blowing off and continued to work with me long after the new roof was put on after Tropical Storm Hermine. For this roof, I was exonerated by TBPE and by a state office of administrative hearing judge, both of which will be discussed in later chapters. Even though I was judged to be innocent on this roof by both TBPE and an SOAH judge, TDI never relented in their persecution of me, and this roof was the beginning of a three-year-plus trial and persecution that is still going on to this day.

Life under Audit

When I received notice that I was being put under audit on every job, I knew this would be the kiss of death for my clients and my company. This would be the equivalent of the IRS auditing every client return of a CPA. The first thing I did was get the commitment from several different engineers to oversee my work. I was able to obtain agreements from several different engineers who would certify my work. This essentially meant that my work would be audited and peer-reviewed on every project from minor reroofs to major projects. These engineers, who will remain nameless to avoid retribution and persecution by TDI, are heroes and took great risks with their own practices. But they all did so because they trusted me and knew my work was as good as or better than any engineer on the appointment list.

The second thing that I did was solicit legal advice. Gerardo Arriaga, who was both a professional engineer and an attorney, referred me to an experienced attorney, George Powell, who had been involved in insurance disputes. I met with Powell in November of 2010. Powell was mainly a personal injury attorney and was partnered with Chuy Hinojosa in McAllen. Hinojosa is currently a ranking state senator in the Texas legislature.

Powell was a University of Texas–Austin graduate and his wife was Chuy Hinojosa's sister. Powell was from North Texas but had made the Rio Grande Valley his home. Powell agreed to assist me and advised me to get my local state legislator involved. Powell also advised me to file a complaint with the board against Nelson for interfering in my projects. Powell thought the best course of action would be to get the backing of the engineering societies and the TBPE to respond to Nelson's heavy-handed tactics.

Upon Powell's advice, I contacted TBPE compliance officer C. W. Clark and described in great detail what was happening to me with TDI. Clark was sympathetic but gave the patented reply, that TDI had the legislative authority to audit engineers. I had no problem with the random audits but challenged TDI's authority to audit every job. Clark did not have an answer for that. When I specifically described Nelson's actions in Suntide III calling three engineers and the homeowners association to take over my work, Mr. Clark had a big problem with that. Clark specifically stated that if I filed a complaint, it would be acted on.

Besides working for TDI, Nelson was a registered professional engineer and was bound by the Engineering Practice Act. Nelson is also bound by the rules of ethics of TBPE. The rules of ethics are spelled out on the TBPE website, and among other things, they state that

> 131.155 (b) (4) the engineer shall: (4) conduct engineering and related business affairs in a manner that is respectful of the client, involved parties, and employees. Inappropriate behaviors or patterns of inappropriate behaviors may include but are not limited to intentional misrepresentation in billing; unprofessional correspondence or language, sale, and or performance of unnecessary work; or conduct that harasses or intimidates another party.

Nelson is certainly guilty of multiple counts of harassment and unprofessional correspondence.

I next turned to my state senator, Eddie Lucio Jr., for help. I had been the engineer of record for the home of Lucio's former chief of staff,

Paul Cowan. I had received glowing recommendations from Cowan. Cowan had retired, and Lucio's new chief of staff was Louie Sanchez. Sanchez did not have near the gravitas as Cowan and attempted to launch an internal investigation into TDI engineers by TDI employees. By the time I requested aide from Lucio's office, Nelson had been persecuting engineers for over twelve years with the aide and assistance of TDI legal staff. Sanchez approaching the TDI legal team was the equivalent of going to Lois Lerner to complain about the Cincinnati IRS field office harassing conservative groups. I have never been told what was said to Sanchez, but after his initial inquiry, Sanchez ceased contact with me and would not return phone calls, texts, or e-mails. Of all the irony, Sanchez's own mother was having trouble with TWIA certifying her windows after Dolly. She enlisted my services, and I got her windows inspected and certified by one of the outside engineers I was using. If I had turned in the windows in my own name, they would have been audited and likely turned down for punitive reasons that only applied to me. Then Sanchez's own mother would have had her home become one of the poisoned properties that could not be certified by TWIA. Sanchez could not help me, but I was willing to help Sanchez's mother. What are the odds?

Part of Sanchez's initial request for me was to write a detailed account of what had occurred between me and TDI. I compiled and produced the following letter:

> Office of Senator Eddie Lucio Jr.
> 7 North Park Plaza
> Brownsville, Texas 78521
>
> *Re: David V. Day, P.E.*
> *Texas Engineering License 82808*
>
> Senator Eddie Lucio Jr.,
>
> My name is David V. Day, PE. I have been licensed to practice engineering in Texas since 1998 and have been on the Texas Department of Insurance (TDI) list of appointed engineers for

windstorm certification since 2001. As you are familiar, the certification process for structures located in the hurricane-prone region of the state consists of fourteen (14) coastal counties. The Texas Windstorm Insurance Agency (TWIA) was created to provide a risk pool for these structures. In order to get insurance through TWIA, the structure must be certified either by a state appointed inspector or a state appointed engineer.

The reason that I am writing to you at this time is because as of October 28, 2010, I have been told by Sam Nelson, PE, of Texas Department of Insurance that all projects that I submit to TDI must have a full submittal turned in when I turn in my WPI-2. This will result in a full audit on every project I work on. This order was given without any written backup or substantiation for the order. I know of no other engineer that has to comply with this kind of scrutiny or intimidation.

Since being appointed in 2001, I have been audited over ten (10) times by TDI. Five (5) of those times were because I took over properties that had been started by other engineers who had either been forced off the appointment list or chose to resign from the list because they were not able to provide adequate plans to TDI.

There is no written policy within TDI that states that when an engineer is being audited on a property and chooses to resign from the appointment list that any engineer who chooses to take on that property will assume the audit of the resigned engineer. TDI has never answered the question if they are auditing the property or auditing the engineer. If they are auditing the property, then they are placing a burden of proof on a property owner that has no control over the process. In all five (5) cases in which I took over properties from resigned engineers, the homeowner had hired a contractor to build his home. The contractor had secured the engineer to perform windstorm design and inspection.

A TDI audit consists of turning all work products to certify a home over to TDI and getting their approval before the home can be certified. This includes but is not limited to engineering plans for all wind bracing and anchorage to foundation, calculations used to develop plans, product evaluations on all components, and cladding attached to the home such as doors, windows, garage doors, vents, and roof cover, and all inspection reports.

The average time for me to complete one of these audits was over six (6) months with the shortest time being three (3) months and the longest time being eighteen (18) months. The time length was not because I had done anything wrong but because it took that long to answer questions and prove my design. On the one project that took eighteen (18) months (46 Whooping Crane in Laguna Vista, Texas), I was told my design was wrong and to do it over. I had to hire another structural engineer, Simon Solorio of Mission, Texas, to peer-review my design. Mr. Solorio's conclusion was that my design was conservative. I also had to make a trip to Austin to defend my design at my expense. After eighteen (18) months my design was accepted, and the WPI-8 was issued by TDI. At that time the home had been complete for over one year, and the owner was forced to seek insurance outside of TWIA while the audit process was being completed. The added cost of this audit was over $12,000.

Because the contractor had gone out of business, I was not reimbursed for these expenses.

Because of this kind of scrutiny, there are no engineers that are willing to take on projects that have been flagged by TDI.

Mr. Nelson's order to me for complete data submittal came two days after one of my clients, the contractor, and homeowner representative for Suntide III Condominiums at South Padre Island, Texas, spoke to Alexis Dick, the deputy commissioner of TDI, after their project was put under audit by TDI.

This project was put under audit because it had lost two roof cover replacements in two years: the first during Hurricane Dolly on July 23, 2008, and the second during Tropical Storm Hermine on September 6, 2010. I was not involved with the roof cover that had come off during Hurricane Dolly. Suntide III received extensive damage during Hurricane Dolly that included doors, windows, privacy grating, and the roof cover. I inspected and approved the roof system that was put on after Hurricane Dolly. The roof cover that was damaged during Hurricane Dolly was a 60-mil synthetic thermoplastic poly-olefin (TPO) membrane that was fully adhered to the tapered extruded polystyrene insulation (EPS) board.

TWIA will only pay for like, kind, and quality for roof cover replacement. Because a TPO membrane had blown off, a TPO product was put back. The product submitted had a Miami-Dade product approval for over 167 psf design pressure, which includes a safety of factor of 2. The maximum design pressure required for the roof is 134.6 at 140 mph winds. TPO membrane is also considered a green roof because no hot asphalt is involved.

Prior to Hermine, South Padre Island also received tropical winds from Hurricane Alex, which made landfall sixty (60) miles south of South Padre Island. After Hurricane Alex I inspected the entire property at the request of the owner and visually inspected the entire roof. There was no damage to the roof at that time, and the TPO membrane had no voids beneath the surface. The day after Tropical Storm Hermine, I was called to Suntide III and found the majority of the roof cover torn loose from the surface and hanging over the building like a curtain. I inspected the roof with Merlin Orr, an adjuster for TWIA and several roofing contractors. The TPO membrane had torn loose from the DensGlass board that sealed the EPS. The fiberglass backing on the DensGlass had been peeled off. The DensGlass board and the EPS board remained intact. This is obviously a product failure and not an adhesive failure.

The roof at Suntide III has two roof hatches, one at the top of each stair landing. The south roof hatch was completely dislodged, and the TPO membrane was still attached to it. The fasteners connecting the roof hatch frame to the concrete roof-deck were severely corroded, and only two (2) on one corner showed evidence of adherence to the concrete. The roof hatch was 3' × 3 ½' or approximately 10 sf. If the roof hatch came loose, it would have caused a peel failure in the TPO membrane. In my opinion this is what caused the failure in the roof system.

A temporary roof cover was placed at Suntide III within one week of the roof failure. I originally recommended that a built-up asphaltic rolled roofing system be installed because it is a heavier system and less prone to complete failure. The built-up system was significantly more expensive than a TPO system, so the decision was made to install a TPO system. The roofing contractor submitted to CASA Engineering a Mule-Hide system over tapered EPS board that would be fully adhered with OlyBond 500 adhesive. I researched this product and found a Factory Mutual (FM) and Miami-Dade product approval for -150 psf with a safety factor of 2. The maximum design pressure on this roof is -134.6 psf.

The Mule-Hide company submitted an independent evaluation report from Trinity ERD giving the same design pressure of -150 psf. I submitted all of this data to TDI and was told that they needed the backup test data that was used to produce the -150 psf rating. There was also a qualification statement from Trinity ERD that reduced design pressure to -120 psf on a tapered system. The process of getting all of the backup data to TDI Engineering Department took weeks, and the contractor and HOA were becoming increasingly frustrated. They repeatedly asked me what the delay was, and each time I told them that TDI Engineering Department needed all of the backup data before they would approve the Mule-Hide system.

On October 26, 2010, I was contacted by the restoration company Triton requesting the contact information for TDI Engineering Department. I advised them that complaining to TDI would more likely inflame the process, but they insisted, and I gave them the contact information.

I received a call from Triton on the afternoon of October 26, 2010, and was told that the HOA manager had spoken directly with Alexis Dick-Paclick. Ms. Dick-Paclick told them the reason their project was being held up was that David Day had not given them a submittal that they could approve.

I was out of my office all day Wednesday and received a message that Sam Nelson had called requesting to speak with me. I returned his call Thursday morning (October 28, 2010). Mr. Nelson, with Mr. Welch Watt present, told me that because of problems with my submittals that I was now required to submit all plans, calculations, reports, product evaluations, and pictures to TDI each time I turned in a WPI-2 certification on all projects. Later that morning I was called by Triton and was told that Mr. Sam Nelson had informed them that they should get another engineer to handle their submittals, and he gave them a list of three engineers that he had already spoken to. I confirmed this by talking to two of the engineers that Mr. Nelson had called. I agreed to work with whatever engineer that Triton chose in an effort to expedite the process.

A reroof was finally started on this building on November 19, 2010. The contractor has elected to go with a built-up asphaltic system that I had recommended in the first place. TWIA has agreed to pay the increased cost of the built-up system because TDI would not grant approval on the TPO system.

The built-up system is not of "like and kind" and cost approximately $150,000 more than the TPO system. As I am no longer the engineer on the Suntide III project, it is obvious that I was not the cause for the delays.

Now every project I turn into TDI has the risk of being held up for months while I answer questions from TDI on the submittal process. I have not received anything in writing from TDI stating why I am being singled out. I know of no other engineer that has to turn in complete work product with each WPI-2 submittal.

Because of the excessive scrutiny that the TDI audit process subjects on engineers, there are very few, if any, that are now willing to take on residences that have been left in limbo by engineers that abandoned the process after the construction on the home was begun. I have been the only engineer in Cameron and Willacy County that was willing to take on audited projects. I lost thousands of dollars in time that I could not bill to the owner for answering TDI questions. Now there are no engineers in South Texas that are willing to take on audited homes. The structural engineers that have been designing large commercial structures for years are subjected to the same scrutiny as engineers who practiced in other areas of engineering prior to being placed on the TDI appointment list. There are very large, very respectable engineering firms that design multi-million-dollar structures but refuse to deal with TDI Engineering Department. Their structures are left to be inspected by small engineering firms such as CASA Engineering.

Having each of my projects submitted to TDI is the equivalent of a CPA submitting all of his work to the IRS. How many clients would be expected to stay with a CPA that would be subject to that type of scrutiny? Like the tax code, the building codes are subject to interpretation, and if my interpretations differ than those of TDI Engineering Department, my projects can be held up for months while the process is being resolved. This process will likely cause great harm to my company. I have been given nothing in writing from TDI and have had no accusations of wrongdoing or incompetence.

The Engineering Practice Act section 137.63, "Engineers's Responsibility to the Profession," states in section (B) (5) the engineer shall: (5) "conduct engineering and related business affairs in a manner that is respectful of the client, involved parties, and employees. Inappropriate behaviors or patterns of inappropriate behaviors may include, but are not limited to, misrepresentation in billing; unprofessional correspondence or language; sale and/or performance of unnecessary work; or conduct that harasses or intimidates another party."

I consider the actions of the TDI Department of Engineering towards me to be harassment, and I do not feel any professional engineer should be subjected to what I have been subjected to by the TDI Engineering Department. Because of TDI's propensity towards retribution on engineers that they feel aren't meeting their arbitrary standards, I feel that a confidential survey of all TDI-appointed engineers should be conducted immediately to determine if any other engineers are being harassed and to also judge the competence of the TDI Engineering Department.

I know of no avenue to address grievances with the TDI Engineering Department, and that is why I am forced at this time to write this letter and copy it to my attorney and to the Texas Board of Professional Engineers for further action.

Attached to this letter is a sampling of the projects that I have had audited by TDI, the reason given, and the outcome. Also attached to this letter are reference letters and correspondence with TDI.

Should you have any questions or concerns regarding this letter, feel free to contact me.

Thank you.

Ironically, I compared my plight to the plight of a CPA having every return audited. This letter should have raised some concerns with Senator Lucio. As requested, a simple inquiry into Nelson's behavior would have revealed dozens of instances where Nelson abused his power. The trouble is that no engineer was willing to go on the record with their complaints against Nelson for the simple reason, they did not want happening to them what was happening to me. The only way to uncover the truth would be to have an independent survey of Nelson's performance from appointed engineers, whose names would remain anonymous. To date, there has been no known outside inquiry into Nelson's behavior.

I followed through with my attorney's advice and filed a complaint with TBPE. The complaint was 140 pages long and gave detailed evidence of Nelson's abuse of office including his intervention at Suntide III and his letters stating that I was responsible for the roof at Plumosa despite the fact that the roof was complete when I first inspected it.

I gave considerably more evidence than TDI ever gave in the numerous complaints they filed against engineers at Nelson's request. Public records show that numerous engineers were sanctioned by the board based on complaints turned in by TDI. I made a habit of calling each engineer who had been sanctioned by the board and got a similar story from the majority of them. The typical complaint filed by TDI is that the engineer of record had filed a WPI-2 on a structure with known deficiencies similar to my handling of Plumosa or that the engineer could not substantiate his design such as TDI attempted to do to me at Emerald by the Sea. I got similar stories from all of the engineers that I interviewed. They had done their job with due diligence, and TDI had audited them and found their work deficient as in shingles with overdriven nails, or the calculations they provided were not enough to meet TDI standards. All of the engineers I contacted felt they were innocent and from the details that they provided, they were innocent. They just didn't have the will or the money to defend themselves. They were offered a minimal fine of $500 to $1,000 and six months of probation by the board. The fee to fight TDI could run well over $100,000 as I was to find out.

The board took over six months to investigate my complaint and did not call one of the witnesses or references that I provided. In the end, I received a letter from C. W. Clark with one paragraph stating that the complaint was dismissed for lack of evidence and that the case was closed. I fired off a letter stating that the law provided for a submittal of additional information and for a full explanation of the boards reasoning.

Civil & Structural Associates

May 18, 2012

Texas Board of Professional Engineers
1917 IH 35 South
Austin, TX 78741-3702

Attn: C. W. Clark, P.E.

Re: Official Complaint against Sam Nelson, P.E. File P-33206

Mr. Clark, I received the attached letter dated April 20, 2012 by mail on April 23, 2012. The letter states that my complaint which was submitted on 08-15-2011 has been denied. I am extremely disappointed in the position taken by TBPE (Board). I spent weeks putting the complaint together with input from numerous Professional Engineers and two attorneys. There were numerous obvious violations of the Engineering Practice Act committed by Mr. Sam Nelson, P.E. I will only cover two in this letter.

The last sentence of your letter states "Please consider this matter closed by this office, effective with the date of this letter." This is a very unfortunate sentence because the Engineering Practice Act (Act) clearly allows me thirty (30) days to provide more information for consideration by the Board. Considering the matter closed is a severe violation of the Board procedures and my due process rights. I have attached to this letter the Complaint/Investigative Process copied from the Board website. Furthermore section 139.17(e) of the Act states "If the board intends to dismiss the complaint because the investigation of the complaint does not produce sufficient evidence to substantiate a violation of the Act or board rules, the board staff will inform the complainant for the rationale for the determination prior to reporting the dismissal to the board." Your April 20th letter offers no rationale for your decisions.

By this letter and with advice and consent of my attorney I am providing more evidence to be considered in my complaint # P-33206.

Prior to my filing this complaint I made several calls to you, Mr. Clark, and described the behavior of Mr. Nelson and the actions that he had taken against me. When I told you on the phone that Mr. Nelson had personally intervened in his capacity as Chief Engineer for TDI to advise my client at Suntide III Condominiums on South Padre Island, TX to cease to use me and offered them the names of three (3) engineers to take my place, you agreed with me that this was wrong and advised me that if I filed a complaint it would be acted on. Not only did you not act on it, your staff neither called any of the witnesses I listed nor did you call me.

1117 N. Stuart Place Rd., Suite E
Harlingen, Texas 78552
Phone 956.428.7900
Fax 956.428.7903
www.casaengr.com
TX Registered Firm F-8483

Mr. Clark, attempting to influence the client of a practicing engineer is not only against the Act it is tortious interference in a contract and is against civil law.

The same violation occurred in Mr. Nelson's letter to me concerning 101 Plumosa. Mr. Nelson stated in the letter that I was responsible for getting a new roof on a structure, that had already been completed when I had it inspected and certified it, or Mr. Nelson would turn me over to enforcement. This is a clear attempt to force a contractual relationship between myself and the roofer and the homeowner. It is the roofer's responsibility to honor his contract with the owner and Mr. Nelson cannot threaten me with retribution if I do not get the roof replaced. Mr. Nelson and TDI were asked by my attorney to provide statutory basis for making this request and they provided none.

It is extremely unfortunate that you have taken the position that this is not a violation of 137.63 "Engineers responsibility to the Profession" b(5) " conduct engineering and related business affairs in a matter that is respectful of the client," and c(2) "maliciously injure or attempt to injure or damage the personal or professional reputation of another by any means." Mr. Nelson's direct unsolicited intervention in a contract between my client and me for services at Suntide III directly damaged my relationship with my client and I was forced to resign as Engineer so that the work could proceed. The witnesses for Suntide III that Mr. Nelson called and that I listed in my complaint stand ready to speak to your investigator when called. The letter from Mr. Nelson requesting me to get another contractor to reroof 101 Plumosa or I would be referred to enforcement was submitted in my complaint and is attached. The owner of 101 Plumosa was not taking any action against me and in fact reached an agreement with the roofer over one year later and had the roof replaced. I had it inspected and certified it at that time. Mr. Nelson was wrong to intervene in the contract between the owner of 101 Plumosa and his roofer and he was even more wrong in taking enforcement action against me in a SOAH court for actions that I had no control over and regarding a roof that was already certified. How is this action by Mr. Nelson making him a faithful agent to TDI and the Engineering Profession? And how is Mr. Nelsons actions in both of these instances not damaging to me both personally and professionally.

By dismissing my complaint you either take the position that intervening in an Engineers contractual relationships with a client is appropriate behavior for Mr. Nelson or you feel it is inappropriate and I failed to provide substantial proof. I feel I have provided substantiating evidence to support the complaint and without you interviewing myself or my witnesses I do not understand how you can reach the conclusion that no violation of the Act has occurred.

Disciplinary action by the board on contract matters is not new and a review of "Enforcement News" in the Issue No. 39 of the TBPE Express contains several.

In the case of Victor S. Medina, P.E., Corpus Christi, TX, Case No. D-32298. The last sentence states "After fifteen (15) months, Medina decided not to perform the inspection and although he refunded his payment back to his client, it appeared that his lack of action indicated he was not a faithful agent or respectful to his client." The board is clearly taking a position on contractual obligations here. Mr. Nelson clearly intervened in a contractual agreement with me, Triton Renovations, and Suntide III Homeowner's Association. By soliciting three engineers to take my place Mr. Nelson clearly caused me to lose a contract that produced over $28,000 in fees for

Aran and Franklin, the Engineering firm that replaced me. Mr. Nelson clearly acted in a manner that was not respectful to me or my clients.

It is more unfortunate that you have attempted to deny my due process by considering the case closed when it is not. I am not the only Engineer that Mr. Nelson has injured or attempted to injure professionally and monetarily. I submitted in my complaint numerous SOAH actions initiated by Mr. Nelson against Engineers and referred to the Board for further action. Many of them were dismissed by the Board for lack of evidence of a violation of the Act. Why is the Board allowing Mr. Nelson to prosecute Engineers on a daily basis on matters of Engineering in a SOAH court? How many more Engineers are you going to allow Mr. Nelson to harm before you sanction him? In his position as Chief Engineer for TDI, Mr. Nelson has the power to audit Engineers. This is the same power that is given to any city or county permit officer. Mr. Nelson does not have the power to intervene in contracts of or practice retribution against Engineers.

By this letter I am requesting an explanation of the investigative process that took over seven (7) months and did not even call me or any of my witnesses. I am requesting in writing the rationale in denying my complaint.

Respectfully Submitted,

David V. Day, P.E.
CASA Engineering, L.L.C.

DVD/ra

Cc: Lance Kinney, P.E. Executive Director TBPE
George Powell, Attorney
Greg Abbott, Attorney General
State Senator Eddie Lucio

Enclosures

To date, this letter has never been given a response from the board.

I filed a similar complaint against Stephen Harp, the lead auditor for TDI, listing numerous errors Harp had made in his audits that cost the engineers and the homeowners hundreds of thousands of dollars in compliance. I specifically cited the case of Bob Burkhart, the engineer who had started the home at Whooping Crane that I had taken eighteen months to get certified.

Burkhart was a very honorable, conscientious engineer who had a full-time job with a municipal utility district. He did his windstorm engineering on his own time. He did all calculations by hand, and all of his detail drawings were hand drawn.

Harp's initial letter to Burkhart stated that Burkhart's calculations were wrong because he used the wrong pitch of the roof from the wind pressure tables in the ASCE-7-05 loads manual and then stated that Burkhart's designs did not meet any standard of engineering.

Burkhart had used a higher wind speed, 130 mph, than what was required, 120 mph. The wind pressures for the higher wind speed would more than offset the pressures for the lesser roof pitch. Harp's criticisms of Burkhart's use of a wrong roof pitch were wrong and irrelevant because higher pressures were used by Burkhart in his design. Though hand drawn, there was nothing wrong with Burkhart's plans and details. All information needed for the contractor to build the home was contained in the drawings. All loads calculated by Burkhart were above what was later verified by me and proven in a subsequent audit of me on the same property.

As a result of this audit and others that Harp conducted on Burkhart, Burkhart could not afford to contest the audits. Burkhart had a full-time day job, and hiring an attorney to aid in fighting TDI would have hurt his full-time job. TDI gave Burkhart the option to resign from the appointment list, and in return they would not bring enforcement action against him and would not file a complaint with TBPE.

TDI has neither the authority nor legal standing to make deals with engineers on enforcement actions. Only the board of engineers can offer enforcement deals to engineers. Yet TDI makes these kinds of deals routinely, and TBPE turns a blind eye and hides behind the legislative authority of TDI. The legislation did not give the power to TDI to make enforcement action deals with engineers; TDI just took this power and will continue to get away with lawlessness as long as they are able to sweep away any opposition with the power of an out-of-control state agency.

Bob Burkhart was one of the better engineers in the program but was forced to resign or lose a lot of money defending himself. Burkhart was fully prepared to go on record and support me in my quest to stop TDI abuse when he was diagnosed with cancer. He passed away six months later. I detailed the incorrect abusive audit that Harp conducted on Burkhart in my complaint against Harp to TBPE. Once again the board dismissed the complaint without explanation.

The Attack Begins

It did not take TDI long to go into full attack mode. On April 1, 2011, TDI filed a motion for a hearing in SOAH court. After listing six audited projects, TDI concluded that David V. Day had "knowingly, willfully, fraudulently, or with gross negligence signed or caused to be prepared an inspection report or sworn statement that contains a false, fictitious, or fraudulent statement or entry."

The charges on their face value were absurd. The sworn statement they refer to is the WPI-2, which is clearly an engineering document. The first line of the WPI-2 is acknowledgment that I am a professional engineer. The last sentence of the first paragraph states, "I do state that I am personally responsible as the engineer of record for the windstorm inspection of this project, and I have provided standard and customary construction review services including an inspection or inspections by myself or an employee under my direct supervision." Standard and customary construction review services do not entail witnessing every nail being driven. Every job that I signed off on, which numbered in the thousands, involved random inspections to assure general compliance with code and/or product evaluations. TDI had absolutely no evidence that I had fraudulently responded on any WPI-2. TDI's standard of proof appears to be if their inspectors found what they called deficiencies and the engineer either didn't find any or disagreed with what they called deficiencies, then the engineer is guilty of fraud.

Of the six addresses listed in the filing, three, Plumosa, Shadowbrook, and Suntide III, have already been covered at length in previous chapters. There were three new complaints that occurred after I had been put under audit on all jobs.

GREENBRIAR

This home was very similar to Plumosa and Shadowbrook, but it involved a roof on a home that was not certified by TDI. There are numerous homes that were built after 1998 that had never gotten certified because they had private insurance. After Dolly and Ike in 2008, the private insurance carriers were dropping out of the coastal areas and putting the wind portion of their policies into TWIA. Several large insurance companies would insure in the private market if they could get the WPI-8 on the roof only. They reasoned that the majority of insurance claims after Dolly and Ike were for roof damage to asphalt shingles. If they could get a certification on the roof, they were at least getting the roof validated by an engineer who had professional liability for the roof. For the roof at Greenbriar, the home was being sold, and the new buyers had requested a WPI-8 on the home. The private insurance company requested the roof certification to write a private policy. Even though the roof would be certified, the home was not eligible for TWIA because the entire structure would have to be certified to be eligible for TWIA.

This job occurred after I was put under audit on all jobs. The nails were checked and were evenly placed, six nails per shingle right above the glue line. This is a safe place for the nails to be, and the CASA employee, Sergio Saldivar, reported back to me with photos showing the nail placement. I saw nothing wrong with the placement and accepted the roof. Once the WPI-2 was turned in, TDI immediately sent two inspectors to look at the roof. The TDI inspectors were Doug Klopfenstein and Michael Cowen. They had come to look at Greenbriar and at another roof on Fannin Street in San Benito.

Doug Klopfenstein reported back that the nails were above the manufacturer's recommended nail location for Greenbriar and were overdriven or crooked at Fannin. I met Klopfenstein at Fannin and went shingle by shingle, looking for damage. Doug Klopfenstein called many nails overdriven that were perfectly okay. I even arranged a demonstration for Doug Klopfenstein where I drove nails in a shingle on a board to what Doug Klopfenstein called overdriven. I then backed the nails out of the board and showed that the shingles were untorn and undamaged. It didn't matter to Doug Klopfenstein because his instructions from Welch Watt were to reject any nails that had the nailhead below the shingle granule surface. Doug Klopfenstein did not even touch any of the shingles he called overdriven. He took pictures from over two feet from the shingle surface. He e-mailed the pictures from his phone to Watt, and I received a voice mail twenty minutes later from Watt stating that they were not going to accept the roof because 66 percent of the nails were overdriven. This was an assessment made on photos in an e-mail taken over two feet from the shingle surface from an inspector who had not physically touched one of the nailheads to determine if it was actually overdriven. I have kept this voice mail and have it to this day.

The next day, I had a meeting at my office with Doug Klopfenstein to discuss Greenbriar and Fannin. The discussion was frank and heated; Doug Klopfenstein had allowed the roofers at Fannin to continue when he knew he was going to reject the roof because they were putting the nails on with a nail gun. Doug Klopfenstein denied it, but the roofer had already spoken to four witnesses from the roofing company who vouched that Doug Klopfenstein did not try and stop the roofer but allowed it to continue without saying anything. I told Doug Klopfenstein that he was wrong and needed to make decisions based on the demonstration that I had given the day before. Doug Klopfenstein stated that he did not have "the luxury to make decisions." The TDI inspectors so feared being reprimanded or terminated by Watt that they would not accept a good roof if it did not meet Watt's incorrect standards.

On Greenbriar, I told Doug Klopfenstein that the home was not eligible to be in TWIA because the entire structure was not certified. Doug Klopfenstein reported back to Watt that I had admitted that the roof was not eligible for certification. This was a flat-out lie that would later be repeatedly stated in trial. It wasn't just my word against Doug Klopfenstein; Manny Ramirez, my employee, attended the meeting and produced a signed affidavit attesting to the fact that I did not tell Doug Klopfenstein that the roof was not certifiable.

I later produced a manufacturer's document that the nail location was acceptable. TDI ignored this document and continued their persecution of me on this issue. The code simply states that asphalt shingles must meet a 110 mph wind test and that nails be installed in accordance with the manufacturer's recommendations. The manufacturer had produced a bulletin that the nail position was acceptable, and that should have been the end of it.

The section of the code on shingles gave manufacturers of AC shingles powers that no other manufacturer had. The number one insurer of products, Factory Mutual, which developed and implemented the majority of roof tests, accepted that all asphalt composition (AC) products were the same, and if tests were passed on one brand of shingle, then it applied to all brands of shingles. The National Roofing Contractors Association (NRCA) had conducted numerous tests and basically concluded that the nail placement was irrelevant as long as they were in the middle area of the shingle. It is the sealant at the edge that determines the effectiveness of the shingle performance. If the shingles do not seal, then no matter how well or at what location the nails were placed, the shingles would not pass a wind test. Unless the nails are actually overdriven, the shingles will pass a wind test if the edge sealant is good.

TDI inspectors even took the ridiculous position that if the contractors used more nails than what was necessary, then the shingles could not be accepted. Doug Klopfenstein stated that if a nail was overdriven, the shingle had to be replaced. He would not allow the roofer to place a good nail next to it. Doug Klopfenstein and I discussed this at length. I told Doug Klopfenstein that one and a half nails were one and a half times stronger than one nail. Doug Klopfenstein refused to accept it.

NORTH SHORE

For this home the windows had been replaced in 2009, and CASA had sent in the paperwork. As frequently happens at TDI, and any engineer on the list will tell you, TDI intake division loses or misplaces numerous documents. Over 2 percent of CASA documents had to be resubmitted because TDI had lost them. All documents went to a centralized location and were distributed from there. How exactly this process occurs can only be answered by TDI, but it is a fact that numerous documents get misplaced. North Shore in San Benito was one of them.

Also as frequently occurs, the homeowner already has private insurance and doesn't have to use TWIA for windstorm insurance. At North Shore the homeowner already had private insurance and didn't need the WPI-2 for their windows. A year later their insurance agent was price shopping and inquired about the WPI-2 for the address. CASA looked into it and discovered that it was never acknowledged by TDI even though CASA had stamp-dated evidence that it had been sent to TDI.

Linda Olvera, the CASA office manager, called TDI Intake and described what had happened. TDI assured that all that was needed was a recent inspection date because it was over six months old. This occurred after I was put under audit on all new projects after October 28, 2010. CASA accepted TDI Intake at their word and submitted the WPI-2 again with a new date. Either TDI lied or another agent received the documents and followed the orders given at Intake that anything from David Day be referred to Engineering. Once Engineering received the WPI-2, they immediately requested all the backup data for this project. I responded with the affidavit from Olvera and stated that certification occurred before October 28, 2010, and was not subject to audit as per Nelson's verbal instruction to me on October 28, 2010.

There was nothing wrong with the windows at this address, and they would easily pass even TDI's arbitrary standards, but I was rightly concerned that if TDI started auditing structures that were completed prior to October 28, 2010, then they could cause great harm to me and my clients by trying to prove the obvious to TDI or not being able to verify and vouch for every nail on the roof or on the sheathing. Though there was nothing wrong with the windows, TDI turned me into enforcement for not providing data on a job that was over one year old, was completed long before the October 28, 2010, mandate, and the owners had private insurance. They did this without ever visiting the site to see if the windows were even installed. I acted on the advice of my attorney not to turn the data in because the owners were not requesting the certification.

East Levee

On this project TDI exercised one of their most egregious abuses of power. The building at East Levee was a six-story stair-stepped bank building in downtown Brownsville that had six different roof covers at six different elevations. The original roofs at all elevations were built up with tar and gravel ballast. Over the years the bank had replaced several roofs with modified-bitumen cap sheets after 1988. The bank wanted to get TWIA insurance, so they employed CASA to do an evaluation of the entire building. I produced a report listing numerous deficiencies to different elevations that would have to be corrected before certifications could be made to any part of the structure. It must be noted here that one certification cannot be done to roof covers that are applied at different dates. The certifications must be by TDI rules for the date the repairs were made.

The bank hired a roofer to begin making the repairs in a phased approach. The roofer started with the easiest repairs on the third and fourth floor, where all that was needed was a proper termination sheet at the parapet wall at third and fourth floor and to correct some standing water areas at fourth floor. All this involved was adding an additional layer of cap sheet at the parapet walls and in the low spots. This is a common repair and done every day in the roofing business. I used the product evaluation for the cap sheet used, which was fully adhered. Since this project occurred after I was put under audit on all jobs, TDI requested full backup information. I sent them the wind pressure calculations, the product evaluation for the cap sheet, and the original report. The repairs were certified separately from the roof as is required by TDI for the date the work is done.

TDI Stephen Harp took exception to the use of the product evaluation being used on an existing roof surface. As with most requests from Harp, this was patently absurd. All products will be attached to existing surfaces that they have not been tested to. Even on new roofs the roof cover will be attached to metal flashing, metal curbs, plastic roof vents, metal scuppers and gutters. On any partial reroof, the new roof will have to tie into the existing roof. TDI has a category for partial reroof on their WPI-2 form. This would indicate that a new product is going to be tied into an existing roof. No one from TDI visited the Levee site to see if there was any inferior work. They just took the wrong position that I could not use a product evaluation for a new product on an existing roof. TDI can accept or not accept anything for any reason, but to accuse an engineer of fraud when there is disagreement is abusive, reckless, and even fraudulent on the part of TDI.

Before the hearing was set, TDI amended the complaint to include two new projects: Guadalajara and Sunchase IV. Both of these projects came up after I had been put under an audit on all projects. After the first seven or eight audits after October 28, 2010, resulted in two of them, Greenbriar and Levee, being referred to enforcement, I stopped sending in projects and relied 100 percent on other engineers to certify projects.

At Guadalajara, Juan Salinas, one of my most trusted inspectors, looked at the roof from start to finish. This was a simple reroof job with Atlas Pinnacle thirty-year architectural shingles. The nails were done by hand, six nails per shingle in the Atlas-approved nail zone, which is a one-inch zone that includes the glue strip. It is never a good idea to nail in the glue strip with a hammer, and most shingle manufacturers forbid it because it disrupts the bonding capacity of the roof cement. The nails were placed at the bottom side of the glue line because the farther down the nail, the stronger the connection. On the final inspection, Salinas noticed some of the nailheads were partially exposed when the succeeding shingle was placed. The amount of exposure was less than 10 percent of the nailhead. Salinas instructed the roofer to apply roof cement to the nailheads if they were even close to the edge.

TDI sent Benito Garcia to inspect the roof. When Garcia saw the tar marks, he said there were too many and rejected the roof. Garcia also told Juan Salinas that his shoes were causing scuff marks on the roof. Garcia was heavier than Salinas and was wearing the same shoes. He also rejected the roof vents because they were nailed with one-and-one-fourth-inch roof nails, and the product evaluation called for one-and-one-half-inch nails.

Stephen Harp sent me a letter asking to correct the deficiencies. I immediately contacted the manufacturer and explained the situation to them. The Atlas representative directed me to their technical bulletin.

 ROOFING CORPORATION

Technical Bulletin

Re: Fastening of Atlas Shingles

Atlas requires the use of roofing nails, to comply with the following installation criteria to install shingles onto a clean roof deck and underlayment. Re-roofing over a single layer of a flat, smooth surfaced 3-Tab roof covering is permitted, but the fastener lengths must be increased by at least ¼".

- The galvanized shingle nails need to be a minimum of 1 ¼" long with nominal 3/8" dia. flat heads for the fastening of the Pinnacle and StormMaster Shake laminated type shingles.
- The nails need to be a minimum of 1" long for the fastening of the GlassMaster 25 shingles.
- The nail head must not cut through the top surface of the shingle when driven.
- All nails must be driven through the double thickness, overlapping laminated area of the shingles.
- The shingle nails may penetrate and/or overlay the sealant strip material to assure that the nail shaft penetrates the double thick area of the shingles.
- Any inadvertent exposure of nail heads may be corrected by applying a minimal amount of caulking gun grade asphalt adhesive to coat the exposed portion of the nail heads.
- The points of the nails must penetrate into the Building Code approved decking materials at least ¾". If the decking is less than ¾" thick, the points of the nails must penetrate and protrude at least 1/8" through the bottom of the decking material.
- The fastener placement and all fastener criteria stated herein, as well as those on the bundle wrappers, must be adhered to in order to receive coverage under the Atlas Limited shingle Warranty. Incorrect or incorrectly placed fasteners will void the Limited Shingle Warranty.
- The use of staples is specifically not recognized as proper shingle fasteners due to the staple's inherent inconsistency in controlling the driven depth and difficulty to consistently drive them parallel to the length of the shingle.
- Following these guidelines will maintain the Atlas Shingle Limited Warranty in effect at the time of the installation.

Atlas Roofing Corporation

2000 RIVEREDGE PARKWAY · SUITE 800 · ATLANTA, GEORGIA 30328

The bulletin clearly states that applying roof cement to inadvertently exposed nails was acceptable and would not void their warranty. I forwarded this bulletin to Harp and also showed Harp that the one-and-one-fourth-inch nails at the roof vents had clearly penetrated the deck and that similar products from the same manufacturer allowed one-and-one-fourth-inch nails. Also the Miami-Dade NOA allowed one-and-one-fourth-inch nails.

Harp accepted the roof vents based on the nail penetration but rejected the technical bulletin and proceeded to give false and misleading statements about how asphalt on the roof would affect the performance of the shingle reflection of UV rays. This was preposterous and had no basis in science and, in fact, was the complete opposite of the truth. The shingles are fabricated with roof cement and rely on it to hold the granules in place.

In order to get the homeowner a roof certification, the roofer agreed to replace the shingles with exposed nails. This work was completed, and I sent the photos to Harp and left the replaced shingles on the ground. TDI sent Garcia again to look at the roof. I met Garcia on the roof. There were numerous roof cement patches on the roof where the nails were not exposed but were close, and the roofer had put the tar just as a precaution. I showed Garcia the technical bulletin from Pinnacle, which stated that inadvertent exposed nails could be covered with roof cement. When confronted by the homeowner, Garcia said he would accept the roof if the engineer accepted it. Presumably he was referring to the TDI engineers. Garcia reported back to Harp, and once again Harp refused to accept the roof cement on the roof and requested that the shingles be removed.

The roofer agreed to remove all shingles with tar marks from the roof and did so. I reported back to Harp that all tar marks were off the roof and the roof should be certified. This time Doug Klopfenstein inspected the roof with Garcia and proclaimed that the roof had too many scuff marks to be acceptable. There is nothing in the IBC codes or within TDI that has any mention of scuff marks. The only mention is on the Pinnacle packaging, which says that granule loss during the first year is to be expected. The shingle granules are broadcast in an asphaltic matrix to bind them to the felt substrate. They will be dislodged at the perimeters with foot traffic. Anytime someone walks on a roof, there will be evidence similar to walking on a carpet. The loose granules disturbed when walking on the shingles will be cleared away with the first rain or wind. And this was the way it was with Guadalajara. Months after the final TDI inspection, the roof looked like new. But TDI had already rejected it and turned it into enforcement to be added to the charges against me. Once again a homeowner was being punished because of a personal vendetta against me by TDI going all the way up to the department manager, Alexis Dick.

The last address brought in the TDI amended complaint against me was Sunchase IV condominiums. Sunchase IV was a multilevel stair-stepped twelve-story condominiums on the southern end of South Padre Island. The roof cover, which was built-up modified bitumen, was damaged during Dolly, and the homeowners association elected to replace it with a single-ply Duro-Last membrane. This membrane is similar to the one employed at Suntide III but is a PVC membrane and not TPO. In this case the manufacturer recommended a mechanically attached membrane fastened with concrete screws to the concrete deck. Duro-Last designs in-house and supplies the membrane already fabricated to the roof dimensions so that the installer just fastens at the seam tabs, and very little field seaming is done.

The roof membrane at Sunchase had eighteen-inch spacing at the seams at the corners and perimeters and at twenty-eight inches OC in the interior. Even with this close spacing there will be uplift during winds between the seams. That is why vents are installed on roof to allow the membrane to go back down when it has lifted. TDI has approved the Duro-Last membrane with seams at ten feet OC. With the seams at ten feet OC, the membrane may rise six inches between fastened seams. At the Sunchase roof with seams at twenty-eight inches OC, the membrane lifted approximately one inch between the seams. This raised questions from the owners on the upper floors, who would look down on the membrane and see it flutter in the coastal breezes. Their own inspector that they hired after Dolly to consult on hurricane repairs, Delton Lee, advised them that the fluttering was natural and okay. The fluttering was brought to my attention, and I also responded in writing that the fluttering was okay. The owners were also concerned that the lightning-rod-protection system was corroding and leaving copper-colored stains on the white membrane. The owners were so upset with the roof membrane and convinced that there was something wrong, they refused to pay the roofer the balance of their contract and called Sam Nelson at TDI to complain about the roof. Nelson didn't bother to call me to see if there was a problem. He just sent out Welch Watt to look at the roof. I had already been turned over to enforcement but was not turning in any new work to TDI to get audited, so TDI now had to go after a roof that had already been certified by me.

Watt visited the roof and reported back to Nelson that the roof was fluttering in the wind and apparently wasn't installed correctly. Watt did agree though that staining from the lightning-rod cable was not a problem for the roof or the roof installer. Nelson and Watt called me together, and Watt expressed concern that the roof was fluttering when it was supposed to be fully adhered. The roof was over one and a half years old at this point, and I had certified hundreds of roofs after Dolly, most without ever seeing them. I told Nelson I would look into it, but Nelson had already sent a letter listing a number of concerns and requesting all backup information on the roof. Mr. Nelson's letter contained five concerns, which were all invalid and proven to be so.

After two months of a letter-writing campaign in which Mr. Nelson repeatedly made incorrect and false statements, all complaints were dismissed with the exception that Mr. Nelson refused to accept the test data that I submitted even though the design exceeded the requirement by over 10 percent. The design submitted by Duro-Last, the manufacturer of the Duro-Last PVC membrane, was for 150 mph. The wind speed requirement for TDI was 130 mph. The field pressures for the roof had test data acceptable to TDI, but the perimeter and code pressures were calculated and had no test data published. The Miami-Dade NOA correctly allowed calculations for the perimeter and corner zones, but the TDI product evaluations incorrectly do not. In layman's terms, the pressures are higher at the building perimeter because as winds come over a roof, they are both positive pressures and negative suction pressures where in the center of the roof there will only be positive or negative pressures in the field. The pressures decrease from the corner and perimeter to the interior, where it remains constant. For this reason manufacturers only run tests on the interior portion of the roof and allow the corner and perimeter zones to be calculated based on the load per fastener. For example, if the pressure on a roof was calculated to be 100 psf at the field, 150 psf for the perimeter, and 200 psf for the corners and the field tests were conducted with the fasteners at 1 foot OC, the load per fastener would be 100 lb per fastener. Using this information, the fasteners would be spaced at 1.5 per square foot for the perimeter and 2 per square feet for the corner zone. The load per fastener remains constant and has already been tested. Mr. Nelson, for whatever reason, refused to accept this and required that the membrane have a test run for the perimeter and corner zones. Because no test existed, I was forced to have the membrane tested in the field with a vacuum box. The trouble is that the vacuum box has dimensions of five feet by five feet and must be at least six inches from the roof edge. The perimeter zone for this roof was three feet wide, so the test box was over two feet into the field zone with fasteners at a greater spacing. The tests validated the field pressures and, by calculation, the perimeter zones, but Nelson also refused to accept this and took the extraordinary step of referring me to disciplinary enforcement with TDI and later with TBPE.

The president of Sunchase IV HOA, Wally Jones, was refusing to pay the roofer for the completion of the roof based on the billowing and staining of the roof. TDI rejected both of these complaints but aided and abetted Mr. Jones's refusal to pay the roofer based on incorrect requirements for test data. This roof was already certified by TDI, and the certification was never pulled even though TDI rejected my submittals and turned me into enforcement.

TDI was allowing Mr. Jones to keep his TWIA insurance and refuse to pay his roofer. If Mr. Nelson truly believed the roof was bad and didn't meet the design pressures, then he was obligated to pull the certification. Mr. Nelson was allowing this large condominium owner to keep their certificate while not extending the same privilege to East Levee, North Shore, Greenbrier, and Guadalajara and required Plumosa and Shadowbrook to be reroofed. Mr. Nelson took the extraordinary step of directly intervening at Suntide III and requested the restoration company that David Day be removed and then solicited three other engineers to replace me.

This is all documented and, in fact, entered in evidence to TBPE in the form of a complaint by me against Nelson to the board. For the aforementioned actions, Nelson certainly deserves to be sanctioned by the board, fired from TDI, and prosecuted in criminal proceedings for directly interfering as a state officer in a civil contract. Multiply this by the hundreds of engineers who received and are receiving the same treatment as me. Nelson's boss, Alexis Dick, knew absolutely nothing about engineering but would defend Nelson no matter how egregious his offenses. She never consulted outside of TDI to determine if Nelson's decisions were correct. Alexis Dick was also not above retribution. The day after Suntide III owners directly complained to Dick, she blamed me, and the next day, I was put under audit on all projects, essentially a kiss of death. An engineer in Galveston County, Harvey Cappell, wrote a letter to Dick complaining about test procedures and immediately received twenty-three audits by TDI.

I would later find out just how bad Dick and Nelson were from insiders within TDI. But first I had to go through the SOAH court hearing before an administrative law judge (ALJ).

The Trial

Even though it was officially a hearing before an SOAH court with an ALJ administering, the impact of the hearing had more repercussions of any trial held in Texas. There had never been a TDI hearing for disciplinary actions against an engineer that lasted more than a day or even a few hours. My hearing would last over two years and produce an extraordinary amount of testimony by TDI employees that underline their willful ignorance of the code, of jurisprudence, and of their statutory authority.

Though the complaint was first made in April 2011, a hearing was not convened until December 2011 and did not conclude until December 2012. The decision would then take five more months. During the trial, TDI would file a complaint to the Texas Board of Professional Engineers with the exact same complaint that was entered to the SOAH court, and TBPE would ultimately reject it in its entirety and completely exonerate me before the SOAH hearing was concluded.

The hearing is a matter of record, and the complete transcript is public record. I was represented by George Powell of Hinojosa and Powell of McAllen, Texas, and his consultant, George Basham of the Weichert Law Firm of Austin, Texas. TDI was represented by in-house council Olivia Connett and assistant. Prior to the hearing, there was some discovery by both sides, but no depositions were taken of me or any party involved in the hearing.

Between the time the charges were leveled against me in 2010 and the beginning of the hearing in December 2011, the Texas legislature convened and passed House Bill 3, which completely changed the engineering-appointment process. The bill revised the TDI certification program and now required TBPE (board) to screen engineers wanting to be on the appointment list. Though this legislation directly conflicted with the occupations code and the Engineering Practice Act, the board nevertheless created a screening process. The bill was signed into law in September 2011 before the SOAH hearing was convened.

In opening statements, Powell presented to the ALJ, Judith Cloninger, the new rules and flowchart which clearly showed that any disciplinary action against an engineer had to be referred to the board and only if the board found any wrongdoing could TDI then take action against an engineer. TDI argued that all of my offenses occurred before the new law was passed, and therefore the new law did not apply. The judge ruled in TDI's favor and allowed the hearing to proceed.

In TDI's opening remarks, they gave very contradictory statements. They first argued that David Day as an inspector had accepted numerous defective work and then that David Day's behavior did not meet proper engineering standards. Throughout the hearing TDI would continue to try and have it both ways. They knew they had no control over engineers, so they claimed they were only condemning my actions as an inspector, but they were accusing me of fraud and negligence for sealing and signing an engineering document, the WPI-2.

When the hearing began in December of 2011, TDI had already filed a complaint with the board in October of 2011. The board would take six months to investigate the charges, and I would not be aware of the complaint until April of 2012. So TDI was fully aware in December of 2011, at the start of the hearing, that they had filed the exact same charges verbatim to the board in the form of a complaint as a violation of engineering. They conveniently left out this fact in their opening statements while they repeatedly insisted that they were only condemning my actions as an inspector and not as an engineer. By filing the complaint with the board, it was clear that TDI considered my actions to be engineering violations. It would be legally prudent to wait for the board to render a decision on the complaint before proceeding with an SOAH hearing.

Except for the charges for Suntide III where TDI relied on a third-party engineer with EFI Global, TDI relied solely on their in-house engineers and inspectors. They did not consult with any experts or third-party inspectors. Even though I disputed every accusation in my answers to their interrogatories and provided evidence to back up my refutations, TDI legal staff did not investigate any of the evidence. They simply relied on the work of their in-house engineering staff as if they were infallible. The engineering staff of TDI relied solely on the word of their field inspectors also as if they were infallible. Of the addresses that were used in the complaints against me, not one did TDI engineering staff visit. They relied solely on pictures and reports from their field inspectors.

I on the other hand personally visited each address and examined the roof coverings, which were the basis of the majority of the complaints. As with the majority of the engineers on the appointment list, I relied on my inspectors to examine the work in the field and made my certifications based on their input. In all cases CASA inspectors were more educated than the TDI field inspectors. Four of them were graduate engineers. None of TDI field inspectors were graduate engineers. When the charges were brought against me, I visited each site and examined the work that my inspectors had accepted. In all cases, I found that my inspectors were correct, and TDI inspectors were wrong. I would later demonstrably prove this in the hearing.

What follows is an account that is so extraordinary and produced such extraordinary results that one would think they are a work of fiction if the parties involved had not lived through them. For me it became a four-year odyssey that led to the writing of this book. What are the odds?

The hearing began with the TDI attorney, Olivia Connett, informing the judge, Judith Cloninger, that she just found out that she was pregnant and was experiencing morning sickness so she might have to be frequently excused. The judge assured her it would not be a problem.

During TDI's opening statement, they repeatedly made references to engineering. The only reason that they had any control over engineers is that they claimed that they were only using engineers as inspectors. This is an absurd statement because the form WPI-2 that the engineer had to sign and seal began with the statement, "I am a professional engineer licensed to practice in the state of Texas."

Powell objected and asked for the hearing to be suspended until the board could rule on my alleged complaints. There was a heated exchange with Connett admitting that TDI intended for the board to rule on my actions (volume 1, page 14, lines 6–13). What Connett did not say is that the same complaint submitted to Cloninger was submitted to TBPE verbatim. Had this important fact been known by me, Powell, or Cloninger, the outcome of the trial may have changed. Legally, you can't accuse an engineer of fraud in his practice as an engineer before an SOAH Judge. Only the board can judge matters of engineering fraud. This hearing should have never happened, and the fact that it did happen speaks volumes about the abuse of the Texas court systems and a bloated bureaucracy, TDI, far exceeding their legal authority.

As with any hearing, the plaintiffs go first in presenting their evidence. TDI's first witness was Sam Nelson, chief engineer for TDI Windstorm Program. As previously stated, Mr. Nelson had been appointed to this position not by qualifications but by attrition, for the previous TDI chief windstorm engineer, Randy Shakelford, was leaving, and Nelson's previous position in the sprinkler-pipe division was being phased out mainly because of Nelson's heavy-handed tactics in the sprinkler system submittal process. In previous testimony in TDI v. TWIA, Nelson had admitted that he only had a two-week transition with Shakelford to learn the ropes of the windstorm program.

Nelson's appearance during the trial was telling of his personality. Everything was impeccable—the creases in his suit, his posture, his seemingly unbreakable concentration, even the way he combed his hair. One small stain or imperfection would probably send him into conniptions. Anytime something did not play to his liking, his façade broke, and he became visibly flustered. He did not like imperfections or complications. This hearing was just that: a complication, an imperfection to his plans and reputation. It was a stain that needed to be removed no matter the cost.

Overall, in Nelson's testimony, he admitted that he never visited any of the job sites in question and had not personally examined any of the evidence. One would think that any professionally run government agency such as TDI would have their key witness examine the facts that he is going to be testifying to if he is to be their chief witness. Mr. Nelson was never presented as an expert witness, only a fact witness, and his knowledge of the facts was appalling. Also, Mr. Nelson made incorrect statements or flat-out lied numerous times.

EXAMPLES OF FALSE STATEMENTS

Volume 1, page 67 states, "Mr. Day signed certification knowing that there were deficiencies."

Fact—this statement was made about Plumosa where the areas that I submitted as evidence were checked by TDI and found to be okay. I later proved to the ALJ that TDI was incorrectly calling gun-driven nails overdriven.

Page 69, lines 22–24 consider fish mouths on shingles (areas where they did not seal) a cause for rejection.

Fact—TDI's own inspector did not reject the so-called fish mouths. There is nothing in the code or manufacturer's literature that lists fish mouths as a defect, and in fact, TDI with Nelson as the primary witness had been over ruled on this exact so-called defect by the ALJ in TDI v. TWIA.

In page 93, lines 7–11, Nelson states that TWIA will be harmed if David Day remains on appointment list—an extremely reckless statement bordering on slander. The fact is that both TWIA and the coastal counties have been harmed by Nelson's actions in denying legitimate certifications.

In page 99–100, Nelson admits that TDI accepts Miami-Dade product approvals but states that they must meet TDI code. This statement reveals Nelson's complete ignorance of the international codes. TDI and Texas and Florida adopted the international code. Florida added two chapters to the codes that go above and beyond the code while TDI added two pages of revisions. There is no Florida test requirement that does not meet the international codes. Florida would be very surprised to know what the chief engineer for the Texas Department of Insurance thinks that the Florida and Miami-Dade product evaluations do not meet the IBC code.

On page 135, line 20–22, when asked if he ever told Mike Scanlon if he had Day's number, Nelson answers no, a deliberate lie. I obtained and submitted a signed notarized affidavit from Vicky Huckaby, who was in the car with Scanlon and listening on speaker phone when Nelson told Scanlon, "Don't worry about Day, I have got his number." Shortly after Nelson made this statement and while the hearing was still in progress, Scanlon would start a telephone campaign to discredit me. Several of the engineers reported back to me about Scanlon's derogatory comments. It was common knowledge that Scanlon was Nelson's mole in the appointed engineering society and therefore would get favorable treatment in audits and was appointed by Nelson to head several committees. What was also common knowledge among the appointed engineers is that neither Scanlon nor Nelson had any credibility.

Nelson repeatedly admitted that there is a difference of opinion between TDI inspectors and David Day. A difference of opinion does not rise to the level of fraud, yet that is what TDI continually and with malice accused me of.

An honest reading of Nelson's testimony transcript would show that Nelson did no damage to me and was frequently discredited by Powell. Nelson's testimony also revealed the complete ignorance of the TDI attorneys about the facts of the trial. When discussing the concealed conditions of the roof covers, they repeatedly asked, "Shouldn't a good inspector have seen these defects?" Even after it was made abundantly clear that all roof fasteners are concealed when roofs are complete, the TDI attorneys kept insisting that David Day should have seen all nails that TDI saw when they lifted shingles even though I wasn't there when the shingles were lifted.

TDI's next witness was Doug Klopfenstein. Doug Klopfenstein had inspected three of the projects, Plumosa, Greenbriar, and

Guadalajara. Unlike Nelson, who was vague, evasive, and lied several times, Doug Klopfenstein was mostly truthful. He honestly believed in what he was doing, and his admissions were astounding.

Some of his more astounding admissions are as follows:

When shown a picture of an obviously overdriven nail with a good nail next to it (volume 1, page 197), Doug Klopfenstein stated that the shingles could not be repaired by adding an extra nail. This statement epitomized the problem with TDI inspectors and TDI in-house engineers. Of course you can repair a bad nail by placing a good one next to it. That is what you are supposed to do, and anywhere else in the country and any inspection entity would find this the right thing to do, but not TDI inspectors. If the nails were not exactly as they were shown on the shingle wrapper instructions, then TDI was not going to accept them. If the wrapper showed four nails and the roofer put five, then TDI would reject it.

In page 222, Doug Klopfenstein could not identify defective nails from his own pictures. When pressed, he could not tell if it was overdriven or underdriven. At first Doug Klopfenstein called it overdriven, and then Powell suggested that it looked underdriven. At that point Doug Klopfenstein admitted it might be. And then upon redirect, the TDI attorney then questioned him about the same nail being underdriven still being a defect. Astounding! First Doug Klopfenstein calls a nail in his own photo overdriven, and TDI attorney says that David Day should have caught it. Then upon redirect, Doug Klopfenstein says the same nail is underdriven, and TDI attorney says that David Day should have caught it.

The truth is that the nail was properly driven, and no one can tell if a nail is overdriven from pictures, but as mentioned previously, on Fannin Street in San Benito, Welch Watt called 66 percent of the nails overdriven from pictures taken at least two feet away. Unless a nail is driven halfway through the shingle, an inspector has to touch it and feel it to determine if a compressed nail has cut or torn the shingle.

In volume 1, page 264, Doug Klopfenstein testifies that the nail does not have to cut or damage the shingle for TDI to call it overdriven and reject it. This is a direct admission that TDI standards are not based in reality but only in the prejudicial standards of Welch Watt.

No good engineer and no good inspector are going to call a nail that does not damage a shingle overdriven and reject it. There have been many good engineers run out of the program because they accepted properly driven nails and TDI inspectors wrongly rejected them. Over 90 percent of all shingles are installed with a pneumatic gun, and TDI inspectors would reject every one of them if they inspected them. That is why all roofers pay engineers to inspect roofs when TDI inspectors will inspect them for free. And that is why when the new legislation was passed in 2011 to have the board screen engineers, 80 percent of the engineers opted out of the program. They did not want to put up with the abuse of nonengineer TDI inspectors rejecting work that they had accepted and then have TDI engineers and attorneys accuse them of fraud for correctly accepting work. And the biggest shame of all is that TBPE accepted improper complaints against engineers for fraud and fined the engineers. Very few of the engineers had the time or money to defend themselves against TDI or the board. They accepted the fine and got out of the windstorm program.

In volume 1, page 273, lines 4–16, Doug Klopfenstein believes he has the authority to reject an entire roof based on one incorrect nail! Not only does he believe it, he practices it every day. With a standard like this, no engineer is safe. Any roof cover—no matter how well it is installed—will have one bad nail, and if the engineer misses it, he can then be accused of fraud for turning in a WPI-2 for a roof with a "known" deficiency.

No one in the private industry could ever get away with a statement like that. It is this kind of mind-set at TDI that started with Welch Watt and spread down to all of the TDI inspectors who wanted to keep their jobs. If you don't like someone, you can find one bad nail and reject their entire roof.

Doug Klopfenstein insisted that the reason that he could reject a roof for one bad nail and the nail could not even be repaired is that the shingles were not tested with extra nails or nails in any location other than what is shown on the shingle wrapper. Upon cross-examination by Powell, Doug Klopfenstein was forced to admit that he did not know how shingle tests were conducted—that he didn't know anything about the test process.

Doug Klopfenstein wrongly rejected shingles on a daily basis on a misguided notion that shingle nail application was an absolute science that couldn't be altered by any slight change of the nail pattern.

The truth is that all shingles are made from the same materials, yet different manufacturers allow different nail locations. If a nail pattern works on one brand of shingle, it will work on all of them. The NRCA has long held that shingles stability depends on the glue strip sealing, and once a shingle is sealed, it doesn't matter where the nails are. On the contrary, shingles that are expertly nailed exactly where the manufacturer intended them are not any good if they do not seal. They will blow up in moderate winds.

After Powell got through with him, Doug Klopfenstein was visibly shaking. By the time of Doug Klopfenstein's testimony, Welch Watt had retired, and Doug Klopfenstein had taken over from Watt as the inspector who rejected shingles or construction, not because it was improperly installed or in danger of failing, but because it did not meet the exact letter of the specification as interpreted only by TDI. Doug Klopfenstein was not used to having his authority questioned. He was very smug when questioned by TDI attorneys but emotionally distraught when repeatedly challenged by Powell. But unlike Nelson, Doug Klopfenstein was not evasive or untruthful. He told the truth, and his admissions as detailed previously should be enough to completely disband the TDI field offices and end the persecution of roofers.

The first day of the hearing ended with Doug Klopfenstein's testimony, and afterward he approached me to shake my hand ,indicating it was nothing personal, that he was only doing his job. Doug Klopfenstein actually respected me but felt that he could not allow anyone to second-guess TDI inspectors.

The hearing was scheduled only for three days, but TDI had only questioned two of their seven inspectors. It was obvious that the hearing was going to last longer than three days. TDI had not had an engineering disciplinary hearing last longer than one day.

Olivia Connett was visibly distressed throughout the first day, and her assistant had to finish the afternoon for her. When all the parties arrived for the second day of the hearing, Ms. Connett was not present. Her assistant explained that Ms. Connett had bleeding and complications with her pregnancy and had to go to the hospital. Though completely briefed on the hearing, her assistant did not feel comfortable continuing by herself and asked the judge for a continuance. Powell and I agreed. What was unknown to TDI and the judge is that Powell's son was in the hospital with a serious ailment that was life threatening. Powell was able to stay in Austin with his son, who made a full recovery.

I welcomed the break because TDI had revealed their entire case with their questioning of Nelson and Doug Klopfenstein. A continuance would give me more time to gather evidence against TDI. No one thought that the continuance would go on for nine months. I never did hear what happened to Ms. Connett. Though concerned with the health of Ms. Connett and her unborn child, it was my opinion that Connett's treatment of me before and during the hearing and her treatment of other engineers deserved her termination of employment for malicious prosecution on "known" innocent and competent engineers. She never once investigated the validity of any TDI accusation. Like any unaccountable bureaucrat, she did her job regardless who she wrongfully harmed.

None of the TDI attorneys, engineers, or inspectors appeared to care that their decisions and actions cost engineers, builders, and homeowners hundreds of thousands, if not millions, of dollars in losses over the frivolous placement of nails or exact reading of a product evaluation that was never intended to be absolute but only as a guide. They were paid bureaucrats who did their jobs, just as Nazi soldiers did theirs.

The Board Action

It would be over nine months before my hearing resumed in September of 2012. Meanwhile I remained under probation on every job that I would turn in a WPI-2 on. So I continued to issue all of my work through other engineers. By doing this, I was effectively being audited on every job, not by TDI engineers who had no practical experience, but by my peers, actual practicing civil structural engineers. In April of 2012 I finally received word from the board concerning a complaint from TDI.

The complaint consisted of the TDI allegations in the SOAH hearing verbatim to the board. The TDI attorneys did not change one word. The entire complaint used in the SOAH hearing in which TDI claimed was only about David Day as an inspector and had nothing to do with engineering was now submitted to the board as a complaint about David Day as an engineer. Connett had indicated this in her opening remarks before the SOAH judge. She indicated that the board would be deciding on Mr. Day's professionalism. What she deliberately did not indicate that first day is that the complaint against David Day in SOAH court as inspector was filed with the board against David Day as an engineer.

The complaint had been entered to the board in September or October of 2011. It took the board six months to investigate the complaint. During that time, no one in my office was contacted nor was any of the clients whose roofs were affected contacted. After six months, I received a registered letter from Charles Pennington with the board. The statement listed some but not all of the complaints in the SOAH charges, but it did list each address contained in the SOAH complaint. The board letter stated that the complaint had been filed and listed the same charges contained in the SOAH complaint. The letter further claimed that the charges had been investigated, and the board deemed them credible, and I had thirty days to refute the charges.

At the time I received the board complaint, I had already filed complaints with the board against Stephen Harp, PE, and Sam Nelson, PE, for incompetence, fraud, and malicious persecution of engineers. In my complaints, I listed witnesses' phone numbers and addresses. The board did not contact any of the people involved in my complaints, yet after six months, they dismissed the complaints as not having sufficient grounds. In TDI's complaint against me, the board, without interviewing or contacting any witnesses, found the complaint to be credible. Is this a double standard? Probably! It certainly shows a bias toward the complainant.

So I was now tasked with proving my innocence and competence to two different state agencies. Fortunately there was now the transcripts of Nelson's and Doug Klopfenstein's testimony, in which both admitted there was a clear difference of opinion between David Day and TDI over interpretations of manufacturer's instructions and product evaluations. I responded to the board through my attorney Powell.

Powell submitted the SOAH allegations in that TDI considered them to be inspector errors and not engineering fraud. Powell then quoted from the trial transcripts, proving the allegations were disagreements. Powell also submitted my responses to the SOAH allegations.

After another sixty days, the board came back with their formal response. Of the eight addresses listed in the TDI complaint, based on Powell's response, the board dismissed six of the addresses as not credible and issued a formal disciplinary action against me for my actions on the roofs at Suntide III and Sunchase IV on South Padre Island. It must be noted here that TDI dropped the charges against me in the SOAH hearing concerning Sunchase IV. The board offered up a $900 fine and six-month probation for the alleged offenses. I had the option of accepting the charges or requesting a formal hearing with the board to defend myself in person.

Usually at this point the majority of the engineers who received fines from the board similar to mine did not contest the charges and accepted the fine. I had interviewed dozens of them over the phone and some of them in person. I usually got the same response: the fine was small, and the engineers did not have the time or money to defend themselves in Austin. Even though the charges were generally baseless or a difference of opinion, the board was routinely fining engineers based on frivolous, baseless, and in some cases fraudulent charges by TDI. As evidenced with my complaint, the board was not doing any interviewing of witnesses. If TDI decreed it, it must be true.

The best case that illustrates the injustice of TDI and board action is the case of Vera Green, PE, of Galveston. Her case parallels my case in fascinatingly similar circumstances. Vera Green was a Czechoslovakian immigrant who had done her undergraduate studies in the Czech Republic. She had fled the totalitarian communist government and gotten a visa to the United States. Ms. Green was a licensed professional engineer in Arizona and Texas and specialized in restoring older buildings. Her engineering emphasis was structural, and she was highly qualified to be on the TDI appointment list and as competent as and more so than any other engineer on the list.

Similar to me, Ms. Green had certified many structures and reroofs after the 2008 Hurricane Ike. Ms. Green lived and worked in Galveston, and after Ike hit, she, as with all engineers in the area, was inundated with roof inspections. Because of the sheer volume of properties affected, many residences got inspected by both TDI and appointed engineers. As previously described at length, TDI will not accept shingle roofs that are applied with a nail gun because of their incorrect interpretation of overdriven nails. Like me, Ms. Green also got crossways with TDI when she accepted roofs that TDI rejected.

Faced with a lengthy fight in Austin or paying for roofs that she had no part in installing, Ms. Green accepted a plea deal with TDI in which she would voluntarily resign from the TDI appointment list, and TDI would drop all charges against Ms. Green and not refer her to the board for disciplinary action. This plea deal was illegal and certainly unethical on the part of TDI, especially the licensed engineers within TDI. If an engineer fraudulently signs a WPI-2 as TDI alleges, then TDI is legally bound to notify the board. They don't have the power to make plea deals concerning engineering. Section 1001.553 of the Engineering Practice Act states: "Report of a Violation—A public official shall report a violation of this chapter to the proper authorities."

By making a plea deal with engineers, TDI is violating the Engineering Practice Act, which is the law in Texas. By accepting the plea deal, Ms. Green assumed that, that would be the end of it. She would no longer certify work for TWIA and would just practice structural engineering. In one of her e-mails to me, Ms. Green stated that nothing in the totalitarian communist country that she fled compared to her treatment by TDI.

What happened next should not happen to any engineer. Another engineer in the Kingsville, Texas, area was found guilty by TDI and by the board of falsely signing WPI-2s. I never interviewed this engineer, Horacio Castillo, so I could not determine the validity of the charges. Once Mr. Castillo was found guilty and had exhausted his appeals, he requested through the Freedom of Information Act all engineers who had made plea deals with TDI. Mr. Castillo then entered a complaint to the board on all of those engineers with the complaint that TDI had brought against them.

Similar to me, Ms. Green received a letter from the board listing the TDI allegations, and the board found them credible. Ms. Green submitted a response, and similar to me, the board came back with a small fine and a probationary period. Unlike me, Ms. Green chose not to fight the fine even though it was baseless and had not been thoroughly vetted. Ms. Green felt that she did not have the time and, more importantly, the money to contest the charges. So Ms. Green accepted the fine and probation, which was much cheaper than hiring an attorney to contest the charges. Had Ms. Green met me prior to the board hearing, she probably would have contested it. Cautionary notes here to any professional accused of fraud or negligence—don't ever accept a fine of any amount if you are truly innocent. The repercussion on your professional career can be devastating.

It was over a year later when Ms. Green experienced those repercussions. With the economy taking a downturn, Ms. Green's business suffered, as did with many professionals. It was at this time that Ms. Green began an investigation of how to get back on the TDI appointment list. She met with Sam Nelson and the TDI attorneys in Austin. TDI gave Ms. Green a totally arbitrary list of demands including working under an engineer in good standing. TDI had no authority to make such demands, but that had never stopped TDI. Ms. Green was not able to meet the arbitrary TDI demands, but when the legislation changed in 2011, Ms. Green was able to get on the boards list, and TDI then placed her on the new list in 2012.

I knew I was innocent and appealed the board decision. A hearing was set in Austin. Once again I had to dole out thousands of dollars to defend myself against baseless charges. The hearing took place in Austin with me and my two attorneys present and my son, Dennis Day. Present for the board were the executive director; the director of enforcement, C. W. Clark, PE; the investigating officer, Charles Pennington, PE.; the board attorney and assistant attorney; and one member of the board, Bobby Balli, PE. The investigating officer, Pennington, presented the board's position.

Powell and Basham then spoke, briefly describing how the investigating engineer with EFI Global who investigated Suntide III had been completely discredited in his testimony against me and that TDI had dropped the charges for Sunchase IV. I then stood up and, with samples from both roofs and the code book and the product evaluations, proceeded to educate the board on what occurred on both roofs. When I was done approximately twenty minutes later, the board members began to question me. I answered all of their questions expertly, and only Pennington, who had brought the charges, seemed unconvinced about the roof hatch at Suntide III not being my responsibility. Even the board members and the executive director had to remind Pennington that the fasteners were concealed and could not have been seen by me or anyone.

Pennington was soft-spoken and came across as nerdy. If Pennington had done any comprehensive investigation or consulted any roofing authority, he would have concluded I was correct. The board has limited resources and limited staff, but no engineer should be made to suffer for that. Engineering is a broad field and consists of many competencies. A small staff cannot investigate complaints without background and knowledge of the specifics in the complaints. Pennington made no effort to consult outside his limited knowledge. His decisions and those of other board investigators have profound repercussions on the lives of the engineers they are investigating.

Anyone can file a complaint against an engineer. There is a link on the website to file the complaint. From my experience, it appears the board gives the benefit of the doubt to the complainant, unless you are filing a complaint against Sam Nelson, and then even with written evidence, the board dismissed the case. Since Sam Nelson took over as chief engineer for TDI, TDI has filed hundreds of complaints against engineers, and Pennington and other inspectors have frequently found them to be credible even though the majority of them are not. And even with overwhelming convincing evidence by me in my hearing, Pennington was still questioning my professionalism. After the brief hearing, no more than a half hour, the board dismissed me while they deliberated. They sent me and my team to a waiting room. While in the room, we felt fairly confident that we had prevailed. Dennis, who had a degree from Collins College in Tempe Arizona in video production and screenwriting, was taking notes on the hearing for the purpose of producing a movie script about my ordeal. I remarked to him to be sure he gave an accurate description of Pennington in the movie. His short stature, impeccably cropped upright hairstyle, wide eyes, and needling behavior gave all present the impression of a troll. We had been in the room less than ten minutes, and right on cue when the term *troll* came out, Pennington himself knocked on the door and announced that the board had made a decision. Just in case he had overheard, Powell mentioned to Pennington that they were discussing trolling for information.

As soon as they were all seated, the board executive director announced that all charges were dismissed. It took the board ten minutes to undo what TDI had spent two years trying to do, and that would be to absolve David Day of any fraud or negligence. Under the current law in Texas passed by the Texas legislation in 2011, TDI would have to run any disciplinary action through the board and honor the board's decision. I had already been put on the appointment roster. All action by TDI should have ceased at this point. The governing board that licenses engineers had just cleared me of any wrongdoing. There is no SOAH Judge who has the capacity to understand the evidence presented against an engineer more than the board that governs engineers. To not even consider the board's decision for me would be both unprofessional and unforgiveable on the part of an SOAH ALJ. I would soon find out that with TDI, there is no justice, only the enforcement of their will.

The assistant attorney for the board, after the hearing, mentioned to Powell that there was an obvious potential product failure that led to the roof coming off at Suntide III and that TDI let the product manufacturers off the hook while they went after David Day. TDI has demonstrated repeatedly that they do not care about the facts or the truth. They are not going to let an engineer get away with challenging their authority.

The Trial Resumes

The hearing resumed on October 23, 2012, ten months after the hearing had opened in December of 2011. TDI was now represented by two new attorneys, Jennifer Loefler and Sara White. I never did hear what happened to Connett, but Loefler definitely had more experience.

The hearing began with TDI dropping the charges on Sunchase IV. This was the claim where the owner didn't want to pay the roofer because they didn't like the way the roof looked because it billowed in the wind. Their claims were unfounded and even dismissed by TBPE, but TDI, in their zeal to get me, were looking for any excuse. TDI refused to accept the product evaluations that were provided even though they were legal and nationally recognized. The product evaluation that was provided allowed for corner enhancement per the testing institution's, Factory Mutual's, guidelines. TDI wanted a test for the corner and perimeter pressures, which are higher than the field pressures. Also, this roof had already been certified by TDI and had a TWIA policy. If TDI pursued this claim, they might have had to defend their dubious policies in court. TDI dropped the claim in SOAH court but left it in tact in their complaint to the board. As previously detailed, the board would also dismiss the charges against me for Sunchase IV.

TDI then challenged my witness list. The witness list included not only fact witnesses, those who had personal involvement in the case, but also included other engineers and inspectors who had personal knowledge of TDI's abusive tactics or had been in similar circumstances as me. It was TDI's contentions that if the witness was not a fact witness, then they should not be allowed. After all, no engineer had ever brought witnesses to their hearing. TDI's attorneys were obviously ignorant of the rules of court proceedings, and the judge disallowed their request.

In volume 3, page 29, lines 6–10, Loefler states, "TDI witnesses are either disgruntled engineers or are individuals who left TDI on bad terms. In lines 11–14, Loefler continues, "Basically the one thing they have in common, they just don't like TDI." What an outstanding admission by Loefler speaking on behalf of TDI. In TDI's myopic view, anyone who disagreed with their multiple incorrect arbitrary decisions was a chronic malcontent who just didn't like TDI. The seven hundred engineers who dropped off the appointment list when the board created the new roster must have done so because they just did not like TDI.

What follows is a little background on David Day's witnesses.

DON LEE

Lee was a state representative from Harlingen who sponsored the legislation that created the windstorm certification program. Lee then left the legislation to run the windstorm division of TDI. It was Lee's intention to run the program similar to Florida but instead use state employees to do the inspections. Lee travelled to Florida, New York, Louisiana, and other states to meet with state officials and review their programs. I never met Lee in person but did talk to him on the phone several times. Lee had left TDI when he had enough state time to retire, but he also did not like the direction the windstorm program was headed with control being transferred to Austin. Lee told me his biggest regret is that he did not fire Welch Watt. Lee wanted to set the record straight, and he penned the following letter to the TDI commissioner.

Texas Department of Insurance
P. O. Box 149104
Austin, TX 78714-9104

January 3, 2012

Commissioner Elenor Kitzman,

My name is Don Lee. I served in the Texas House of Representatives from 1981 to 1987 for District 38 and 51. In 1987 I was a supporter of the legislation that created the Windstorm Certification Program for Texas Department of Insurance (TDI). The intent of the legislation was to provide an affordable program for the residences of the 14 coastal counties that insured homes were built to resist the higher winds from hurricanes.

In 1988 I joined TDI as the manager of Wind Pool Operation. I served in this capacity until 1992. From 1992 to 1995 I served in the position of liaison between TDI and Texas Windstorm Insurance Association (TWIA).

During my 1988 – 1995 tenure as TDI Manager, I visited state agencies in Florida, South Carolina and New York to research effective affordable windstorm insurance. At TDI we were attempting to pattern our risk pool management similar to that of Florida. We wanted local control of building practices and established local offices to provide timely affordable inspections to these builders and homeowners that wanted insurance through TWIA.

In our seven regional offices there was a good working relationship with the builders and homeowners. The exception was the Angleton office that was managed by Welch Watt. There were constant complaints from this area due to Mr. Watt's excessive rejection of new construction and reroofs.

As personnel in Austin changed in the Windtake Division, the focus and intent of the program changed completely. Instead of enforcing standard codes, TDI began to dictate design and construction procedures through prescriptive guides that were treated as code. They also used their power to control local Engineers. Under the leadership of Mr. Watt, the majority of local TDI inspectors left the program and the majority of windstorm inspection was transferred to private Engineers and inspectors. This was never the intent of the original legislation.

The process in affect today is expensive, harmful to homeowners and subject to wide spread abuse. TDI Engineering Department under the supervision of Sam Nelson, P. E., has completely destroyed the original intent of the program to help homeowners. Mr. Nelson is abusing his power and using the

Administrative Law Court (ALC) to accuse Engineers with fraud who disagrees with him on matters of Engineering.

I have become familiar with the case of TDI vs. David Day, P. E. of Harlingen, TX. I have read the complaints against Mr. Day and the replies from Mr. Day. Mr. Day's case and all others like them are an abuse of the ALC system. If Mr. Nelson has a problem with Mr. Day's or other Engineers engineering decisions, he should get an opinion from the Texas Board of Professional Engineers (TBPE).

At present Mr. Nelson has no adequate supervision or oversight. When I was manager of Wind Pool Operations, I would never have supported Mr. Nelson to take the actions that he is taking.

The TDI is allowing Mr. Nelson to illegally prosecute Engineers. This action will lead to class action suits against TDI. It is my understanding that Mr. Nelson currently has two formal complaints against him being investigated by the TBPE with more likely to come.

TDI needs to stop the abusive practice of using ALC's to take actions against Engineers. Mr. Nelson should be relieved of his duties until the TBPE evaluates the complaints against him. All ALC actions against Engineers should cease until the TBPE has evaluated the Engineers for any alleged wrong doing.

I am willing to attend any meetings or hearings to discuss the TDI Windstorm practices, past, present or future.

Respectfully submitted,

Don Lee

Don Lee
2001 Parker Lane #128
Austin, TX 78741
Ph: (512) 965-6863

The man who sponsored the legislation that created Sam Nelson's position had stated in his letter that Nelson's position and that of all the TDI in house inspectors were no longer necessary. Do you think Don Lee wrote that letter because he didn't like TDI? What Mr. Lee did not like is what TDI and the windstorm program had become—an abusive, bureaucratic, bloated entity. Mr. Lee was right, the TDI oversight of TWIA needed to go.

Unfortunately Mr. Lee passed away in the summer of 2012. His letter to the commissioner is his legacy, and he specifically interviewed and promised me he would do all he could to correct the injustices of the TDI Windstorm Program under Welch Watt, Sam Nelson, and Alexis Dick.

HENRY SEGURA, PE

Mr. Segura, like Vera Green, underwent the same abuse as me, and his case remarkably parallels mine. Mr. Segura, unlike some of the engineers on the appointment list who never practiced structural engineering full-time before getting appointed, had always practiced structural engineering and was extremely competent and practical.

As the result of abusive audits in which, like me, TDI refused to accept his design information even though it was correct, charges in an SOAH courthouse were brought against Segura. TDI engineers', particularly Harp and Nelson's, favorite line is that the audited engineer failed to provide substantiating calculations or product information. The problem with Harp and Nelson is that the information they were rejecting is routinely accepted in Florida, California, and everywhere else in the country.

Segura showed up to his hearing with only his attorney and was his own witness. TDI also relied only on their in-house engineers and inspectors. The SOAH ALJ not only sided with Segura, who was able to walk the judge through all the evidence and accurately described why TDI was wrong and out of line, the judge admonished TDI and stated that the harassment needed to stop.

The TDI attorneys in their final written statements to the commissioner reiterated the false accusations against Segura and that Segura was guilty of fraud, but they would respect the ALJ's wishes.

I observed that no matter how much TDI's evidence is refuted, they will never admit they are wrong.

TDI left Segura alone for a few years until, according to Segura, a real estate inspector filed a complaint with TDI on one of the homes Segura had inspected. TDI put the home under audit and once again refused to accept Segura's design even though it was correct, and once again TDI put all of Segura's projects under audit and filed a second complaint against Segura in an SOAH court. This time Segura got a different ALJ. The evidence was similar to first hearing with baseless charges of fraudulently sealing a WPI-2. Once again Segura defended himself, but this time the ALJ ruled in TDI's favor. TDI removed Segura from the appointment list and then filed the same charges with the board. As with me, the board found Segura in violation of the Engineering Practice Act and gave a small fine and probationary period. Like me, Segura appealed the ruling and had a hearing in Austin. Like me, after presenting his evidence, Segura was exonerated, and the response that he got from the board was that it was apparent that Segura was being picked on. They even asked Segura if he wanted to file a complaint against TDI Engineering. At this point Segura was burned out from the whole process. Mr. Segura continues to practice structural engineering in the Houston and Galveston area, but his designs are certified by other engineers—the very same designs that TDI said could not be substantiated. So Mr. Segura was another witness for David Day who "just didn't like TDI."

DELTON LEE

Delton Lee was son of Don Lee but was an ex–naval officer and worked for the TDI, Harlingen, Texas, field office as a field quality control inspector. He was one of the original groups of TDI inspectors who were charged with enforcing the TDI prescriptive guide. Unlike many of the inspectors, Delton had experience as a general contractor, a framing carpenter, and a roofer.

Delton witnessed firsthand the change that occurred when Welch Watt took over as manager of the windstorm division of TDI. Prior to Watt, TDI inspectors could make decisions and interpret the code and manufacturer's directives as they were generally interpreted by roofers and the majority of the country. After Watt took over, it became Watt's way or the highway. Watt brought in his myopic interpretation of the code and roofing standards. Watt was in no way an authority and where the code did not address a situation, Watt made up rules that were not in writing but nonetheless enforced, as for an example, scuff marks. What was even worse, if a roofer added more than what was needed, as in adding an additional nail to a shingle, Watt would reject it with the lame excuse that it was not the way that it was tested. Anywhere else in the world, more is better when it comes to adding nails to shingles.

Delton Lee went from being a respected inspector to having to constantly look over his shoulder to see if he was going to be second-guessed. He witnessed TDI quality control managers come behind him on a roof that he had accepted and continue to lift shingles until they found what they called overdriven or crooked nails. Lee watched as TDI inspectors were disciplined and threatened with termination until they either left TDI or would not accept anything for fear of being second-guessed.

That is why engineers got into the business of certifying roofs. TDI would inspect roofs for free while engineers even in the late nineties would charge $200 plus for a reroof certification. Roofers started getting rejected for work that had been previously accepted by TDI inspectors and in fact was correct. They were now being rejected by inspectors under the iron hand of Welch Watt. They just couldn't repair the roof, which is totally acceptable, they had to replace the entire roof. TDI inspectors went from inspecting over 90 percent of roofs to less than 10 percent of roofs.

Delton lee had enough time with the navy and the state to retire, so rather than put up with further abuse from his fellow employees at TDI, he took early retirement and walked away to resume his career as a general contractor.

Delton Lee became good friends with me because I was one of the few engineers who knew what I was doing and also had an abundance of common sense. Lee visited the sites at Fannin, Greenbriar, and Guadalajara and confirmed that TDI was involved in a concerted effort to target me and oust me from the windstorm appointment list. It was an obvious witch hunt. The roofs at Greenbriar,

Fannin, and Guadalajara were as good as or better than any in the country and had been routinely approved by TDI inspectors before Welch Watt became manager. So Delton Lee was another witness for David Day who "just did not like TDI."

What Delton Lee, Don Lee, Henry Segura, and Vera Green all have in common is that they were subjects of abuse by TDI personnel and that Sam Nelson, Welch Watt, or Alexis Dick did not like them. Nelson, Dick, and Watt were the only ones who could authorize continuous audits or disciplinary action against an engineer or a TDI inspector.

The ALJ dismissed TDI's concerns about my witness list and allowed them all to stay on. Unfortunately, because of TDI's two-year delay in my hearing, two of the witnesses, Don Lee and George De La Matyr, PE, had passed away, and one potential witness, Bob Burkhart, PE, passed away before the hearing began. What are the odds?

Next in the hearing, Powell introduced the case of TWIA v. TDI. During the ten-month delay in the hearing, I had discovered the TWIA hearing from one of the many engineers that I would interview when I found their name pop up on a TDI disciplinary action. The TWIA v. TDI hearing is the epitome of the abuse of TDI Enforcement Division and a prime example of government overreach in general.

A Brief History of TDI v. TWIA

After Hurricanes Dolly and Ike in 2008, thousands of frivolous claims were being turned in. Many homes that sustained no damage or minimal damage were filing claims for complete reroofs through public adjusters. The claims process works as follows: The property owner will file a claim with his insurance company, who will then send out an adjuster to access the damage. The adjuster will visit the home and record any damage that is related to a windstorm event, such as shingle loss, impact damage to glazing or finishes, and interior water damages from a storm-created opening. The adjuster will then write up an estimate and, depending on the policy, will include depreciation and then subtract the policy deductible and turn in his estimate to the insurance company, who will then cut a check for estimate amount. Many times the damage is for roof coverings only, and with a 2 percent deductible, the balance will only pay for half of the roof replacement.

In an effort to increase the insurance payout, many homeowners turn to attorneys or public adjusters who are private adjusters for hire, and they perform their own inspections. A roof with only a handful of shingles blown off would not meet the deductible. The public adjusters were lifting the shingles to determine if they were still sealed. If the shingles were not sealed, the public adjusters were calling it wind damage and were giving estimates for complete reroofs. TWIA denied the claims and even put out a memo stating that unsealed shingles were not an insurance claim unless there was evidence that the wind broke the seals and lifted the shingles. If shingles lift during a storm, there would be evidence of debris beneath the shingles. Many shingles over time will lose their seal, and many that are placed during cold weather may never seal. For unsealed shingles, TWIA recommended resealing them.

Many of the claims denied for unsealed shingles had been certified by TDI inspectors. TDI objected to the TWIA claims that shingles that were not sealed were not an insurance claim. TDI's position is that if TDI certified them, then they were sealed and could have only been loosened by high winds.

TDI filed a complaint in an SOAH court to force TWIA to pay the claims. This was an absurd complaint and once again a significant overreach by TDI to affect the commerce of a semiprivate agency.

In the hearing, TDI arrogantly relied solely on their in house staff of Sam Nelson, PE, and Welch Watt. TWIA brought in roofing experts, PhDs, and roofing manufacturers. TDI's testimony was that the shingles were checked for sealant as part of the certification but at the same time admitted that they checked shingles after the roof was complete before the shingles were sealed. In other words, it would be impossible to lift shingles and check the nails if the shingles had already sealed. Even Watt was forced to admit that it may take several days to a week for the shingles to seal and that TDI inspectors did not make return trips to verify the shingles had sealed.

TWIA produced testimony from experts that shingle sealant is activated by heat and that shingles installed in cold weather may never seal. Even manufacturer's warranty literature states that if shingles do not seal within one year, to seal them with roof cement. It was TDI's contention that sealing with roof cement was not proper because that is not the way the shingles are tested. Once again TDI and Watt were trying to split hairs with reality. The seal and strip that comes on all shingles is composed of the same roof cement that is used to repair shingles. Asphalt sealant is asphalt sealant whether it comes on the shingle or is applied afterwards.

Some of the more extraordinary testimony came from TWIA management, who stated that TDI took unilateral action against TWIA without any meetings or even correspondence to discuss the issues. The ALJ noted that TWIA testimony was much more credible than that of TDI and stated in the written opinion that Welch Watt admitted under oath that his only roofing experience was as a laborer for a roofing contractor, and Sam Nelson's only experience as chief engineer for the windstorm division was a two-week transition period with the previous engineer. The ALJ specifically ruled that neither Nelson nor Watt could back up their opinions.

The ALJ ruled in TWIA's favor that their contention that shingles may not seal is correct and that unsealed shingles can be repaired by sealing them with roof cement. Powell presented compelling evidence that even though TDI had already been ruled against in SOAH court for sealing shingles, TDI still charged Day with improperly sealing shingles at the roof at Guadalajara.

The hearing then resumed with Stephen Harp, PE, as the next TDI witness. Harp testified for the remaining of the first day and into the next, not because of all the questions that were asked of him but because his answers were excruciatingly slow. Even with his own attorneys coaching him, Harp gave a very poor performance. He was prone to one gaffe after another. When Powell cross-examined him, he was unintelligible.

In volume 3, page 37, Harp begins his testimony by describing his duties as making sure engineers' performances are improved. Improved? Compared to what? Harp had one short-term job working with a home designer, less than a year. This in no way would make him eligible to meet the board's new requirements of two years of structural experience to be put on the windstorm roster. And it certainly does not give him the experience to be auditing engineers and improving their experience. Mr. Harp was hired into TDI eight years prior into one of the worst environments an engineer could be placed into. He was placed among engineers, especially Sam Nelson, who had no structural experience yet were very vain in thinking that they knew more about the code than the rest of the code experts around the country. The TDI engineers were continually reinforced in their perception of themselves as being infallible by the appointment engineers who continuously sought out their opinions. The appointed engineers did this not because they believed the TDI engineers knew what they were doing but because if you challenged or disagreed with Sam Nelson, you could be charged with fraud. Nelson had already admitted under oath that there was a difference of opinion between David Day and TDI. Yet I was being charged with fraud for signing a WPI-2 that the majority of the engineers on the appointment list would sign and do sign on a daily basis.

The first home that Harp testified on was Shadowbrook. On this file, the TDI inspector had visited the home three times: two times during the first day and one more time after the roof was completed. He issued a fourth report stating that the file was closed. Harp testified that the inspector made four trips to the home. This was significant in that Harp did not understand his own inspector's field forms and that the TDI attorney did not understand them either. Yet these were the two people who were passing judgment on me based solely on evidence submitted by TDI field inspectors. Harp never visited any of the sites that he sat in judgment of me on.

On Volume 3, pages 47 through 49, Harp discussed at length overdriven nails at Shadowbrook. There were no photos taken by the TDI inspector for the Shadowbrook residence. Harp was indicting me based solely on the word of the TDI inspector without any evidence to back up the claim. Also on page 48, lines 24 and 25, Harp states that the shingle must be torn or damaged to call nails overdriven. There certainly was no evidence of a torn or damaged shingle submitted by TDI, but more importantly, this testimony conflicted with Doug Klopfenstein and Nelson, who said that the shingle did not have to be torn or damaged to call the nail overdriven.

On Volume 3, page 91, lines 11–14, Harp states that warranty and building code requirements are separate criterion. He even called them apples and oranges on pages 10 through 14. This is incorrect for the sole reason that the building code for shingles only states that they must be installed in accordance with the manufacturer's instructions. The warranty covers additional items, such as mold resistance, but all of the building code criteria are contained in the warranty.

For the Guadalajara roof, TDI repeatedly tried to dismiss manufacturer's warranty information because I produced a manufacturer's bulletin that stated unequivocally that inadvertent exposed nails could be covered with roof tar, and it would not affect the warranty. When this bulletin was produced, TDI should have dismissed their complaint for Guadalajara, but the truth is they were not concerned about the roof; at this point they were doing everything they could to get me in trouble and find fault with my work.

For the Shadowbrook roof, in which corrections had been made to the roof before certifying it, Harp repeatedly stated that my actions were suspicious because I gave a photo of the roof receipt instead of producing the receipt. What was suspicious about this? As I would later explain, the roofer produced his receipt at the jobsite; I took a photo of it for my records and submitted it to TDI. What is the difference between taking a photo and photocopying the receipt? With the technology these days, I could have scanned the receipt with my phone and transmitted it directly via e-mail to TDI, but somehow Harp stated that this activity was suspicious. As I observed repeatedly from previous audits, Stephen Harp did not approach an audit to verify compliance; he approached it with the sole purpose of seeing what he could find wrong. He would go to the extreme of making things up as he did when he stated in his correspondence that the roof cement used to cover the nails at Guadalajara harmed the shingles because it blocked the granules from reflecting UV rays. The roof cement applied in the area the size of a penny on a black shingle is not going to do anything to harm the shingle and is the same cement used to seal the shingles. Mr. Harp just made this up because he never produced a source to back it up when I requested it.

When questioned about the Miami-Dade NOAs that were produced, on page 92 and 93, Harp states, "We can't just assume that you know, the Miami-Dade County people that wrote these reports, you know, provided factual or true information." This is a very damning statement on the part of Harp and TDI in general. Miami-Dade is the most respected product evaluator in the country, and they set the standard for the rest of the country. They have engineers in-house who actually know what they are doing. For Harp to say that Miami-Dade evaluators might not know what they are doing would be equivalent to saying that the Kelley Blue Book cannot be trusted for evaluating cars or Dun & Bradstreet cannot be relied upon to evaluate credit.

Harp should be fired or at least reprimanded for making such a foolish statement, but he continues to this day to make similar foolish statements.

As stated earlier, Harp's statements were extremely slow. Harp took almost twenty minutes to describe a ridge of roof while drawing a picture on a poster sheet. A ridge can be described with a simple sentence, "Where two slopes of roof come together," and he could have placed his hands together to demonstrate.

After over a half day of questioning by his own TDI attorney on information that should have been covered in less than one hour, Powell finally got to cross-examine him. Harp was defensive, red-faced, and strained during his entire cross-examination.

Harp had repeated in correspondence and in testimony stated that I was to have the roof at Guadalajara corrected. After repeatedly being asked who is responsible for having the roof replaced, Harp finally admitted that it is the owner's prerogative. I could not touch that roof without the owner's permission.

Harp stuck to his guns when asked about the legitimacy of Miami-Dade and still stated that they may have illegitimate documentation (page 161, lines 17 through 25). But on page 162, lines 17 through 25, Harp admits that an engineer relying on Miami-Dade is fairly widespread.

After repeatedly stating that a roofer has to rely only on the shingle wrapper to meet code, Harp was forced to admit (page 148, lines 2 through 14) that the code does not reference the shingle wrapper.

This was the same question that embarrassed Dough Klopfenstein when he was questioned by Powell. One would think that the TDI attorneys would have prepared Harp for this question. But TDI was totally vested in their scripted story that if it wasn't on the shingle wrapper, then it must be rejected, even if the shingle is not damaged and is okay with the manufacturer.

For the East Levee job where I had certified repairs to an existing roof, Harp's testimony was almost comical. First, Harp was unaware that the roof covering that was repaired did not have gravel ballast. Harp compared putting a patch on the roof to putting a bumper sticker that was meant for a car bumper to putting a bumper sticker on a tree trunk (page 28, lines 15–25). The distinction that Harp and TDI try to make is that if you put a Brand X cap sheet on a Brand Y cap sheet, it is equivalent to putting a bumper sticker on a tree trunk. This could not be further from reality. A more appropriate description would be comparing putting a bumper sticker to a Ford or a Chevy.

It was Harp's and TDI's contentions that you could not place a cap sheet repair on an existing roof unless the complete tested assembly was applied. TDI fails to realize that tested assemblies can only be done in a lab on new material. You cannot test existing material in a lab. If Brand X cap sheet wants to be used commercially, it will have to be tested over different substrates and insulation boards and felt layers. All of these can be interchangeable, and the deck will always be different. Only in TDI and Harp's world does the cap sheet have to have the full tested assembly for every square inch that is applied to. This never happens in reality, and even the ALJ was incredulous at some of Harp's replies. On any given roof, the cap sheet will be attached to any number of substrates, the base sheet, the adjoining cap sheet, metal flashing, concrete and masonry walls, and plastic vents. To say that it has to have the complete assembly for every square inch it is applied is ludicrous and would preclude any repairs to any roof.

If you take TDI's case against David Day for the Levee roof in saying that new material cannot be applied to existing material, then it would prevent any roof from being repaired unless all roofing material is removed and a complete new assembly is installed. A homeowner could not replace tree-damaged shingles on one slope unless all shingles are replaced because at some point, a new shingle is going to be covered by or cover an existing shingle, and as Doug Klopfenstein and Harp would state, that is not the way it is tested.

If TDI audited all roofs the way they audited Levee and Guadalajara, then no one's roof, including the roofs of the TDI engineers, attorneys, inspectors, Welch Watt's roof, Alexis Dick's roof, the ALJ's roof, the governor's mansion, and the office that houses TDI could pass inspection. Harp even made the outrageous statement that no roof could be accepted that had scuff marks from foot traffic (volume 4, page 8, lines 1–8). You have to walk on a roof to install it, and the majority of the shingles will have scuff marks. This is equivalent to walking on a new carpet and leaving a footprint. By TDI standards, that carpet would have to be rejected.

Powell, in his redirect, asked Harp, "If scuff marks were truly damaging to shingles, wouldn't the damage still be present two years later?" And Harp replied that it would be the same or worse (page 52, lines 1–7). Powell asked him if the shingles at Guadalajara still showed scuff marks, and Harp didn't know. This is important because TDI was indicting me on scuff marks that are not even a code or manufacturer defect and no longer existed at Guadalajara. They washed off with the first rain, as the manufacturer's literature stated.

On the same home, Guadalajara, Harp argued that the exposed nails would corrode and damage the roof and argued that covering them with tar is not acceptable even though the manufacturer had issued a bulletin stating it was acceptable. Harp dismissed this bulletin because he said it wasn't in the code. All the code states for asphalt shingles is that "they will be installed in accordance with the manufacturer's requirements." A bulletin issued by the manufacturer's would meet the "manufacturer's requirements." The nails used at Guadalajara were corrosion-resistant nails and would last as long as the shingles if they were totally exposed. Harp had claimed that metal cannot be exposed even though the roof had metal vents and metal flashing exposed that had the same zinc or galvanized coating.

Harp's entire testimony totally lacked credibility and was prone to outlandish statements such as comparing a roof cover to putting a bumper sticker on a tree and saying that Miami-Dade test evaluations could not be trusted. No experienced attorney would have ever put Harp on a witness stand. He came off as a cartoon character, and even the ALJ would frequently question his replies. She did this with no other witness, only Harp. Harp's demeanor was reminiscent of Johnny Galecki's character, Leonard, on the television show *The Big Bang Theory*.

The TDI attorneys were not experienced attorneys. They were totally ignorant of the facts of the case and had either not talked to any of their witnesses or had not adequately briefed any of them. A legitimate court and a legitimate judge would have never allowed the case against Day to be brought. But as Day would find out, there is no justice within TDI and the control they have over the SOAH courts. Harp was a joke as a witness, and no good attorney would have put him on the stand. TDI was so used to getting their way with using their in-house staff, they put up as witnesses whoever was involved in the case no matter how incompetent.

The next two witnesses were TDI field inspectors, Benito Garcia and Daniel Cantu. Garcia had only been involved in Guadalajara, and Cantu was involved in Shadowbrook and Guadalajara. Garcia was up first and had no problem embellishing the truth or just flat-out lying.

Garcia began his testimony by stating that he began working for TDI in 1998. This happens to be the same time that Sam Nelson and Welch Watt were promoted to chief engineer for Windstorm and director of inspections respectively. Garcia described his duties as doing inspection verification on the TDI field inspectors. It must be noted that during this time, the TDI field inspection staff went from over fifty to approximately fifteen. If a TDI inspector did not do Welch Watt's biding and rejects nails installed with a pneumatic gun, then he would soon be forced out of TDI. Benito Garcia and Doug Klopfenstein were the chief enforcers of Watt's will.

Garcia began his testimony on Guadalajara by describing some information he had obtained on the Atlas Pinnacle website that addressed exposed nails (page 68, lines 20–25). The TDI attorney pressed on and attempted to use this information to indict my acceptance of the nails that were partially exposed. It must be noted that the TDI attorneys had spent three days with three witnesses, Nelson,

Klopfenstein, and Harp, emphatically stating that only the information on the wrapper could be used to judge shingle installation, and now they were saying that information they had found on the Internet could be used against me.

When asked if the roof at Guadalajara was acceptable, Garcia stated that he had told Juan Salinas and Day to tear the roof off and start over (page 103, lines 1–12). This is completely untrue. No one at TDI, including Nelson and Watt, will ever tell a roofer or engineer to tear a roof off. Even Garcia's and Harp's letters and reports stated that corrections needed to be made. In fact, in the presence of Salinas and the homeowner and me, when Garcia was given a copy of the Atlas bulletin stating the nails could be covered with roof cement, Garcia stated, "If the engineer accepts it, I will accept it." In fact, he repeated it several times.

Garcia also stated he never talked to the owner (page 112, lines 4–6). This is also blatantly untrue. As stated above, he told the owner he would accept the roof if the engineer accepts it. The homeowner was trying to find out from Garcia if he was going to accept the roof. Garcia would not tell the owner the result of his inspection.

Garcia then contradicted himself and stated that it was inappropriate for TDI to advise a roofer to replace a roof after it is finished (page 116, lines 1–10). It was my opinion that TDI did this deliberately. They would never tell a roofer to replace a roof. They would just put in their reports that corrections needed to be made, and this is what they did at Guadalajara. They would just refuse to accept it until the roofer replaced it. They would also tell the roofer that they could get an engineer to accept the roof. This is, at best, an unethical policy and possibly illegal. If TDI feels the roof is unacceptable, they should be legally bound to state so. Telling a roofer or a homeowner that he has the option to get an engineer to accept it is an untrue statement. At this point the roof is already an open file at TDI and cannot be approved unless TDI inspectors or TDI engineers accept it. Telling a roofer or homeowner that an engineer can accept it is an untrue statement. Only TDI can accept the roof once they initiate an investigation. This frequent and abusive process should be grounds for termination for the entire windstorm inspection and engineering division, legal staff, and supervisors. It amounts to nothing less than entrapment for engineers who disagree almost universally with TDI on what constitutes an overdriven nail from an air gun.

Garcia also stated in his testimony (page 117, lines 1–13) that it is inappropriate to lift shingles after they have sealed. Garcia lifted numerous shingles in the presence of me and Salinas at Guadalajara.

The most blatant lie from Garcia is when he was asked by Powell if he had seen the Atlas Technical Bulletin on the jobsite, he replied, "No, sir" (page 129, lines 11–13). Garcia was handed the bulletin by me at the jobsite in the presence of the homeowner and Salinas. This is when he told the homeowner that he was not aware of the bulletin, and if the engineer accepted it, he would accept it. If Garcia did not remember getting this bulletin and talking to the owner, he should have said so instead of lying under oath.

While being questioned by TDI, Garcia said he would accept some exposed nails, "fifteen to twenty." I knew this was not true because Garcia accepted a roof in the Corpus Christi area that I had turned down because Doug Klopfenstein had rejected it for over-driven nails. When another engineer took it over, Garcia allowed him to make corrections and put tar on exposed nails. I sent Chris Hamby from CASA to look at the roof, and Chris found over two hundred exposed nails and nails covered with tar.

When questioned under oath, Garcia stated he accepted it because it only had twelve exposed nails (page 132). Garcia either missed over two hundred nails or he was lying. The roof still stands as is with the exposed nails.

One of the more egregious statements by Garcia both in his reports and in testimony (page 136, lines 18–23) is that Salinas's shoes were causing scuff marks. Garcia and Salinas were wearing the same Sketchers sneakers.

Garcia constantly stated that the roof was unacceptable because of all the scuff marks, and if he were the owner, he would not accept it. It must be noted that the homeowner never objected to the roof appearance and wanted TDI to accept it. When asked by Powell if the code addressed scuff marks, Garcia admitted that it did not (page 144, lines 3–8).

Garcia was such a poor witness and contradicted himself so many times that after Powell got through with him, the TDI attorney did not offer any redirect. A judge would normally take this into account, but as we would later find out, apparently not by Cloninger.

The next witness was Daniel Cantu. In my opinion Cantu was the only TDI employee who gave an honest testimony. He made no attempt to discredit me and even validated my contention that repairs were made at Shadowbrook. Cantu's testimony did more to validate me than harm me. Upon having to make numerous admissions that TDI had no written policies on scuff marks or sealing shingles during Powell's cross-examination, TDI once again chose not to redirect.

The fourth day of testimony ended with Cantu's testimony. The hearing was originally scheduled for three days in January 2012 for a complaint that was brought in October of 2010. TDI had presented five witnesses, all TDI employees, and still had two to go: the engineer who evaluated Suntide III after Tropical Storm Hermine blew the roof cover off in September of 2010 and a TWIA representative to testify on Suntide III.

The Fifth Day of
Hearing: Round 5

The fifth day began with TDI calling the engineer who had written the report for Suntide III after the roof blew off during Tropical Storm Hermine. I had read the engineering report after it had been given during discovery. The report was full of errors and was not meant to be a report of causation. The investigation was done at the request of TWIA to determine if the roof claim was an insurable claim by TWIA. The report concluded that wind caused the roof cover to blow off, and it was an insurable claim. Based on the engineering report, TWIA paid the claim.

I had encountered this engineering company twice before, and each time incorrect conclusions of fact were made. After Dolly, one of the high-rise condominiums had suffered extensive damage to the parapet walls. The storm had severely pitted the parapet wall, which is the five-foot wall around the roof concealing the rooftop. The pitting left large water blisters on the parapet wall where wind-driven rain had been driven beneath the wall covering. There is no doubt that water was beneath the parapet wall cover and no doubt that water would migrate below the roof cover, but somehow the inspecting engineer found no evidence of damage on this roof, and based on his report, TWIA denied the claim. The homeowner appealed the decision, and eventually TWIA was forced to pay to replace the damaged parapet walls covers.

The second encounter was on an automotive repair shop in Port Isabel that had sprayed-on polyurethane roof over a metal deck. The storm had dislodged large chunks of roof cover and severely scarred the remainder of the roof. The owner, to mitigate the damage, had made temporary repairs to the worst areas that were leaking. The repair contractor had done isolated repairs where they sprayed new foam to seal the leaking areas. The repair areas were obvious, and the bucket and lid that contained repair material were still on the roof when I looked at the roof over six months later.

TWIA had sent the same engineering company to evaluate the roof in October of 2008, three months after the roof had been repaired. By that time the repairs had weathered and were covered with dust, but were still obvious. The inspecting engineer concluded that the repairs were pre-Dolly, and that was evidence that the storm caused no damage.

In an SOAH hearing held in a Harlingen courthouse, the public adjuster presented the contractor who had made the repairs and TWIA's own photos taken in 2007 showing the roof with no scarring and a report that listed the roof in fair condition. It must be noted that the representative from TWIA under oath dismissed this report because, as he stated, "The employees who produced these reports for TWIA were paid $60 per roof and could not be trusted." So TWIA will take the insurance payments based on these reports but will not pay claims based on the same reports because they say that they cannot be trusted. All TWIA policy holders need to know this.

When the inspecting engineer was called up to testify, he was forced to recant the evidence in his report and was forced to admit that damage was done to the roof during Dolly. His only excuse was that the repairs looked old. The hearing should have ended at this point and the roof repairs awarded to the shop owner. Unfortunately, in a horrific decision issued months after the hearing, the SOAH judge, Stephen Rivas, ruled for TWIA and stated that the engineer for the shop owner, David Day, had admitted that the damage was prior to the storm. This is completely untrue and the exact opposite of the evidence presented. The ALJ had ruled completely opposite of the facts, either deliberately or out of complete ignorance of the evidence. In either case, he should be disciplined for such a blatantly incorrect ruling, and the shop owner should be reimbursed by TWIA for all his expenses and a new roof.

It was with this track record that the engineering witness was called as a witness to testify on the Suntide III roof. If this roof cover had not blown off, it is very likely that I would have never been put under audit on every job which precipitated the witch hunt against me.

I had read the engineering report, and it was obvious that the inspecting engineer did not realize that the roof cover TPO membrane had taken the fiberglass backing off the DensGlass cover board that it had been glued to in the field. This had not been mentioned in his report. I had fully briefed Powell on why the roof had come off and the fact that the engineer had not written about the DensGlass fiberglass backing coming off.

When the TDI attorneys questioned the engineering witness, they did not ask about the DensGlass coming off even though I had written exclusively about it in my reports and in my rebuttal to their report. It was obvious that TDI had not given the inspecting engineer my report or rebuttal.

When Powell questioned the witness, he showed him the small areas where the green fiberglass backing on the DensGlass was still present and asked him what it was; the witness answered that it was the underside of the DensGlass (page 39, lines 5–10 and pages 40–42).

More importantly, the witness agreed that the roof hatch that came off had corroded screws that would not hold it in place under wind pressure (page 50–51). The witness was testifying by phone, but he had the same photos in front of him that Powell was questioning him about. The engineering witness's testimony helped me and severely hurt TDI's case. When Powell was done, once again, there was no redirect.

The last witness for TDI was Patrick Mills, a TWIA claims adjuster. Mills's purpose was to emphasize the amount of damage that the roof cover coming off at Suntide III caused. Mills's testimony would have been very damaging to me if I had in any way been responsible for the roof cover coming off. Instead, Mills's testimony benefitted me and further indicted the motives of TDI.

It was now obvious that the roof failure was at the interface between the DensGlass and the factory-applied DensGlass cover board. This was a product failure and a roof hatch failure; neither of which would be my responsibility or capability to verify. TDI could have used their resources to determine the cause of the DensGlass failure, but instead they concentrated on pointing the finger at me. They never hired a product engineer or forensic specialists to determine if the DensGlass was faulty or, as stated in my reports, had been subjected to the pressure created when the hatch came loose that was greater than the design properties of the DensGlass fiberglass backing. Instead TDI chose to go after me for the purpose of forcing me out of the program by bringing up one bogus claim after another that would have rendered any engineer in the country and any roof in the country as a failure.

Under Powell's cross-examination, Mills admitted that they relied solely on EFI report and the report of a roofing company that did not even install TPO roof covers to assess blame for the roof membrane blowing off during the Tropical Storm Hermine in September of 2010.

Once again, after Powell's cross-examination, there was no redirect by TDI. The state now rested, and it would now be the defense's turn. It had been four and a half days of state testimony in which I was made out to be a thoughtless, careless, negligent engineer who, according to the state, "knowingly and willingly fraudulently signed and sealed WPI-2s on seven different properties," allegations that, if true, should not only have cost me my appointment on the TDI Windstorm list of appointed engineers but also my engineering license and even criminal prosecution. But none of it was true. It was now my turn to set the record straight.

David Day's Turn

After Patrick Mills's testimony, the state rested, and the judge recessed for lunch. During lunch, Powell, Basham, me, and my son, Dennis, discussed strategy. The state had presented their witnesses and evidence in the approximate order of the SOAH complaint culminating in what they thought would be their grand finale, the undoing of me over Suntide III roof failure. Powell had already inflicted mortal wounds to the state case against me for Suntide III.

It was my recommendation that they begin by presenting Suntide III first while it was fresh on the judge's mind and let me bat it out of the park. Powell readily agreed, and the plan was set in motion to undo any damage that the state had thought they had inflicted on me.

I had been a spectator for four and a half days of state testimony and had been Powell's constant advisor. Unlike the state, I had brought actual evidence with me and not just photos that TDI engineers had relied on to pass judgment on me. Neither of the two TDI engineers who testified, Nelson or Harp, had visited any of the jobsites that they testified about. More importantly, I had brought a copy of the IRC and IBC codes and was very familiar with their contents. In fact, TDI borrowed it the first day of testimony when both

Klopfenstein and Nelson were forced to admit that the code does not mention the shingle wrapper.

The TDI witnesses were constantly handed the code book that I had brought and asked to find the information that they had just testified about. In all cases they could not find it in the code because it was not in there, and I knew this. Every time a TDI witness misquoted the code, I would whisper to Powell that it was not in the code, and Powell, upon cross-examination, would hand the witness the code and ask them to find the passage, and repeatedly, they could not do it.

I repeatedly watched the color go out of the face of Nelson and the TDI attorneys as Powell destroyed their testimony. While the engineering witness for Suntide was testifying, I could see that Nelson was visibly upset as the engineer could not identify the green fiberglass backing on the top side of the DensGlass. He actually called it the bottom side. Several times I saw the color go out of the face of the TDI attorneys as their witnesses were constantly challenged by Powell as to what was in the code and then were handed the code and were not able to find it in there.

I had to watch as a spectator as TDI repeatedly misidentified evidence and repeatedly asked their witnesses, "Shouldn't a good inspector have seen that?" when referring to concealed nails beneath shingles.

It was obvious to me that the TDI attorneys were extremely ignorant of the facts of the hearing, and now it was my turn to prove it to the judge.

After lunch, I took the stand and would stay on the stand for a day and a half.

Powell began his questioning as all attorneys do with their expert witnesses by establishing David Day's credentials, which, when summed up, were greater than all of the TDI witnesses' combined. None of the TDI witnesses had ever worked as a quality control engineer outside of TDI. I had over thirty years of quality control experience including large power plant construction and working at a nuclear power plant construction job in Bay City, Texas, where code enforcement is at its strictest.

I actually taught code and inspections at Texas State Technical College, where I was program chairman of the welding technology program for three years in the nineties and was now an adjunct instructor. I also taught metallurgy for welders and machinists. Besides being a registered engineer, I was also an American Welding Society (AWS) certified welding inspector (CWI).

My actual degree from Louisiana State University (LSU) was in construction under the civil engineering department. This made me much more educated in construction than Nelson, Harp, or the EFI engineer, the three engineers who testified against me.

I had managed a testing lab for nine years, Professional Service Industries (PSI), when I came to the Rio Grande Valley in 1987. My whole professional career dealt with codes: welding codes, building codes, and testing procedures. I knew how to interpret the codes and knew when TDI incorrectly interpreted them.

After Powell walked me through my experience, he then turned to Suntide III. Powell would ask his questions in a way that required more than yes or no answers. He would allow me to expound on answers and provide explanations and create a narrative. My experience as an instructor at TSTC allowed me to be comfortable explaining things methodically so that I did more than answer questions. I was actually educating the TDI attorneys and the judge so that when she went back and read the testimony, she would have a clear, concise narrative.

After years of lecturing and giving presentations, I had developed the ability to be an excellent extemporaneous speaker. I would often do guest lecturing and presented PowerPoint presentations to business groups, service clubs, and professional groups including giving windstorm presentations to insurance companies, engineering companies, and city building officials. When I did these PowerPoint presentations, I would put together a series of slides to illustrate points, and then without rehearsing, I would present the information, creating a narrative for each slide. So when I was presented an exhibit at the hearing, I could provide a thorough explanation and give real life examples, unlike Harp comparing a roof patch to putting a bumper sticker on a tree trunk.

After establishing the history of the roof cover application after Dolly at Suntide III, Powell then turned me loose to explain what happened to the roof cover during Tropical Storm Hermine. We had brought two samples of the roof assembly taken from the roof after the roof cover TPO membrane had come off. The samples contained the insulation board with the DensGlass cover board fully adhered to it. The green fiberglass cover membrane was still attached. This sample was taken where the TPO membrane was still adhered to the west wall and part of the floor. I then showed the photos that had been taken by the EFI engineer and blown up by TDI in an effort to show the magnitude of the damage. Instead, these photos showed the roof-deck with over 99 percent of the green fiberglass backer pulled off.

I then produced a sample of the TPO membrane taken from the roof that had come off during the storm. The sample still had the green fiberglass backer still adhered to the TPO membrane. I then walked the judge and TDI through the evidence. Everything that I had been responsible for during the application of the roof assembly was still intact.

The insulation board was still adhered to the roof. The Dens deck cover board was still adhered to the insulation board. The TPO membrane was still adhered to the green fiberglass backer. The failure had been almost exclusively at the green fiberglass adherence to the Dens deck gypsum board. This is a factory application, and the DensGlass board had been part of the tested assembly.

There was no field applied adhesive failure, only a factory applied adhesive failure. This should have been obvious to both the inspecting engineer and TDI. Given that the inspecting engineer was not tasked with finding the cause of failure, only if it was an insurable wind-related event, and given that the inspecting engineer may have not been familiar with the DensGlass makeup (after all, during his inspection, it was almost universally white instead of green), it is understandable that he would not have noticed this important fact. TDI, on the other hand, had been told this by me, and it was in my first report and subsequent reports. They made no effort to investigate this failure of the factory-applied DensGlass fiberglass backer. Instead they chose to go after me and put all of my jobs under audit so that they could find something, anything, they could use against me. This was a bona fide witch hunt by an unaccountable bureaucracy. This was either extreme incompetence on the part of TDI or gross misconduct. In either case, some heads should roll for this travesty of justice against me.

So why did this roof fail? I had given the explanation in my first report to the restoration contractor two days after Tropical Storm Hermine. The day after the storm when Merlin Orr, the public adjuster for TWIA, and I looked at the roof and found the roof hatch still fastened to the TPO membrane but pulled loose from the concrete, it was obvious that this was the cause of the failure. The roof hatch had been attached when the building was constructed in the early 1980s. The roof hatch was aluminum and attached to a two-by-four frame, which was fastened to the concrete deck with concrete screws every eight inches. Because that hatch was located over an open balcony, over time the salt moisture had gotten to the fasteners and corroded them. Of the twenty fasteners, only three showed any evidence of adherence to the concrete, and they were all in the same corner.

I was asked in court by the SOAH judge and when I appeared before the board of engineers why I had not seen the corroded fasteners. The answer was simple. It was because they were not visible. They were two inches away from the wood-frame edge of the hatch that you climbed through when you accessed the roof surface. The two-by-four frame showed no sign of wood rot. The concrete deck showed no sign of salt-induced spalling. The hatch aluminum frame was in good condition. The hatch frame and fasteners had gone through Hurricane Dolly two years earlier without any damage to the frame, though the hatch cover had come off. You could not observe the fasteners without dismantling the frame. This could not be done without destroying the frame. The second roof hatch on the north side of the building did not come off and did not have completely corroded fasteners.

The south roof hatch fasteners had reached a level of corrosion to where they were no longer holding. If they had not come off during Tropical Storm Hermine, they would have come off with the next big wind event, which could be a strong northern rainstorm when the winter fronts came through from the north. These storms produce winds of forty to fifty miles per hour, and there have been roofs come off on South Padre Island during northers. As I explained in court and in my initial report, the roof hatch had an area of ten square feet. The sixty-mile-per-hour winds would produce upwards of twenty pounds per square foot of area. For ten square feet of area, this would be two hundred pounds of pressure on the roof hatch perimeter. With the roof hatch fasteners corroded, the hatch lifted from the two hundred pounds of pressure on the roof hatch perimeter. With the roof hatch fasteners corroded, the hatch lifted, and the two hundred pounds of pressure exceeded the design pressure for the TPO membrane. The apparent weak link in the assembly is the green fiberglass backer on the DensGlass cover board. It was my opinion that the DensGlass board was not faulty, but the design pressure was exceeded when the roof hatch came up.

Once the TPO membrane got air beneath it, it became like a kite and ballooned up until it reached the walls, and the pressure at this point was enough to cleanly tear the TPO off at the batten strips at the base of the parapet wall and at the top of the parapet wall. Both the EFI engineer and the roofing company hired by TWIA had stated in their reports that the batten straps were deformed and had failed. This was entirely untrue. The batten strip at the top of the parapet wall remained intact, and the strip at the bottom of the parapet wall was over 99 percent secure.

The termination batten bars had not failed; the TPO membrane had not failed. The only two things that had evidence of failure were the roof hatch and the bond between the DensGlass cover board and its fiberglass backer—two things which I had no control over and could not verify. I should have never been blamed for this roof cover coming off, and TDI was extremely negligent and irresponsible in bringing this charge.

It took me less than an hour on the stand to dismantle TDI's number one case against me. Three years of my life had been spent dealing with abusive audits or paying other engineers to certify my work to avoid abusive audits. I had spent countless hours defending myself and over $100,000 in legal fees and administrative fees. In one hour I had destroyed TDI's credibility, but when you are dealing with a bureaucratic state agency funded by taxpayers' dollars, one does not need credibility.

Powell next turned to Plumosa. This reroof was next in order in the SOAH complaint. More importantly, this roof had the whole credibility of David Day v. TDI on the line. Who was right, TDI and Welch Watt cronies or David Day and all engineers on the appointment list who I was indirectly representing? For the majority of the engineers on the list had approved similar roofs. In fact, any engineer who dealt with AC shingles dealt with shingles secured with pneumatic-gun-driven nails. This was the majority of the appointed engineers. I was now going to expose TDI's windstorm inspection department for what it was, an incompetent, punitive, and bully organization that had an atmosphere of fear and retribution among their field inspectors. You had inspectors who would absolutely not make a decision contrary to the Welch Watt directives. As Doug Klopfenstein had told me during his meeting in 2010, "I don't have the luxury of making judgment calls." Imagine that, one of the lead inspectors for TDI considered making judgment calls a luxury.

Powell walked me through the inspection process for shingle roofs that are already complete. I explained the random sampling process where the inspector, at random, selects locations and lifts shingles without tearing them to reveal the placement of the nails. If the randomly selected areas representing different areas of the roof are all okay, then it is assumed that all areas are okay. I had run a testing lab for nine years, and all field testing is done using random sampling. Only constructions such as structural steel where all connections are exposed have 100 percent inspection.

I then turned to a demonstration on shingles that would have made Perry Mason proud. I had brought with me a full section of a roof complete with rafters, plywood decking, felt underlayment, and multiple courses of overlapping shingles. Prior to coming to court, I had used a pneumatic nail gun to install nails in the constructed sample adjacent to hammer-driven nails. I had made sure the nails represented the nail placement that I had personally witnessed TDI inspectors, including Doug Klopfenstein, reject.

I then selected one of the many shingles that I had brought with me. I demonstrated to the judge and the TDI attorneys how a shingle is constructed. All shingles, no matter the manufacturer, are constructed the same. The base layer is asphalt-saturated felt. Felt comes in varying thickness that is labeled by its weight per one hundred square feet. So fifteen pounds felt would weigh fifteen pounds per one hundred square feet of coverage. Shingles have a base of ninety-pound felt. The base felt is then saturated with asphalt bitumen and coated with granules of crushed stone. The granules have no structure. They are only a protection layer for the base felt. The granules protect the base felt from UV rays, from debris impact, and also serve as ballast or weight to give the shingle added weight to hold them down and aid in weighting the shingle down so that the factory-applied glue strip adheres to the shingle above.

Because the granules are not structural but only individual grains held together by the asphalt, on fresh shingles the granules will come off during handling and foot traffic, and the shingle wrapper even states so.

The granule layer is approximately ⅛-inch thick and will compress 1/32 inch to 1/16 inch when contacted by the hammerhead. This compressed area will be the entire diameter of the hammerhead. I demonstrated this in court by striking a shingle with a hammer and then using a straight edge to show the depression created when I had struck the shingle. I then turned to the prepared air-gun-driven nail sample that I had brought. I placed the straight edge over the air-gun-driven nail and showed the same 1/32-inch depression. Because the air gun only compressed the shingle in the area beneath the nailhead, the nailhead was submerged below the granule surface at the same compressed depth as a hammer-driven nail. And this is the way it has to be; otherwise, under high wind pressures, an air-gun-driven nail that did not compress the shingle, when driven, would compress it when the shingle uplifted during a windstorm. What TDI was having the roofers do who dared to use air guns was to back the air pressure off to where the nail would not compress the shingle. This is incorrect, and this nail would be underdriven. When the nails correctly compressed the shingles, TDI inspectors under the direction of Welch Watt were calling them overdriven. And if an engineer certified these nails, TDI would bring disciplinary actions against him in an SOAH court, and thus I was now standing in this court having just demonstrated for TDI attorneys, the ALJ, and Sam Nelson why they were wrong.

So why did TDI enforce something that was wrong? In my opinion it was all because of an artistic depiction of nail placement that had been around since the 1950s or earlier.

I then proceeded to reproduce this diagram on the display pad that the court had provided. This diagram is found on most shingle packages and roofing manuals. The diagram shows the four conditions of nail placement, and these four placements are exaggerated for clarity.

1048   The NRCA Roofing and Waterproofing Manual—Fourth Edition

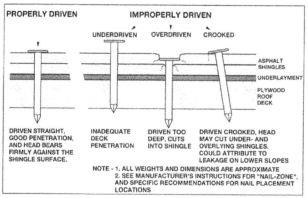

Figure 13 Example of fastener set for shingle nails.

C.   Re-cover roofing (the application of new asphalt roofing materials over existing asphalt roofing materials), requires the use of longer nails that will extend through all layers of roofing and penetrate the substrate, providing sufficient attachment to the roof deck.

D.   Generally, the nailing of hips, ridges and some roof accessories (e.g., some roof ventilators) requires the use of longer nails, as the fastener must penetrate through more layers of roofing and/or material. However, if more than sufficient length nails are used in the field of the roof, then the same length nail may be adequate for attachment of hip and ridge shingles, providing the nails penetrate the deck per the requirements as noted above, and as set forth by the shingle manufacturer.

Note: If properly applied, either hand-nailed or pneumatically (power) actuated nail applications are acceptable.

E.   For individual full-width three-tab shingles, a minimum of four nails are required. For some areas and climatic regions (i.e., areas where building codes dictate or where high wind regions require), six nails per full-width three-tab shingle are required. (See Figures 14 and 15.)

From left to right, the diagram shows a properly driven nail with the nailhead bottom above the shingle surface. The second nail is listed underdriven and has nailhead above the shingle over a one-eight inch. The third nail is listed as overdriven and shows a nail driven halfway through the granule surface with distress marks or cuts shown in the shingle ninety-pound felt. The fourth is listed as crooked and shows nail at an exaggerated angle approximately thirty degrees.

TDI interprets and enforces any nail placement other than the exact placement of the first nail as being improper and in need of rejection. This is an extreme view and an incorrect view for air-gun-driven nails that compress the granules in the vicinity of the nail-head. This diagram has been around since before the pneumatic nail gun was put into use.

A literal interpretation of the four-nail diagram would have any height of nailhead less than nail 2 or higher than nail 3 or at a lesser angle than nail 4 as being acceptable because by TDI's interpretation of the nail placement of nail 1 being the only correct position of the nail, then the nail would have to be in the exact same position as the other three placements to be considered improper. The truth is that these pictorial representations are only intended to be a guide and not a literal, exact placement chart for determining properly driven nails. But when TDI inspectors do not have the luxury of making judgment calls, they will cling to this diagram and reject any shingle that does not exactly match the depiction of the properly driven nail. They may lose their job, and TDI inspectors have lost their jobs for not rejecting nails that vary from the diagram. Even if the manufacturer tells them the nails are okay, they will still reject them.

As I summed up the shingle demonstration, I compared the gun-driven nails to fastening a shingle with a bolt, nut, and washer. TDI's depiction of the properly driven gun nail would have the washer resting on the surface of the granules, but this would not be an appropriate placement because the shingle could still compress under wind loads. To be appropriately secured, the nut would have to be tightened to compress the shingle surface and get a secure connection. When the washer compresses the surface, the bottom of the washer would be below the surface of the granules, and even though this is correct, TDI would reject it.

The code would not require that these nails be rejected, and TDI is only tasked with enforcing the code. No manufacturer or insurance company would say these nails are rejected because more than 90 percent of shingles in the country, including Florida, are installed with nail guns, and the shingles are not being rejected. Only the fifteen or so remaining TDI inspectors who did not get run off by Welch Watt would call these nails rejected.

I did at Plumosa what any respectable engineer would and does do on a daily basis: I accepted properly driven nails. And for this I was accused of negligence and of fraudulently signing a WPI-2. I ended the demonstration by stating in a raised voice "that TDI has the right to set standards with their employees, but when they don't put these standards in writing and these standards are not contained in the code, to call an engineer negligent for disagreeing with them is unforgiveable."

I ended the first day of testimony by defending my actions at Shadowbrook, where CASA employees had been given the original TDI inspection report that stated corrections were needed at the eves. The corrections had been made, and other areas of the roof were checked and found to be okay, and the roof was accepted. Because TDI had previously inspected this roof and found defects, they asked me to provide evidence that the corrections had been made. The roofing company for this roof was run by Caesar Sauceda, a very honest and very competent roofer who had been selected and approved by Lowe's, the national lumber and hardware store, to install the shingles.

The fact that TDI required corrections of Sauceda does not mean that the shingles were improper or unsafe. As already previously demonstrated, TDI's standards are far and above the code or the manufacturer's requirements. The shingles as originally installed would have passed any manufacturers field inspection, but the TDI inspector was following strict edge-distance nail placement and rejected the nails at the rake edges, which is the edge of a roof along a gable end.

At the time CASA inspector Chris Hamby had inspected these shingles, the corrections had been made, and Chris inspected several more locations and found no deficiencies, so he turned in his report listing the shingles as acceptable. Chris Hamby was more than a typical inspector. Chris had attended Texas Tech University in Lubbock, Texas, and received a BS in biology with the intention of going to dental school. When he decided dental work was not for him, he transferred to University of Texas–San Antonio and received a BS in civil engineering. Chris had worked for large construction firms and had his own licensed and bonded construction company, H2O. He certainly had the luxury of making good judgment calls, and I trusted his judgment.

When I was asked for evidence that the corrections had been made, I produced Hamby's report, a new report that I had personally done, and a photo of the shingle receipts that was presented to me by Caesar Sauceda at the jobsite. When Harp testified, he called this a suspicious activity. In fact, Harp called all of my actions on Shadowbrook suspicious (page 63, lines 19 to 24). There was nothing done that was suspicious at the Shadowbrook residence. In fact, I repeatedly asked TDI to visit the site to verify that the corrections had been made. As stated in my testimony, "Why would I ask TDI to come to the site if I had anything to hide" (page 217 and 218)?

After Sauceda agreed to reroof the roof so the owner could get his certificate, he asked for TDI to do the inspections so that he would not have TDI second-guessing an engineer. At this point Welch Watt called me and asked to send a letter rescinding the WPI-2 so that TDI could inspect the new roof. This was totally unnecessary, but I complied and wrote a letter to Welch Watt that began with, "As per your request." The TDI attorneys made a big deal about this, indicating that I was doing something underhanded by writing this letter requesting the WPI-2 be rescinded. This was an extraordinary position for TDI attorneys to take because their own employee, Welch Watt, had requested the letter, and I stated so in the letter.

As with Plumosa, the Shadowbrook roof was replaced and certified by TDI. Neither one of these residences should have been used against me because both roofs had been replaced. Any decent judge would have dismissed the charges at Plumosa and Shadowbrook because they were both certified. But decency and fairness are not two attributes of TDI or, for that matter, the SOAH court system.

The first day of my testimony ended, and I was still being questioned by Powell and had only covered three of the six addresses used in the SOAH complaint. Because only three days had been scheduled and Harp took up a day and a half of it, we were forced to have the trial postponed again for the third time. No TDI hearing on disciplinary actions against an engineer had ever gone on more than one day, and now I was having my hearing postponed for the third time and would now enter the fifth day of testimony.

The Fight Continues: Round 6

The hearing resumed on November 8, 2012. The testimony began where it left off with me discussing Shadowbrook and the letter I sent to Welch Watt requesting to rescind the WPI-2. Even the ALJ asked why I had written the letter, and the reply was that TDI and Welch Watt had requested it because they were taking over the inspection of the new roof.

The testimony then turned to Guadalajara. It was on this roof that TDI went to extremes to reject the roof. They fabricated evidence (scuff marks); they ignored exculpatory evidence (the Atlas bulletin); and in the case of Benito Garcia, he flat-out lied. He stated he had never met or discussed the roof with the homeowner when he had done both. He also claimed he had not seen the Atlas bulletin when it was given to him by me at the jobsite.

I discussed the scuff marks at length and compared them to walking on a carpet. The footprint on the carpet and the displaced granules caused by foot traffic on the roof will also go away and did go away, and I produced photos of the roof two years later, showing absolutely no scuff marks.

At Guadalajara, TDI, in their zeal to get me, took a perfectly good roof and refused to accept it. They ignored manufacturer's directives on exposed nails and lied about or misrepresented the quantity of the nails that were exposed. They stated that they would allow some exposed nails but steadfastly refused to say how many or express it in terms of a percentage, which any product code authority would do. Instead they forced the homeowner and roofer to make needless repairs in an effort to get TDI to accept the roof.

TDI tried to insinuate that the fact that repairs were made on the roof was an admission of guilt on my part, that the original certification was false. Nothing could be further from the truth. To get a WPI-8 certification, it doesn't matter what David Day, the roofer, the homeowner, or even the manufacturer believes. It only matters what TDI accepts. The roofer and the homeowner did not replace shingles because they were unacceptable; they replaced them in an effort to get TDI to accept them. The board of engineers was copied with all correspondence, and at no point did the board indicate that I had done anything wrong.

After replacing every single shingle that had a tar mark on it, whether it was covering an exposed nail or not, TDI refused to accept it because of the scuff marks on the roof even though they had no written policies or manufacturer's literature which states that scuff marks are a rejectable defect or even a defect. In fact, I read directly from the Atlas wrapper, which stated that granule loss was to be expected.

I then debunked Harp's assertion that the exposed nails would corrode and leave holes in the roof. I had experience in the galvanizing or zinc-coating process because of my experience teaching metallurgy to welders. I produced a FEMA bulletin that clearly stated that galvanized nails are good for the life of the product and then gave the example of metal buildings which last fifty years. The shingles on this roof were rated for thirty years. The galvanizing coats the steel nail with zinc. The zinc acts as a sacrificial liner and will totally consume before the steel corrodes. As stated before, this is a process that can take twenty to fifty years, depending on the amount of zinc coating applied.

Powell then turned to East levee and Northshore. The amazing thing about both of these projects is that neither had a TWIA policy, and there was no risk to TWIA if either had failures. What was also amazing is that TDI did not visit either site and produced no evidence that anything was wrong with either structure. These two projects were all about paperwork or, in the case of Northshore, the lack of.

TDI's actions at Levee were particularly egregious because the certifications produced by me were part of a comprehensive repair plan for a six-story building that needed many repairs and modifications before it could get a policy from TWIA. The work was being done in phases by different roofers, and partial roof certifications were issued as a repair was completed. The drive-through teller had already been certified by CASA and had a WPI-8 when TDI audited me on the roof repairs. Remember, TDI was not auditing this job at random as is their only legislative authorized requirement; they were doing this because they had illegally put me under audit on all projects after October 28, 2010.

TDI requested all data, and I complied. TDI would not accept the partial repairs because they stated that the product evaluation used was for a new assembly. Keep in mind that there is no such thing as product evaluation for existing construction. All products are tested in a laboratory on new materials. Unless it is a new construction, roof products will always be placed on existing structures. Yet TDI allows for reroofs and even has a separate category for reroofs and alterations listed on the WPI-2 form that the engineer signs.

In the case of East Levee, at the third and fourth floors, the roofs did not have proper terminations at the parapet walls, and the fourth floor needed some drainage modification to correct some standing water. This work was accomplished by adding a cap sheet at the parapet wall at the third floor and placing ten feet to twelve feet lengths of cap sheet at the fourth floor to build up some low areas to provide drainage. When this work was done, it completed the contract for this part of the roof, and I issued a WPI-2.

What was done on this roof was totally acceptable, it is industry standard, and it is done nationwide. The cap sheet used was a self-adhering cap sheet from Liberty placed over a clean, primed surface. The Liberty cap sheet was tested in an assembly over concrete that consisted of multiple layers of insulation board, base ply, intermediate plies, and the cap sheet. This in no way implies that any or all of the assembly has to be used on every square inch of the roof and, in reality, cannot be used on every square inch because, as I explained (pages 86 and 87), the cap sheet will get adhered to any number of substrates on any given roof that are not part of the tested assembly. This would include the parapet walls, any vent housings, AC curbs, and any roof penetration. Cap sheet to cap sheet is part of the tested assembly and is approved in the TDI product evaluation RC-121.

At Northshore, TDI was asking for all information even though the work was done in 2009, prior to the illegal mandatory audits and in violation of Nelson's directive that there would be no audit on work that occurred prior to October 28, 2010. No one from TDI had visited the site, and the owner was not seeking TWIA insurance. The whole thing came about when the homeowner's insurance agent called CASA and inquired about the certification on the windows that had been installed on the home the prior year. The agent was seeking options for the owner, and TWIA was one of those options. The owner already had private insurance outside of TWIA. When CASA called TDI to inquire why a WPI-2 that had been submitted a year earlier was still active, they were told that the WPI-2 had never been received. CASA had a fax receipt of the WPI-2 that was stamp dated. TDI had received it but had either misplaced or lost it. This was not a onetime occurrence. It happens frequently on more than 2 percent of WPI-2s. Linda Olvera of CASA specifically asked the TDI employee if it was going to be audited if it was sent in again. Linda was told that all that was needed was to resubmit the WPI-2 with a new inspection date because it had been over six months. So CASA resubmitted the WPI-2, and another TDI employee forwarded it to engineering with no explanation, and I received an audit letter from Sam Nelson requesting all the backup information on the windows on this home.

I replied to the request and provided a signed affidavit from Olvera stating what had occurred with this WPI-2. It didn't make a difference to Nelson. He still wanted the information. I was very concerned at this point that TDI would start auditing all of the projects that were already completed. I sought the advice of Powell, who I was already consulting with over the illegal audits. Powell asked me if I had the information, and I stated that I had the information from the time the project started. Powell then asked me if the home-owner insurance was going to be affected, and I responded that the homeowner already had private insurance and didn't need the WPI-2. Powell's response was that TDI didn't need it either. I responded to Nelson that the job was completed in 2009 and not subject to audit per Nelson's instructions.

The information was given to TDI when subpoenaed, and TDI had it in its possession for over a year before the hearing began.

For the Greenbriar roof, TDI had rejected the roof because they said the nails were nailed above the manufacturer's recommended nail zone. They also said I was not able to name the shingle in the field and, when asked, gave the name of a three-tab shingle and not the architectural shingle that was present. This was really a stupid position for the TDI attorneys to take because correctly naming the shingle in the field from memory is not a rejectable offense. The correct shingle had been listed in the report that had already been turned into TDI. I also produced a manufacturer's enhanced nail zone that applied to all architectural shingles. The nails all fell within this enhanced nail zone. TDI did not dispute this evidence; they just refused to accept it. There is nothing in TDI's rules which allows them to ignore manufacturer's instructions, to enforce some but not others. And what is worse, their attorneys ignore it also.

The most extraordinary claim that was made against me is that I stated that I had certified the roof at Greenbriar knowing that it was not certifiable. This lie was started by Doug Klopfenstein and repeated by all of TDI including in correspondence from Alexis Dick. This lie originated when, in a meeting at my office, I stated that the home was not eligible for TWIA because the entire struc-ture had not been certified. I said nothing about the roof not being certifiable. Present during the meeting was my employee, Manuel Ramirez, a graduate engineer. Ramirez signed a sworn affidavit stat-ing that I never said in the meeting that the roof was not certifiable. The bottom line is that TDI's evidence was refuted, and the shingles at Greenbriar were acceptable.

TDI and Nelson in his testimony stated that I should have not certified the roof when the home was not certified. Once again this is a prime example of the left hand not knowing what the right hand is doing. It was clearly TDI's policy to allow roofs only to be certified, and it was clearly written on the WPI-2 that was turned in. The language that CASA used was given to them by none other than Welch Watt, who stated to write on the WPI-2 that the certification is for new construction but for roof only. This was not the first roof that I had certified this way, and I was not the only engineer to do it. In fact, the 2011 legislation also created the WPI-12, which was solely for a roof only on new construction. It was always TDI's policy to allow certification of a roof only on new construction, but apparently this had never been told to Sam Nelson or the TDI attorneys.

I concluded my direct testimony by stating under oath that I wouldn't be sitting there if I had paid for all of the roofs out of my pocket, as other engineers had done to stay in TDI Inspection Department's good graces. All of my work was correct, and I stood by all of my certifications.

It was now TDI's attorney's turn to cross-examine. Strangely, they began their questioning by challenging my assertion that I was on the new list. TDI had been trying to skirt the new legislation by stating that all of my transgressions occurred prior to the new legislation. Cloninger had granted their every request to keep the hearing under the pre-2011 rules. The trouble is that I was now on the new list, which would go into effect January 1, 2013. The whole hearing should have become moot at that point because the appointment list that they were trying to take me off of was now being superseded by the new list, and I was already on the new list granted by TDI and sent to me in a letter signed by none other than Sam Nelson.

I had noticed that back in September, when I first began testifying and Powell had asked me if I was on the new list and I stated that I was, Nelson appeared very agitated and immediately conferenced with the TDI attorneys. Apparently, Nelson did not realize that he had allowed me on the new list. The first thing the TDI attorney did was hand me the letter and asked me if this was the letter I was referring to when I stated I was on the list. They had me to read from the second paragraph, which stated, "As a qualified inspector…" And then they asked me if this paragraph was why I thought I was on the list. I answered that it was, and there was in fact a new list, and my name was on it. It must have been a shock to TDI that I was on the new list, but the legislative language was very clear: if the board placed an engineer on their list, then TDI *shall* appoint the engineer as an inspector. This was a very important point that TDI and the ALJ would ignore for the remainder of the hearing.

The TDI attorney then challenged me about the nails at Guadalajara. The attorney Loeffler held a sheet of paper in front of her and asked facetiously if that meant that she was no longer visible. Her comparison in of itself was laughable. An eight-by-eleven piece of paper would no more conceal her than a granule of sand would cover a nailhead. The nails at Guadalajara were properly concealed just like Loeffler would have been if she had held up a tarp in front of her. This was reminiscent of Harp's "bumper sticker" analogy. I answered that the nails were only partially exposed. If Loeffler had used the sheet of paper and asked if it covered her nose, then that would have been an appropriate analogy. I then grabbed the sample board that had shingles placed exactly how they were nailed at Guadalajara. I showed this to TDI, and the ALJ asked to let the record show that I was using my roof sample to demonstrate the nail placement at Guadalajara.

I stated (page 137) that if the manufacturer would have asked me to have the nails removed, I would have asked the roofer to remove them. But the manufacturer, being fully aware of the situation, provided me with the bulletin and highlighted the part that said the warranty would not be violated. The law and the code on this are very clear. The code simply states that shingles will be installed in accordance with the manufacturer's instructions. If the manufacturers allow it, it is acceptable, end of story, whether TDI likes it or not. If TDI wants to go above and beyond the code, they can do so legislatively, but they cannot do so by proclamation of Welch Watt, Sam Nelson, Alexis Dick, the commissioner, or anyone else.

The TDI attorney then asked why I made corrections at Guadalajara if I felt the roof was correct (page 150–151). I explained that the corrections were made at the request of TDI because they reserve the right not to certify a roof, and whether they are right or wrong, if the owner wanted TWIA insurance, he had to meet TDI's approval. It must be noted that TDI can be completely wrong as they were in every single complaint they brought against me in the SOAH hearing, as the board of engineers verified that I had done nothing wrong, but TDI can still refuse to accept a WPI-2. I had bent over backwards trying to get TDI to accept Guadalajara, and anyone reading the correspondence could see that.

As stated before, if TDI does not want to accept a WPI-2, legally they have the right not to. But they do not have the right to accuse an engineer of fraud and negligence for disagreeing with them.

The two addresses that TDI spent the most time on were East Levee and North Shore. It is ironic that they spent time on these two addresses because no TDI employee visited either site, and neither owner had a TWIA policy. TDI has no say if an owner has private insurance. They are only tasked with enforcing windstorm compliance for an owner seeking TWIA policies. If a home or building is built in complete violation of the building code but has private insurance, TDI has no say or jurisdiction over the engineer or building official who accepted it.

They repeatedly had me read from the code or the appointment rule, trying to entrap me, but because of my experience and knowledge of these two documents, I would answer them by pointing them to another passage right before or after their selected passage and explaining why the code or appointment rule allowed me to do what I did (pages 154–158) or why TDI cannot do what they are doing to me in auditing every one of my projects (pages 170–181). I even turned the tide on TDI and asked them why they were auditing me on every job, and the TDI attorney responded that I had a history and pattern of certifying structures incorrectly, and I responded emphatically, "I think I have proven just the opposite" (pages 181, lines 1–11).

The universal rule of attorneys is never asking a question that you do not know the answer to. After I just got through asking the TDI attorney a question and then corrected her, Powell then took over and asked me why I thought I was audited on every project. They had just turned me loose to explain TDI motives, and I did just that (pages 183 and 184, lines 1–7). I compared TDI's actions at Fannin, where I was forced to replace the roof cover twice before TDI accepted it, and Shadowbrook, Plumosa, and Guadalajara, where corrections were made, and in the case of Shadowbrook and

Plumosa, the roofs were replaced by the roofer and accepted by TDI. Why would TDI not take disciplinary action against me at Fannin but take action on the seven addresses that they brought against me? In my opinion, it has to do with TDI and Sam Nelson specifically being able to extract a price from an engineer in an effort to punish them.

None of the owners involved in the addresses had accused me of wrongdoing or blamed me for not getting their WPI-2. They all blamed TDI. In the case of Fannin, a complaint was filed against TDI for their handling of the rejections. TDI had lied about telling the roofer to stop when they observed him using a nail gun. They had also climbed on the roof without the owner's permission, and when she came out and asked what they were doing on her roof, they lied and told her that they had knocked on her door. The owner was sitting in her office next to the front door when she heard the TDI inspectors on her roof. The inspectors had not knocked on her door; they just climbed on her roof. This was typical behavior of TDI inspectors, which would later be revealed in a secret video that I would receive.

Prior to Nelson and Watt taking over as TDI chief engineer and inspection manager, TDI never went after engineers through the SOAH courts. This was simply not their job. Engineers were governed by the board of engineers, and any disciplinary action should have been sent through the board. After Nelson and Watt took over, TDI started bringing complaints against engineers in SOAH court and even doled out monetary fines. The board eventually stopped the fines in the early 2000s, so at this point, the only way TDI could hurt an engineer was to extort them into paying for a repair or by removing them from the list.

TDI simply has no legal authority to ask an engineer to repair or replace anything, and if they do so as they did at Plumosa with Nelson putting in writing that I was to have the roof repaired or disciplinary action would follow, it is nothing short of extortion. Nelson can and should be criminally prosecuted for writing that letter. And he certainly should be disciplined by the board.

So as I explained at the hearing, when I replaced the roof at Fannin, no action was taken against me, but when I refuted TDI and even if the roof was replaced, as at Plumosa and Shadowbrook, TDI still took action in the form of an SOAH complaint against me. If TDI didn't extract their pound of flesh from an uppity engineer, then they would have him removed to set an example to any other engineers not to defy TDI. For no matter how wrong they are, the legislature has empowered them with the right to be wrong. As I summed it up, "If I had paid for those roofs out of my pocket, I would not be sitting here today" (pages 183 and 184). I paid for Fannin because my inspector had made an error, and my inspectors and I personally got on the roof and replaced it.

I then explained how a built-up roof at Levee is installed with multilayers, and each layer is adhered to the layer beneath it. It was obvious throughout all of the TDI attorneys' questioning of both TDI employees and me that they did not understand how roofs are installed and why the TDI employees, especially Harp, were so wrong in their answers. They kept stating that the cap sheet was adhered to the concrete deck when in no instance was the cap sheet adhered to the concrete deck. In all instances, built-up roofs have one or more plies of felt or insulation board between the cap sheet and the concrete.

I finished the questioning by debating partial roof repairs. I explained that by TDI actions on Levee in stating that a repair had to be a fully tested assembly (pages 195 and 196), then no repairs could be done on any roof. I then compared it to Suntide III, stating that if that single ply membrane had been torn from impact during a storm or even from some careless maintenance man dragging a sharp object across it, then by TDI's accusations, the whole roof would have to be replaced. Because by what TDI was stating at Levee, you could not repair just the cap sheet; you would have to go all the way to the concrete and tie in to only new material.

This could not be further from reality. There is not a roof expert or consultant in the world who would agree with TDI. You repair surface damage on any flat roof by adhering a new cap sheet to cover the damaged or low area, as was the case at Levee.

If all engineering jobs were audited by TDI, then there would not be one partial repair, only complete replacements. But as stated as I wrapped up testimony (page 196, lines 1–5), TWIA and other insurance companies are not going to pay for a complete reroof for minor damage. They will allow it to be patched.

TDI had just had their whole case refuted and had me asking them questions. When they had their turn to recross the man they had been after for three years, they declined and retreated. In any legitimate court before a legitimate judge, this action to not recross me would have been a direct admission of defeat.

The Two Vickis

Although there were numerous people on my witness list and many more who were helping me behind the scenes, Powell made the calculated judgment that no expert witness could do a better job of explaining the facts than I could. This had been proven out in my testimony, which had just concluded and obliterated TDI's complete case. What was needed now was a witness or witnesses that could validate the unfair treatment of me by TDI. Powell chose the two Vickis, Vicki Leggett and Vicky Huckaby.

Powell had vetted both of them and was not only impressed with their knowledge of the relevant facts, he was more impressed with the passion they expressed in describing TDI's treatment of me. Powell would use the two Vickis to provide testimony of those who witnessed the witch hunt against me.

I had worked with Legget since my first days as a professional engineer. Vicki was a homebuilder who parlayed her knowledge of real estate and interior design to start her own construction company, Leggett Custom Homes, where she specialized in building large-scale custom homes. Vicki Leggett took great pride in her work and made sure homes incorporated all of the requirements of the code and would have all of her work certified for windstorm compliance. When design became mandatory in 2003, Leggett had all of her homes designed, inspected, and certified by David Day. She did this until she retired from home building in the late 2000s and started selling real estate.

Vicki Leggett was the one who had called me to certify the home at Greenbriar. Even though the home was not on the TDI list of certified homes, some private insurance companies would give a discount if the homeowner certified the roof only. This was allowed by TDI even though TDI attorneys and Sam Nelson seemed to be ignorant of this fact. Welch Watt himself had given CASA the language to use on the WPI-1 and WPI-2 to show that it was for a roof only on new construction.

Leggett told this story to Powell under questioning. She then went on to state that Nelson had called the homeowner and told them that they would never get insurance unless they replaced their roof. This was totally unprofessional, and Nelson had lied about it when he was questioned about the call. Nelson had stated that the homeowner had called him, and he was returning their call. The homeowners did not know Nelson and had not asked for him. They had simply called TDI Intake to inquire about the status of their roof certification. They had spoken to one of TDI's intake people. Because I was under audit, the call had been referred to Nelson. Nelson telling the homeowner that they had to get the roof replaced or they wouldn't get insurance was a lie. The home had insurance at that time, and the home still stands to this day with the same roof, and the owners have insurance. More importantly, even if the homeowner had replaced the roof, they would not have gotten insurance through TWIA because the entire structure had never been certified. So Nelson had no business calling the owner on a home that was not listed on the TDI Windstorm list of certified homes and then lie to them about them having to replace the roof.

The homeowners were very upset with this call and Nelson telling them it was uninsurable (page 215, lines 1–16). They called Vicki Leggett immediately after the call and described the whole conversation to her. Leggett's testimony was given by phone. This was very unfortunate because Vicki was very professional but also very animated when she spoke and would have made a good impression on the judge.

Powell turned Vicki Leggett over to TDI for cross-examination, and this is where a class could be taught on what not to do when questioning a hostile witness. For when TDI and Nelson went after me at Greenbriar, they also went after the homeowner and Leggett. It never seems to cross TDI's mind that when they audit an engineer, what they are really doing is auditing the property owner, who is an innocent victim of TDI's pernicious audit practices in which they turn ignorant uninformed bureaucrats loose on an unsuspecting public, and then these inspectors do what they have been trained to do, and that is to find something wrong or face disciplinary action.

When the homeowner called the state to inquire about the status of their roof certification, they were called back by none other than Sam Nelson, who told them their home was uninsurable. Leggett testified that the homeowner was very upset and immediately called her after they had gotten off the phone with Nelson. Leggett emphatically let the state know that what they did was uncalled for and inappropriate, and all they did was alarm the homeowner with the lie that the home was uninsurable.

TDI was trying to get out of Leggett that TDI's response to the owner and to Leggett was appropriate because Leggett had written a letter to her state senator complaining of TDI's actions. Leggett let them know emphatically that it was anything but appropriate and needlessly alarmed her client, the homeowner. She had described TDI as being a bully (page 209, lines 7–11).

Without any more embarrassment, TDI passed the witness, and Powell, sensing the damage that had been done, then called Vicky Huckaby.

I had first met Vicky Huckaby when she was working for Mike Scanlon, PE, at Norex Engineering, and they were working on Emerald by the Sea in Galveston, Texas. Huckaby was doing the research for the tests that would be used to test the stucco cladding on the building. She became increasingly alarmed with the requests that TDI was asking for of the building and the contractor. Ms. Huckaby could not find any justification in the code for TDI's requests.

Huckaby left Scanlon because she didn't like his tactics and disagreed with him on the test protocol for the Emerald stucco. Instead of Scanlon doing his job and determining if the stucco was sound, Scanlon was doing everything he could to prove the stucco was unsound despite the overwhelming tests that were needlessly done which validated the obvious—that the stucco was sound. Scanlon had even gone so far as to accuse the test lab of falsifying the tests.

When IBC Bank severed ties with Scanlon for refusing to cooperate, they turned the project over to me because I already had extensive knowledge of the building. When I eventually certified the building, Scanlon turned in his own WPI-2 and checked the box "Does not comply." The state rules are for an engineer to provide evidence for checking this box. Scanlon provided none, and TDI did not require him to. This is at best unprofessional and possibly criminal. But no action was taken against Scanlon, and TDI put me and the owner through a two-year audit that cost the owner hundreds of thousands of dollars before the overwhelming evidence that the building was sound, and Scanlon was wrong and forced them to accept it.

It was with this knowledge that Vicki Huckaby had witnessed firsthand the lengths that TDI would go to keep a project from being certified. She had worked with a "professional" engineer, David Day, and an unprofessional one, Scanlon, and she saw firsthand which engineer TDI preferred to work with.

Powell then asked Huckaby if she had an occasion in which she was with Scanlon and overheard a conversation between Nelson and Scanlon (page 219, lines 24 and 25; page 220, lines 1 and 2). Huckaby then responded:

> Yes, as a matter of fact, that was the day that I actually met Mr. Day for the first time. When we left the meeting, Mr. Scanlon was concerned because he didn't want—he was concerned about having another engineer come in behind him and maybe agree or disagree or discredit what he had been doing. And as we left the meeting, we rode together, and he called Mr. Nelson on

the phone, and we weren't able to get in touch with him. And we had been working with him pretty closely already, trying to decide what's next. And so we went to a meeting in town, and as we were leaving there to go to another meeting that evening, Mr. Nelson called back, and I don't think he knew that I was in the car or it was on speaker phone, that that—at that time Mike, Mr. Scanlon, had told him that he was real concerned about this guy. He didn't know who he was, and he thought he might come in and make him look bad. And Mr. Nelson, who knows Mr. Scanlon well, basically said, you—well, actually, he literally said, "Don't worry about him, I can take care of him because he can't do anything without me approving it." (page 220, lines 3–25)

Nelson had already been asked if this conversation occurred, and he answered no. It is obvious Nelson was once again lying. This conversation belied the arrogant power of Nelson. No one in Windstorm could do anything without his blessing. It was never the intention of the legislature to give any unelected and unappointed individual this kind of power. It should be obvious to anyone reading this book that this abusive power needs to end.

Powell then passed the witness to TDI, and once again TDI allowed the witness to question TDI's motives. TDI was attempting to get Huckaby to admit that she didn't have any direct information on any of the seven addresses in the SOAH hearing, and each time Huckaby would emphatically state that she knew David Day and had worked with him and saw how he was being mistreated. She even stated that other engineers were also being mistreated but were afraid to speak out because they were afraid that the same would happen to them—what was now happening to David Day (page 224, lines 7–11). TDI had to cut off Ms. Huckaby before she could do any further damage, and the testimony was over.

The passion that was displayed in the voices of both Vickis, who both testified by phone, would have swayed any jury. They both made it emphatically clear that TDI was out to get David Day, and it was clearly obvious by TDI's actions.

The hearing concluded the next morning with the testimony by phone of Juan Salinas. Juan had worked for me from the time he had graduated from TSTC with an associate degree in computer-aided drafting and design. Juan had continued his education and, while working for me, attended Texas A&M at Kingsville and received a bachelor of science in civil engineering. Juan had also gotten his ICC code inspector's certification, the same certification that TDI claimed set their inspectors apart from the private industry. Juan had gotten this certification by taking an online course and completing an online exam. No experience, particularly field experience, was necessary. The certification that TDI claimed set their employees above private industry was an online certification offered by International Code Council (ICC), the governing body that writes the codes. The certificate demonstrates that they are able to read and interpret the code, not that they have any experience in the field or even know what they are looking at, as I had so clearly demonstrated with my demonstrations of shingle-nail placement, which TDI inspectors failed to properly inspect.

Juan Salinas's testimony seemed almost anticlimactic compared to Leggett's, Huckaby's, and mine. Juan was soft-spoken and also testified by phone.

What Salinas did do was give a firsthand account of what happened at Plumosa and Guadalajara, which corroborated my testimony and corrected the lies told by Klopfenstein and Benito Garcia.

Doug Klopfenstein had said that he did not lift shingles, and Salinas testified that he lifted shingles in ten areas (page 236, lines 22 and 23).

Benito Garcia said that he had not seen the Atlas technical bulletin stating that inadvertently exposed nails could be covered with roof cement. Salinas testified it was submitted to him (page 245, lines 3–5).

Benito Garcia testified that Salinas's shoes were damaging the roof. Salinas testified that he and Garcia were wearing the same shoes. When TDI questioned Salinas, they asked one interesting question (page 247, lines 5–6), "Are you a qualified inspector with

TDI?" Salinas answered yes, and then TDI asked, "Are you appointed by TDI as a qualified inspector" (page 247, lines 13–14)? This is an interesting question because the only individuals who can be appointed by TDI as qualified inspectors are registered professional engineers. But if you are hired by TDI directly, you don't have to have any qualifications except that after six months, you have to pass an online ICC inspectors exam, and Salinas had completed this exam as well as being a graduate civil engineer and a licensed engineer in training (EIT). He also had eight years of experience working under two different engineers, Day and Durivage. These credentials put him far and above the TDI inspectors Dough Klopfenstein, Benito Garcia, and Daniel Cantu.

So here, TDI is insinuating that you're not qualified if you do not work for TDI directly or are an appointed engineer. The Engineering Practice Act and TDI rules allow for qualified individuals to work under the direct supervision of an engineer, so Mr. Salinas was a qualified inspector and far and above more qualified than Doug Klopfenstein, Benito Garcia, and Daniel Cantu and, in my opinion, more so than Sam Nelson, Stephen Harp, and the EFI engineer.

The hearing concluded at 9:40 a.m. on November 9, the seventh day of testimony, though no testimony was given on the second day, when the hearing was postponed due to health issues of Olivia Connett.

It must be noted here that immediately after the hearing concluded and Judge Cloninger went off the record, she stated, "I call Angelina Jolie." This was off the record, but everyone in the room could attest to it. The ALJ, Cloninger, said this because my son Dennis had attended the last five days of the hearing, and Powell had introduced him to the court, stating that Dennis had a bachelor's degree from a film school, Collins College in Tempe, Arizona. Powell stated that Dennis was working on a script for the hearing for what his father was going through.

Dennis was very helpful during the hearing by researching memos and correspondence and manufacturer's literature while the hearing was going on. As the hearing progressed, Dennis would let each hearing personnel, including the stenographer, know who he thought would be a good actor to play them in the movie. They were all somewhat caught up in it for when Cloninger called Angelina Jolie, the TDI attorney, White, who was very petite and could have been a college cheerleader, stated she wanted Angelina Jolie. I assured her that Eva Longoria would be a better choice, and she agreed.

At this point and with those statements, I felt very confident that the hearing would be decided in my favor. If it had been a jury trial, I had no doubt that it would have been decided in my favor.

How an SOAH hearing works is after the hearing convenes, each side, TDI and the accused party, have to present their final arguments in writing. This is typically thirty days but can be extended as it was in my case because of the holidays. Then each side gets to rebut the other side's final argument.

When the final arguments are given to the ALJ, the ALJ then has sixty days to issue a ruling on the hearing. Each side then gets to weigh in on the judge's ruling before the commissioner gets to make a ruling on the ALJ's ruling. Once the commissioner makes a decision, each side has the chance to appeal it before it becomes final. While all of this was taking place, several events occurred that would reveal just how damaging TDI's actions were to the public and how insidious their employees, especially Sam Nelson, can be and how far they would go to squash dissent.

Corpus Christi Caller Times

As a result of the 2011 legislation, Windstorm appointed engineers now had to recertify and go through a screening process that included a supplementary experience record (SER), which included two years of structural design of wind components, and passing an online exam with 90 percent or better. Even though this was in direct conflict with the aforementioned Engineering Practice Act, which stated, there will be no requirement placed on an engineer other than his license, the TBPE capitulated and enforced the new policy. This was essentially a slap in the face to all engineers who were currently appointed. They now had a standard placed on them that no other engineer in the state of Texas and probably in the country had. An engineer in Texas could design a three-hundred-foot-tall building in El Paso but could not design a one-story home in La Feria, Texas, if he was not on the appointment list.

Many engineers took the opportunity to not renew their certifications. Most had been through the audit process, and if they had any other work that did not involve Windstorm, they concentrated on that and dropped out of doing windstorm design. Engineers who practiced structural engineering exclusively in coastal counties did not have that luxury and were forced to recertify if they wanted to stay in business.

TDI and TBPE were tasked with introducing the new requirements to the engineers who were already on the list, approximately nine hundred engineers. They held seminars in the Houston area, the Corpus area, and the Rio Grande Valley. I attended the hearing in Corpus with all of my staff. The new regulations went over like a lead balloon. There was almost unanimous consent from the engineers present that the new requirements were not fair and in fact were considered unconstitutional. Apparently the appointed engineers were not consulted in drafting this legislation. The feelings were so strong that one individual stood up and recited all of the education, experience, and requirements that he went through to get and maintain his engineering license. He then issued an expletive and stormed out of the room. I called him the next day, and he said that he was dropping out of the program. In all, 75 to 80 percent of the appointed engineers opted out of meeting new requirements. Not because they were difficult to obtain, they were just the opposite, but because it was an unjust burden from a board that would not protect their engineers from abuse by TDI.

It was during this time that a local structural engineer in Ingleside near Corpus, Raymond Stone, contacted the local newspaper, the *Corpus Christi Caller Times*, to inform them of the alarming rate of engineers dropping out of the program. Stone was near retirement and had had enough of the bureaucratic incompetence of the TDI audit process. Stone had had his share of run-ins with Nelson, Harp, and others in Austin, and he also had to go before TBPE and successfully defend himself.

The *Times* responded and appointed Rick Spruill, a local reporter to cover the story. When Spruill interviewed Stone, he was given the names of several builders and engineers to talk to including David V. Day. It was in December of 2012 when I met Spruill. Ironically, I was on my way to Austin to defend myself before TBPE. Outside of Stone, the thirteen other engineers that Spruill talked to did not want to go on record. They were fully aware of TDI's practice of retribution and did not want their name in an article critical of

TDI. I, on the other hand, agreed to go on record with my name. I wanted the world to know the abuses of the windstorm certification program. I even supplied the *Times* with my copy of Don Lee's letter to the commissioner. By doing this, I was granting Lee's wish posthumously that the TDI abuse be exposed.

Spruill and I corresponded several more times, and on February 17, 2013, a full front-page article came out exposing the TDI Windstorm abuses and the alarming rate of engineers leaving the program. The article was followed by a full column editorial. The Spruill article was entitled "Windstorm Engineers Dropping Certification in Droves," and the editorial was entitled "Texas Legislature Needs to Un-Act Some Regulations Pronto." The Spruill article quoted the only two engineers that were willing to go on record, Stone and Day, though it referenced thirteen more who had been interviewed. The article quoted me stating that an engineer could design a nuclear power plant without any special certifications, but if he wanted to design a thousand-square-foot home in a coastal county, he had to be certified by TBPE and appointed by TDI. The article also went into great detail how a local builder, Bill Underbrink, went bankrupt because he could not get a certification on homes he built due to their flagged status at TDI. As I had always stated, TDI's abusive audit process didn't just harm the engineers, it harmed the builder, the potential homeowner, the lending institution, the realtor, and even the local insurance companies.

The editorial went even further and compared the "nightmarish" treatment of engineers fleeing the program to the 1950s novel from Ayn Rand, *Atlas Shrugged*, Just like the late Ayn Rand warned, "Engineers are taking their rigorously licensed know how elsewhere rather than have it second-guessed by auditors whose background is insurance rather than engineering." The editorial concluded by stating, "The coastal economy is in peril until the legislature remedies the situation with less regulation. Whether the governor declares it or not, this is an emergency." To this, as a Catholic, I would respond, "Amen."

So now TDI's abusive practices were finally being exposed. A large city, Corpus Christi, was being harmed by those practices, and the editorial board of the local newspaper was bringing it to light.

TDI had always tried to dismiss complaints against their program as the whining of incompetent chronic malcontents who couldn't get their way. Now a major newspaper was calling them out. Perhaps the *Caller Times*, as attorney Loffler for TDI had stated at the SOAH hearing, "just didn't like TDI," or maybe now those engineers, builders, and owners who complained of their treatment by TDI were finally getting their voices heard.

The Call

The hearing was concluded, and then each side had to wade through well over one thousand pages of testimony and give their summary and final statement to the ALJ. After the hearing convened and before the final statements were given, I appeared before the Texas Board of Professional Engineers (TBPE), and as detailed earlier, I was completely exonerated. It is a shame that this did not happen before the hearing began as it should have been because Nelson and TDI would have had to answer under oath why they were accusing an engineer of fraud and negligence who had been cleared by TBPE of any wrongdoing.

This board ruling would become the cornerstone of my final argument because the hearing began with Powell giving TDI and the ALJ a flowchart issued by TBPE which showed no disciplinary action could be taken by TDI against an engineer without going through the board. The ALJ and TDI kept insisting that all of my alleged transgressions occurred prior to the new law and the flowchart going into effect. But that list went away as of January 1, 2013, prior to the final written arguments. Besides the overwhelming evidence that TDI was wrong factually and legally in every complaint they brought against me, the list that TDI was seeking to remove me from no longer existed as of January 1, 2013.

The final arguments through Powell laid out the evidence for each address and why it should be dismissed. Powell addressed TDI's evidence and the fact that Doug Klopfenstein could not identify improper nails from his own photos and that Doug Klopfenstein, Nelson, and Harp all testified that there was a disagreement with me over the evidence in the case. Nelson, Harp, Doug Klopfenstein, Benito Garcia, and Cantu all admitted that there is nothing in the code or in TDI directives that addresses scuff marks and that TDI produced no evidence to dispute the Atlas technical bulletin at Guadalajara or the enhanced nail zone bulletin for Greenbriar. At East Levee and North Shore, TDI produced no evidence anything was wrong at these addresses and in fact had never visited either site.

TDI's arguments, on the other hand, were written as if the hearing never happened. They did not address any of the evidence that I submitted even though it completely contradicted their evidence. They didn't address it and disprove it. They did not even address it at all. They just rehashed their complaint and basically stated that I was guilty because they said so despite all evidence to the contrary.

These arguments were submitted and rebutted, and the final arguments went to the ALJ. All parties had to wait on Cloninger's decision and ruling. It was after this final submittal that I got "the call."

I would later recall that it appeared to be divine intervention. I am a practicing Catholic and had just left my office on Ash Wednesday of 2013 to go to a five o'clock Ash Wednesday service at my parish church. While driving, I received a text to call my office immediately. I called and spoke to Linda Olvera, who informed me that she had just spoken to Russel Sheffield, the current manager of TDI windstorm inspectors. Sheffield had stated that he was aware of TDI's mistreatment of David Day, and he had some important information for him.

I knew who Sheffield was, the new manager of windstorm inspections who had taken Welch Watt's place, but I did not know anything about him. I had seen Sheffield at the hearing the day that

Garcia and Cantu testified. I remembered that Sheffield was a very large, imposing figure, and the day he was at the hearing, he appeared very somber.

I pulled off the road and called Sheffield. When Sheffield answered, he stated that he had been waiting for my call. Sheffield went on to explain that he had been aware of TDI's mission to get me and that he was not going to be a part of it. His voice was shaking with emotion as he told me he didn't care if he got fired, he was not going to sit back and let TDI railroad an innocent engineer out of the windstorm program.

This caught me off guard, and I even thought that it might be a setup. I asked Sheffield if he was on the level. Sheffield described the day of the hearing where he and I had come face-to-face but had not spoken. He described having seen me and my son at the courtroom. He then went on to describe what prompted his call.

While he waited outside with his two inspectors, Garcia and Cantu, while Harp was taking forever to testify, Garcia called him aside and told him he had to get something off his chest. Garcia told Sheffield that TDI inspectors were being persecuted if they didn't do the will of Welch Watt and that Watt and Nelson were using TDI inspectors to punish engineers and some contractors. He stated specifically that he had been told by Welch Watt to go find something wrong with the Guadalajara roof. Garcia also stated that many of the other inspectors felt the same way and did not feel secure in their jobs because they were constantly being second-guessed by their superiors. This is ironically the same thing that Garcia had done to me at Guadalajara.

Sheffield stated that it was that conversation that prompted him to start doing his own investigation into my SOAH action. What Sheffield found was a concerted effort by TDI to get not only me but other engineers for the mere fact that Watt, Nelson, or Alexis Dick did not like them. I had embarrassed them at Emerald by the Sea in Galveston, where I constantly showed them up and proved them wrong. Sheffield stated that during in-house meetings at TDI, Nelson would refer to me and other persecuted engineers as "eng-gone-eers."

Sheffield also stated that Nelson would refer all work to one engineer (you guessed it), Mike Scanlon. I stated to Sheffield that I knew from experience that no inspector or engineer in the windstorm program was safe, but they were all afraid to speak out. Sheffield replied that he had gotten affidavits from several of the inspectors describing the TDI abuse, and more importantly, he had in his possession a videotape taken by one the TDI inspectors that clearly illustrated the abuse.

My heart was pounding at this moment, and I told Sheffield that I wanted to meet with him as soon as possible and would drive to Waco, where Sheffield lived, and discuss it with him. I told Sheffield I was beginning to go into church and would call him as soon as I got out.

The call lasted maybe fifteen minutes, and I entered the church with a lot on my mind. Ash Wednesday is the Catholic holy day marking the first day of Lent, the forty days before Easter which Catholics treat as a time of fasting. The ash service is to remind all Catholics that from dust they came and to dust they shall return. I contemplated that my persecution by TDI paled in comparison to the persecution that Christ endured on the cross. It occurred to me that Christ's suffering was not without purpose; it was the ultimate sacrifice by God to save all people from sin. I resolved that my persecution by TDI would not be for naught. I resolved to do everything in my power to expose what Sheffield had just described to me as nothing less than evil, the treatment that was doled out to me, TDI's own inspectors, and other engineers such as Henry Segura and Vera Green.

After the service, I called Sheffield back, and we agreed to meet that weekend. Dennis lived in Austin, so that Saturday, Paz, daughter Cristina, and I drove to Austin, picked up Dennis, and then drove to Waco to meet Russell Sheffield. We arrived at Sheffield's home late morning, and for the first time we met face-to-face.

Sheffield was an imposing figure, larger-than-life. He had played defensive tackle for the Baylor Bears and ironically played on the Liberty Bowl team that beat LSU in the last minutes when Sheffield stopped LSU's all-American running back and caused a fumble. Baylor won that game, and I remembered watching it on national television.

Though Sheffield was much larger than me, he appeared nervous in my presence, almost as if he were meeting a mythical figure. Sheffield was risking his job meeting me, and I had to assure him that our meeting would be worthwhile for both of us. Even though Sheffield was the most imposing figure to ever work at TDI, he was also one of the most honest and independent. He was not one of them; he had come from the outside and slipped through the system without them detecting that he was not a ruthless man. Welch Watt was also a big, imposing figure, and he was just as ruthless. When Watt left, TDI hired Sheffield because of his size, no doubt, thinking that he would be just as ruthless as Watt. Instead, Sheffield quickly saw that TDI was not about serving the public. Their goal appeared to be to deny as many windstorm certifications as they could.

The first thing Sheffield had tried to do at TDI was to stop the practice of TDI supervisors from scrutinizing and overturning their own TDI inspectors' work. After Garcia's confession to him during the hearing, Sheffield had asked Garcia to put it in writing, and then one by one Sheffield had solicited and received statements from five of the fifteen inspectors. It was at this time Sheffield had become aware that one of the TDI inspectors, Wesley Clepper, had secretly taped the TDI abusive practices and his own mistreatment.

During our meeting, Sheffield went into great detail how Nelson and Dick would express their distaste and their desire to get me and several other engineers out of the program. Sheffield considered their complaints against me, petty, and in fact disagreed with them over their accusations against me. Sheffield had witnessed firsthand what the TDI inspectors were rejecting and had been attempting to put a stop to it. Sheffield had been trying to get his inspectors to give some tolerance to their inspections and not reject roofs that did not meet their idea of perfection.

Sheffield then showed me the affidavits submitted by his TDI inspectors. The statements all had one common theme: the inspectors were being forced to do things they considered unethical or risk losing their jobs. They complained they were being overly scrutinized and had to reject work that otherwise would have been found acceptable. The most important statement came in Garcia's statement, where he stated unequivocally, "I was told by Welch Watt to find something wrong at Guadalajara." I now had direct evidence that TDI was targeting me with the intent to harm me.

But the most important piece of evidence that Sheffield presented during our meeting was a copy of the videotape made by Wesley Clepper. Sheffield wanted me to have all of this evidence because he was not going to stand by and watch an innocent engineer get railroaded by TDI while he had the power to do something about it. Our face-to-face meeting had convinced Sheffield that I was a qualified professional engineer who had done nothing more than repeatedly challenge TDI's incorrect denials of properly constructed homes, roof, and commercial structures. After meeting me and talking to me and hearing my horror stories of TDI's oversight policies, Sheffield became convinced that I and other engineers like me knew what we were doing and it was the TDI inspectors and engineers, particularly the ones who had testified against me, Nelson, Harp, and Klopfenstein, who were guilty of incompetence, negligence, and fraud.

Though Sheffield was giving the evidence to me with full knowledge of its potential harm to his employment at TDI, he was willing to take that risk. He did request that I seek the evidence through the Freedom of Information (FOI) process from TDI. Sheffield told me that all of the evidence had been presented to TDI management and therefore was discoverable public information, which in fact it was. By law, once the statements and videos were voluntarily turned in by the TDI inspectors to TDI, they became public information. I agreed to make the request through the Freedom of Information Act.

Sheffield and I departed on a handshake, and during the ride back, I listened to the entire Clepper video. Wesley Clepper was a TDI inspector who worked in the Angleton office. Prior to working for TDI, Clepper was a contractor and a roofer. He had installed many roofs under TDI oversight, and when a field position opened in TDI in the late 2000s, Clepper took the opportunity to work for a state agency that offered a salary and benefits and holidays.

While working for TDI, Clepper had experienced firsthand the unwritten rules that TDI was attempting to enforce on me, such as the one dealing with scuff marks. What is worse, Clepper would be given conflicting directives from different TDI supervisors with an individual giving one order and another giving a contradictory order and both being able to discipline Clepper if he followed the order of the other or if he ignored both of them and did what he had been trained to do as a roofer by various roofing products manufacturers and by their written instruction on their wrappers. Clepper had seen firsthand how irresponsible and punitive some of TDI's actions had been toward roofers and engineers and how they attempted to get both in trouble.

Clepper would later relate a story to me about how a roofer had installed shingles with a perfect four-nail pattern, exactly as was shown on the wrapper, and then, for added security, had added an extra nail at the center of each shingle. Anywhere else in the universe, this would have been a good, commendable, conscientious act, but TDI, with their foolish, irresponsible policy of not accepting a roof if it varied one iota from the shingle wrapper and Welch Watt's unwritten standards, rejected this roof because the nails were installed in a manner that had not been tested.

Any legitimate, responsible organization would not allow such a foolish policy. Any legitimate engineer or roof consultant would tell you that anything above the minimum is better. Five nails will always be better than four, and in my case, where roofers were instructed to put six nails where only four were required, the roofs were 150 percent safer. To reject a roof because the roofer put five nails instead of four is not only irresponsible for a state agency, it is clearly beyond their legitimate power.

When it became clear to Clepper that TDI did not have his best interest at hand, Clepper began secretly recording the abuse, the contradictory statements, the targeting of roofers and small specialty contractors, and blatant racism within certain TDI senior inspectors. The video was particularly damning to the Angleton office employees, supervisors Mike Babin and Larry Johnson, Welch Watt, and Doug Klopfenstein. Doug Klopfenstein is clearly shown in the video targeting a roofer by name, saying that "he just doesn't like them."

The video is the most damning piece of evidence of a dysfunctional state bureaucracy that I had ever seen. Clepper had caught TDI with their pants down and at their absolute worst. Everything that I had witnessed in their effort to get me was clearly shown in this video as TDI basic field office protocol being directed by Watt out of Austin with the full aid and support of TDI Engineering, the director, Dick, and TDI legal enforcement. It also reached as high as the ombudsman.

Sheffield had just given me a gold mine of evidence to use in defending myself, and he did so for no other reason than seeing that justice was done. From a call that came on Ash Wednesday, I had discovered that I had a brave ally within TDI. What are the odds!

Retribution

The following Monday morning, the first thing I did was to file a Freedom of Information request for the TDI inspector affidavits and the Wesley Clepper video. I then turned over all the evidence to my attorney. Though all final arguments had already been turned into the ALJ, no decision had yet been rendered. Though Powell considered all of the evidence in the affidavits particularly damning of TDI in general, the only statement directly related to TDI case against me was Benito Garcia's admission that he had been told by Welch Watt to find something wrong with the roof at Guadalajara. Though the statement was unsigned and Garcia was now retired from TDI, I did manage to contact Garcia and get a text-message reply that he stood by his statement.

After he retired from TDI, Garcia remained in contact with Sheffield and appeared willing to back Sheffield in his quest to expose the abuse within TDI. Unfortunately, Garcia naively believed that his written statement would remain confidential and not be made public. A cautionary reminder for any state employee is that anything you give a superior regarding policy immediately becomes public record and subject to review by the public through the Freedom of Information Act. When Garcia found out I had a copy of the affidavit, he was upset and at that point stopped communicating with Sheffield.

Powell immediately filed for an injunction with the new evidence of Garcia's statement. One would think that with this statement and the direct evidence that TDI had a pattern and practice of abuse of power, the TDI attorneys would have reexamined the evidence, but instead they attacked Powell and me for contacting one of their employees. The only problem for them was that Garcia had been retired for three months.

Cloninger also did not look at the direct evidence of TDI's vendetta against me. Instead she only was concerned if Garcia would have made the same findings if Welch Watt had not told him to find something wrong with the roof. She granted a limited reexamination of Garcia's testimony by direct examination or affidavit. Keep in mind that Garcia would have never looked at the roof if TDI were not illegally auditing me on every job, and also TDI inspectors find things wrong with their own inspectors' work, as was shown in the body of Garcia's statement.

Garcia issued a statement saying that he stood by his testimony and the exposed nails were rejectable. Powell requested Garcia be put under oath, but Cloninger rejected his request. Of course, Garcia had to stand by his testimony. To do otherwise would have opened him up to perjury. Garcia had already lied about having met the owner of the home at Guadalajara or had previously seen the Atlas bulletin that was handed to him in front of the owner he claimed to not have met. Cloninger did a terrible disservice to me by not opening up his testimony to further cross-examination by Powell.

So now the cat was out of the bag that I knew about the TDI inspector statements and the Clepper film. Sheffield told me that when Alexis Dick found out about the statements, she broke down crying, saying she had no idea that TDI was targeting engineers and even their own inspectors.

Russell Sheffield would later release a statement:

April 1, 2013

To whom it may concern,

I, Russell Sheffield, Former manager in Regulatory Policy Division at Texas Department of Insurance, Windstorm Inspections Office depose and say:

When working as TDI Windstorm manager, Ben Garcia a Quality Control Inspector stated to me that Welch Watt , prior manager of windstorm inspections, put him up to going out on engineer oversights for TDI and finding things wrong with engineered inspected and approved roofs regardless. I had a conversation with Alexis Dick my Director at the time of the incident and asked her if Garcia were to testify that statement on the stand, what would happen to the final decision of this SOAH hearing? Her answer, as she was frantically biting down on a rolled up napkin and fumbling for her cell phone to contact Sam Nelson at the hearing, she stated it would have an effect on all the cases pending.

Shortly after she had to tell her boss C.H. Mah this news, she announced that she was retiring from TDI. My working relationship with Alexis Dick and Sam Nelson after this event turned to the very worst as meetings took place to ask Sr. Inspectors and protected oversight inspectors about the regime of management style. Her extreme emotions adjourned these meetings crying and sobbing.

If you have any more concerns please contact me.

Russell Sheffield

Dick left TDI at the end of 2012 and so did Benito Garcia. That would leave Nelson as the only remaining individual in the governing trio that reigned over TDI since 1998 with Alexis Dick's support and blessing. Watt had left at the end of 2011. Of course, Dick knew about TDI's vendetta against me. Nelson had stated in his testimony that the order to put me under audit had come directly from Dick.

Dick had already authorized an outside independent study of TDI by University of Texas–Austin in 2002. The study was the result of the initial complaints against appointed engineers. The authors interviewed TDI engineers, appointed engineers, and insurance agents. The report was sixty-two pages long and basically concluded that the audit process was dysfunctional and recommended scrapping the whole process. From this report, Dick was fully aware of the problems with the audit process. This report should be required reading by all state legislators who hold the key to eliminating the abusive audit process.

Dick had hired Sheffield apparently without Nelson's approval, and since Dick had left, Nelson was appointed in her position as interim director of Windstorm Inspections. Nelson immediately put pressure on Sheffield to take and pass the ICC inspector test. Nelson also repeatedly asked Sheffield if he was communicating with Day's camp, as if I was an enemy. The fact is that my new knowledge was the absolute worst news for Nelson. Nelson no longer had Dick to protect him, so he could not have anyone exposing him or questioning his authority. It was also obvious that Nelson was very worried about the outcome of my hearing. The *Corpus Christi Caller Times* article also was shining a revealing light on TDI Windstorm. It was during this time that Nelson was feeding information to Scanlon about the trial and must have been very worried about having lied under oath about telling Scanlon that he would take care of Day.

Neither Nelson nor Scanlon knew that I was in daily communication with numerous engineers who were advising me and hoping that I would be successful. Scanlon began calling these engineers and, unsolicited, would discredit me, saying that I had undermined him at Emerald Condominiums in Galveston and had taken money without ever visiting the condos. Scanlon also attempted to discredit Vicki

Huckaby, saying she was incompetent and worse. What Scanlon did not know is that these engineers immediately phoned me to let me know what Scanlon was saying. The statement about Emerald was the most outrageous because when Huckaby and I first visited the office of GT Leach, the contractor for Emerald, to examine all of the records and submittals, we asked if Scanlon had been given the same information. We were told that Scanlon had never visited GT Leach or requested any records. Scanlon had done his entire investigation of Emerald without once ever consulting with the contractor who built it. Remember, it was Scanlon who submitted his own WPI-2 for Emerald and checked the box "Does not comply." Scanlon's WPI-2 submittal was done so without getting any records from the contractor. His underhanded act cost the homeowner's association hundreds of thousands of dollars proving that Scanlon was wrong.

With TDI's case against me unraveling, Nelson had to stop the inside damaging information from continuing. Nelson new that both Clepper and Sheffield were studying for the ICC exam. As with any exam, those who have taken them will inform their colleagues of the types of questions that are on the exam. This information would be shared by all colleagues who would take the exam. Sheffield's inspectors who had taken the exam would describe to him the questions they had encountered or had even written down what they remembered. This is not uncommon or unethical, but it was this action that Nelson used to place both Sheffield and Clepper on probation. Sheffield and Clepper were accused of illegally obtaining a copy of an ICC exam. They were accused without one shred of physical evidence. From what Sheffield told me, one of the clerical overheard Sheffield say he was going to be studying one of the tests that Clepper had given him. As just stated, it is not uncommon for colleagues to share test questions from their personal experience or even practice tests that they have taken. There was never any evidence that an official ICC exam had been obtained because it simply didn't happen.

Both Sheffield and Clepper were put on probation, suspension, and banned from their offices and given an onerous list of demands, including no contact with TDI employees. Upon leaving the office, Sheffield called one of his field offices to let them know that he was going to be out and who they could contact while he was away. When TDI got the phone bill later and discovered the phone call, they immediately fired Sheffield for violating a probation that he had been illegally put under.

Clepper, on the other hand, had his office computer confiscated, and on the computer was some personal data that Clepper had long forgotten was even on the computer. TDI used this information to immediately fire Clepper. The Clepper video clearly shows other TDI inspectors playing games on their computers and company cell phones, yet nothing was done to them.

It is normally extremely difficult to fire a state employee. Due process and hearings and reviews have to be conducted. Sheffield and Clepper were illegally put on probation on invalid, trumped-up charges and fired for violating the terms of their probation. This action needs to be investigated by agencies outside of TDI.

It was clearly obvious to Sheffield, Clepper, and me that this action by TDI was clearly retaliatory for having exposed the corruption within TDI. What TDI and specifically Sam Nelson had done to Sheffield, Clepper, and me was far worse than anything the three of us were accused of doing. And it was obvious that Nelson would stop at nothing, including using the full authority of the state to persecute individuals who had done nothing more than question his authority and his competence.

Nelson had risen to power because he had a boss, Alexis Dick, who needed him to run the engineering department because she knew nothing about engineering and didn't want outside professionals involved after receiving the UT report. Alexis Dick had worked her way up from a clerk position and had no engineering or inspection background whatsoever. Vain, narcissistic people should never be allowed to be in a position of power, and Nelson's years of incompetent running of TDI Windstorm Engineering Program had left scores of victims, which now included Sheffield, Clepper, and me. What was worse than having Nelson run amok in a state agency is that the state agency including the legal department, the ombudsman, and the commissioner let him.

Nelson could not have done any of his wrongdoing without the blessing and the support of his superiors. Inventing unsupportable charges against Sheffield and Clepper is nothing less than criminal. Using those charges to place them on probation is nothing less than abuse of office and corruption. Terminating them for trumped-up charges is as onerous an act as has ever been enacted by a governmental entity. And now my fate rested in the hands of a state agency that had just shown it to be totally corrupt.

Clepper's secretly taped video had exposed the seamy underside of the workings of a dysfunctional state agency. The knowledge that I had seen this video led to the termination of the two people who had allowed for me to see it. In one of the final scenes in the video, the TDI ombudsman is interviewing Clepper, telling him that what he had done in making the video was unethical but legal. He assured Clepper that nothing would happen to him for making the video. By the time I saw this video, Clepper had already been unethically fired by the same man who had assured him nothing would happen to him.

When I requested the video through the Freedom of Information Act, I was stonewalled and then denied it. The argument that the TDI legal used to keep me from getting the video was that I was involved in a hearing with TDI, and the video was edited and appeared to show TDI in an incriminating light. The state attorney general, in their ruling, determined that TDI did not have to give the video to me, but if I got it through any other means, then they could do nothing about it.

The video was not edited to give the appearance of incriminating activity; the criminal activity was caught on camera by Clepper without any embellishment by Clepper. He did not need to. TDI practiced abusive retribution activity on a daily basis, and it didn't take any creative editing by Clepper to expose it. All he had to do was to turn on his camera and record on any given day, and the dysfunctional nature of TDI would manifest itself without any prompting or editing.

I now had an original copy of the video given to me by none other than Clepper himself. I had copies of statements exposing TDI abuse given to me by Sheffield before he was let go. I had seen how far TDI would go to squash dissent. I had presented a defense of myself in a seven-day hearing when no other hearing had lasted more than a day. I had supplied the ALJ with one of the statements from Ben Garcia that included the charge that Welch Watt had instructed Garcia to find something wrong with my certification of Guadalajara. I had exposed TDI's incompetence during my hearing and showed that Doug Klopfenstein could not even identify improper nails in his own photos. Through Powell, I had gotten Klopfenstein, Nelson, Harp, Garcia, and Cantu to admit that their findings against me were not supported by the code or by TDI written policy. Powell had gotten Nelson, Klopfenstein, and Harp to admit that there was a disagreement between TDI and David Day. It is highly inappropriate and even possibly illegal to accuse an engineer of fraud and negligence for disagreeing with the state. I had done all I could to show why TDI was wrong. And now all I could do was to wait for their decision.

The Decision

The ALJ, Cloninger, had resided over the case for almost two years from the time the charges were filed in May of 2011, through a seven-day hearing that started in December of 2011 and concluded in November of 2012. She was presented with evidence at the beginning of the hearing that the law had now changed, and TDI could not take action against an engineer without input from TBPE. Cloninger should have dismissed all charges at that point because any decision she rendered would be made moot by the new law.

The whole purpose of TDI's action against me was to remove me from the appointment list I was on prior to 2011. That list had gone away on January 1, 2013, and I was appointed by none other than Nelson himself to the new list. Cloninger had maintained through her rulings that she was only judging on the old list. She repeatedly ruled that the new law and the new list did not apply to her hearing. When the old list went away, so should the purpose of Cloninger's hearing have gone away. Powell had given Cloninger every opportunity to correct the record and cancel the hearing because the old list no longer existed.

How Cloninger would rule had been a mystery to everyone involved. Her demeanor during the trial had seemed to favor me.

She constantly questioned TDI's testimony, and her only questions to me were to confirm what I was saying. She had even rebuked the TDI attorney Loffler when she questioned my making statements as an expert. She stated emphatically that she considered David Day an expert and then proceeded to recite my education and experience and then stated she definitely considered David Day to be an expert in his field. Cloninger had made no such statements about any of the TDI witnesses.

During my demonstrations, Cloninger had gotten out of her seat to examine the evidence and made sure that the TDI attorneys saw the same thing that she was looking at.

I felt very confident that if Cloninger would have had to make a decision on the final day of the trial after verbal arguments that she would have sided in my favor. Her last statement as soon as the hearing ended had been that she wanted Angelina Jolie to play her part in the movie of the hearing. That is not the kind of a statement a judge would make who intended to rule against the accused. But then her decision arrived.

The decision came on May 29, 2013, and was 110 pages long, complete with table of contents. The opening paragraph, entitled "Proposal for Decision," ends with the following sentence: "After reviewing the evidence and arguments in this case, the Administration Law Judge [ALJ] finds staff proved some but not all of the allegations against Mr. Day and recommends revocation of Mr. Day's appointment as a Qualified Inspector." The remaining 106 pages were Cloninger's reasoning for her decision, but she let it be known in the first paragraph that she recommended Mr. Day have his TDI appointment revoked.

This is the equivalent of recommending an attorney be disbarred. Even if 100 percent of the charges against me were true, this would be the equivalent of taking away a driver's license for getting a parking ticket. I was aware that ALJs were capable of making completely wrong decisions. As referenced earlier, I had been involved in and read the decision of another ALJ, Stephen Rivas, in the case of the auto repair shop where the TWIA engineer had denied the roof damage because he reasoned that the roof had been repaired multiple times. When the engineer found out during the SOAH hearing that the repairs were mitigation repairs done after Hurricane Dolly, he rescinded his denial of the roof damage and admitted that the roof was damaged by Dolly and needed to be repaired. The ALJ denied the claim and used as his reasoning that the roof damage was old. His reasoning was the exact opposite of the testimony, and he cost the building owner thousands of dollars in denied insurance money. In that case, the hearing was held at the Harlingen City Hall, and there was no stenographer, only a tape recorder. That judge may have heard several cases that day. In the case of the auto repair shop in Port Isabel, the ALJ had gotten the facts and the conclusion completely wrong based on a two-hour hearing recorded with a tape recorder.

Cloninger, on the other hand, had over one thousand pages of testimony and over one hundred exhibits to base her decision on. There was no excuse for her to arrive at the wrong decision and then to recommend a punishment that far exceeded the alleged crime. Cloninger, in her final argument, actually made the statement (page 87), "Due to the serious and repetitive nature of these violations, no sanction less than revocation of Mr. Day's appointment will adequately 'protect' the insurance consumers in the State of Texas and the TWIA risk pool." Imagine that, I was a threat to the insurance consumers of Texas, and the TBPE had totally exonerated me on exact same charges. In Cloninger's 110-page assassination of me that bordered on slander, there was not one mention of the TBPE decision.

The decision may well have been written by Nelson, Watt, or Dick with Cloninger's expressed disdain for me. She had just accused me of knowingly, willingly, and fraudulently affixing my signature and seal to an official state document—a statement that, if true, would be grounds for revocation of my engineering license and possible criminal charges. And yet the state body that governs engineers and is tasked with protecting the public had 100 percent exonerated me on the same charges.

So where did Cloninger go so wrong? The answer could be found in her opening statements. On page 2, first full sentence, "It is important to note that TDI is seeking revocation *only* of Mr. Day's appointment as a *Qualified Inspector* and not his *professional engineer's license* issued by the Texas Board of Professional Engineers [italics added]." Notice Cloninger capitalizes *Qualified Inspector* but fails to capitalize *professional engineers*. When used as a title Professional Engineer should be capitalized. Besides this statement being entirely untrue, Cloninger seemed to imply that the "qualified inspector" status was more important than my registration as a professional engineer.

The statement was entirely untrue because TDI, at the same time the SOAH hearing was proceeding, had filed the exact same charges verbatim with TBPE. TBPE had accepted the charges for investigation, indicating they did consider the charges to be in the practice of engineering, and TBPE had dismissed those same charges and exonerated me. This decision was given to Cloninger in the final closing statement by Powell. So Cloninger had full knowledge of the TDI's filing with TBPE against me, yet she made the statement that TDI was not seeking to revoke Mr. Day's engineering license. Had Cloninger knowingly, willingly, and fraudulently made an incorrect statement in an official state document? By making this false statement, was Cloninger a threat to the insurance consumers of Texas? The case can be made. The remaining one hundred pages contained similar misstatements, lapses of reasoning, and flat-out egregious, incorrect statements.

An entire book can be written on the incorrect statements in Cloninger's 110-page decision, and in fact, all of the evidence discussed in the body of this book sufficiently establishes the background and the correct facts and circumstances.

Not all of Cloninger's 110 pages of findings was a complete indictment of me. In fact, it could equally be seen as an indictment of TDI. On the major sustentative issues, Cloninger in fact agreed with me in all cases.

Primarily on the roof certification that triggered my being put under audit on all jobs, the blow-off roof membrane at Suntide III, Cloninger sided with me. She accepted my argument and the evidence that the roof coming off was due to long-term corrosion of a roof hatch's fasteners. It is important to note that all of the ALJ's detrimental findings were on certifications done after the continuous audit requirement of me. If TDI would have done their due diligence, they would have arrived at the same conclusion as TBPE and

Cloninger. But this was never about arriving at the truth; it was as Russell Sheffield had so clearly said—this was TDI's openly expressed desire to get David Day off the appointment list.

In a slamming indictment of Welch Watt and the TDI inspectors, Cloninger agreed that the nails that TDI were calling overdriven were not overdriven. I had successfully demonstrated during the hearing that the nails that TDI were calling overdriven were in fact properly driven. There have been thousands of roofs rejected by TDI for what they called overdriven nails. And even after this ruling by an SOAH judge, TDI is still calling them overdriven. Replacing the roof at Plumosa cost the owner or the roofer over $15,000. What is even more important, at Shadowbrook, Cloninger ruled that Nelson could not require me to take any action on a roof. Nelson had put in writing that I had to bring the roof at Plumosa into compliance, and I had challenged his legal authority to do so. Cloninger ruled that Nelson had no legal standing to make such a request. When I filed my complaint against Nelson with TBPE, part of the basis of the complaint was that Nelson was requesting for me to bring a roof into compliance. TBPE had ruled that my complaint had no basis. Now they have a ruling from an SOAH judge.

At Shadowbrook, Cloninger agreed that I had done nothing wrong in certifying the roof. The areas that CASA had checked were indeed good and verified by TDI Inspector Cantu. The small area that Cantu found with high-placed nails could have been replaced, but the roofer elected to replace the whole roof. These nails were in a location that has been approved by other shingle manufacturers, and no manufacturer would have required that these shingles be replaced because they were well sealed.

So the three jobs that TDI used as justification to place me under onerous illegal audits had all been shot down by the facts and by an SOAH judge whose decision would be used to revoke my appointment. Placing me under audit on all jobs with the TDI inspectors who had just been proven wrong on all accounts is the equivalent of a police chief ordering his patrol officers to trail me and fine me every time my speed exceeded the limit by one mile per hour even if I were rolling down a hill.

No engineer should be audited more than once, yet I and other engineers who practiced windstorm engineering on residences were audited on a yearly basis. This is not at random. I had been audited eight times prior to be putting under audit on all jobs, and my designs and certifications were all found acceptable—not a bad track record for a man who Cloninger deemed a threat to the insurance consumers of Texas and TWIA. If the IRS had audited me eight times and found no wrongdoing after the first two, would that not be considered government overreach and harassment?

So what did Cloninger find me guilty of? In a severe travesty of justice, Cloninger had found me guilty of "failure to timely respond to TDI's inquiries." TDI had alleged this in their complaint but during the hearing did not mention it one time, which would not be protocol for an entity wishing to have a complaint ruled on. Because it was not alleged during the trial, my attorneys had offered no defense of this allegation. My attorneys and I believed then and believe now that the compliance requirement found in TDI administrative code section 38.001 does not apply to engineers.

As stated earlier, section 38.001 applies to reasonable inquiries to insurance agents and gives them 10 days to respond.

In the hundreds of inquiries given to me, none of which were reasonable, I may have missed the ten-day deadline four or five times and never deliberately. When the certified inquiries came, they were signed for by the office staff, and in some cases, I did not see them until a second notice was issued. TDI had no evidence nor presented evidence that I had seen the inquiries on the day they were received at the CASA office. I knew of one case of George De La Matyr, who is now deceased, that received an inquiry while he was out of the country for two weeks, but his office staff had signed for the certified letter. He was accused of being nonresponsive.

Does the section 38.001, which is found under the insurance code in chapter 38, "Data Collection and Reports," apply to professional engineers? The section of the insurance code 5.4604 was very specific in that only what was contained in section 5.4604 could be enforced on engineers. Engineers are governed by the Engineering

Practicing Act. Immediately before she said I was guilty of violating section 38.001 of the administrative code on page 10, Cloninger had just stated in the first paragraph, "The ALJ further notes that, as previously discussed, 28 Texas Administrative Code 5.4604 [f] [l] [c] which allows for the imposition of a fine as a sanction, does not apply to professional engineers licensed by the TBPE, such as Mr. Day. Therefore, even though the aforementioned law is cited in the second Amended Notice of Public Hearing the ALJ finds it irrelevant to this case." Cloninger was correct to rule that this section does not apply to engineers, and she is just as equally incorrect in stating that section 38.001, "Inquiries," does apply to engineers. Nothing in the administrative insurance code other than the one section dealing with windstorm, applies to engineers, and that section is in direct conflict with the aforementioned Engineering Practice Act, which clearly states that no requirement can be placed on an engineer to use his seal.

There were two things that TDI did not want to discuss during my hearing. The first was the allegations concerning Sunchase IV. This was purely a matter of engineering that if TDI lost on, they would face multiple counts of improperly rejecting roofs for using Miami-Dade NOAs. TDI dropped all allegations against me in the SOAH court concerning Sunchase IV but kept it in their complaint with TBPE, where it was rejected.

The second was the ten-day-response requirement. TDI had been disciplining and even fining engineers for years for failing to respond within ten days. For the same reason that TDI cannot fine engineers, they cannot put time limits on engineers' responses. Only TBPE can do that. The TBPE time line for answering a complaint is thirty days, and that is when an official complaint is filed. In no case with TBPE was a complaint filed by the public. None of the owners involved in any of the addresses involved even blamed me. They all blamed TDI for the lack of certification.

Cloninger was extremely irresponsible in ruling on a legal matter that had not been discussed in her court. And furthermore, her ruling that I was negligent for not timely responding was as wrong as it was irresponsible. Section 38.001 simply does not apply to professional engineers.

What was even more egregious in Cloninger's ruling was her statement on page73, "Even though the due date was on a Saturday and Mr. Day responded on a Monday, he was nonetheless nonresponsive." Even if the rule did apply to an engineer, this would be an extreme enforcement of it that should carry no sanctions.

Where else did Cloninger go wrong? In order of her ruling, the following is a synopsis of the findings.

EAST LEVEE, BROWNSVILLE

Cloninger bought TDI's, specifically Stephen Harp's, allegations that the roof product evaluation RC-121 that I relied on, was for a complete roof assembly and did not pertain to the cap-sheet-only portion of the tested assembly. She ruled that I violated the code by using a product that had not been tested and therefore should be sanctioned.

This is extremely flawed logic and underscores why SOAH judges should not be hearing evidence on engineering matters. The product evaluation RC-121 did indeed test the adherence of a cap sheet to a cap sheet and would meet pressures far in excess of those incurred at the East Levee building. Cloninger even made the following foolish statement on page 23, paragraph2, "While, as attested to by Mr. Day, the partial reroof may meet engineering and NRCA requirements, those are outside the 2006 IBC." Where did Cloninger get this idea? Was she now an authority on the 2006 code more so than engineers and the NRCA?

By making such a foolish ruling, Cloninger now sets precedence that could put TWIA in the position of paying for complete reroofs when there is only partial damage. As I stated numerous times, there is no product evaluation that tests existing conditions to new conditions.

Therefore, theoretically, one shingle could not be replaced without replacing all shingles because there is no test that would account for a new shingle to an old one. These are decisions that are made by engineers on a daily basis, and I correctly allowed the new cap sheet to be applied to existing cap sheet because the existing cap sheet was in good condition to receive a new cap sheet and was repairable.

What is more important is that TBPE had already ruled on this, and Cloninger did not take the TBPE decision into account. There is not one mention of the TBPE decision in the whole 110-page ruling. Even if both TDI and Cloninger believed that the product evaluation submitted did not apply, they both could have asked that the cap sheet be tested in place, and I would have done so. Just like at Emerald by the Sea, the test would have easily passed. This roof repair is still in place and can still be tested.

The Levee address had private insurance when the complaint was brought and has private insurance continuous to date. The certification done by me was part of a multipart remediation at a six-story building. If, as Judge Cloninger stated, the roof blew off, the building would be covered by private insurance, and TWIA would be held harmless. A partial certification will not make a structure eligible for TWIA insurance. Both TDI enforcement attorneys and Cloninger refused to grasp this simple concept. TDI should not have been bringing any disciplinary action against any engineer where TWIA was not involved.

GREENBRIAR RESIDENCE REROOF

Cloninger spent eleven pages covering the Greenbriar roof and produced no evidence that the roof was incorrect, unsound, and not in accordance with manufacturer's recommendations. She also failed to grasp that the home has private insurance to this day. The home has never had a TWIA policy and was not seeking one. TDI did then and does now allow for parts of structures to be certified, such as roofs, windows, and doors. In case the owner ever does wish to pursue a TWIA policy, they would have that portion already covered. This was the case at East Levee and is the case at Greenbriar. Nelson was either ignorant of his own agencies' policies or flat-out lied about the TDI policy of allowing certifications of roof of structures that do not have a windstorm certification. The Greenbriar roof was not the first roof that I had certified on homes without a WPI-8, so it obviously was not incorrect to do so.

Cloninger spent a great deal of ink dwelling on whether I knew what shingle was installed at the time of the inspection at the home with Doug Klopfenstein. The shingle had been properly identified in the inspection report submitted prior to Doug Klopfenstein's visit. So whether I properly named it in the field is irrelevant. There are over one hundred brands of shingles, and knowing them all by name is not a requirement to be a TDI inspector. If I had called it a three-tab shingle instead of the heavier architectural shingle, which it was, then TDI could have at least made a case against my knowledge, but none of it would change the fact that the existing shingles on the roof were installed properly, and I presented the evidence that proved it, and TDI did not refute that evidence.

One of the most egregious and onerous proclamations by Cloninger was buying the lie started by Doug Klopfenstein and repeated by Alexis Dick that I knew the roof was not eligible for certification (page 35, second sentence), "Nevertheless, staff proved Mr. Day submitted a WPI-2 BC-2 for a roof that he knew was ineligible for TWIA coverage." This statement is as outrageous as it is factually untrue. There was no evidence submitted by TDI other than Nelson's testimony that a structure that is not certified cannot have a roof certified. They produced no written policy or directive that stated that this was true. On the other hand, I gave direct testimony of Welch Watt giving the language for the policy and the previous certifications that had been accepted. Vicki Leggett also gave testimony that the owner could get a discount by having a roof certified, as it was obviously common practice. Cloninger dismissed this evidence, stating that the intake division had erred when they accepted these certifications (page 34, last paragraph).

If TDI told me that certifying a roof only of a structure was okay and I followed their instructions, then how could I be guilty of violating anything?

As far as the placement of the nails, I provided clear written documentation that the nails were in the correct manufacturer-tested zone. My document superseded TDI's old, outdated data, and Cloninger completely and irresponsibly ignored it. More importantly the "enhanced nail zone" documents that I produced contained statements that went straight to the heart of the matter. The bulletin submitted stated, "Installation rejections…by code officials and consultants who are assuring compliance with what are overly restrictive manufacturer application directives." Even GAF realized that their shingles were needlessly being rejected. Once TDI and Cloninger saw this enhanced nail zone, that should have been the end of it. GAF now has an expanded nail zone entitled "Separating Myth from Reality" about nailing GAF laminated shingles. This new bulletin allows nails up to 8 ¼ inches, over an inch above the double laminate, and tested to over 110 mph.

The bottom line is that the roof is eligible for TDI certification, and the nails are properly placed. Once again, TDI and now apparently Cloninger, in an unprecedented effort to taint an innocent engineer, had harmed an innocent homeowner.

GUADALAJARA

Anyone who read my correspondence with Harp, with every letter being copied to TBPE, could see that TDI was clearly out to get me. The statements by the TDI inspectors and Harp were not only wrong, they were outrageous. Harp just continuously made up charges, such as the roof cement was detrimental to the shingles that were the complete opposite of reality. I bent over backwards and went way beyond reasonableness to protect the owner from TDI's wrath, but TDI and now Cloninger are throwing another innocent homeowner under the bus in their zeal to get me.

Cloninger spent fifteen pages covering the Guadalajara roof when it could have been summed up in two sentences: The 2006 IRC clearly states that the shingles will be installed in accordance with the manufacturer's instructions. The manufacturer, by providing a technical bulletin explaining inadvertent nails can be covered with roof cement, clearly indicated that they accepted this roof.

Everything else is irrelevant to the Guadalajara roof. The roof vents had already been accepted by Harp and should not have been rehashed at the hearing. The scuff marks are not a defect even recognized by the code and, as predicted, went away. There would have never been any scuff marks if TDI inspector Benito Garcia had properly accepted the roof on his first trip. Benito Garcia had already admitted that he was told to find something wrong with the Guadalajara roof. Also, Garcia admitted at the hearing that he had accepted another roof with exposed nails. Garcia said that there were ten to fifteen exposed nails at this residence when in fact there are still existing over two hundred exposed nails.

Instead of taking the Atlas bulletin at its simple meaning, Cloninger, on page 51, third paragraph, stated, "The applicable building code is silent as to the number of acceptable exposed nails but requires shingles to be installed according to the manufacturer's instructions. The manufacturer of the Guadalajara reroof issued a bulletin stating that inadvertently exposed nails could be covered with roofing cement, which implies to the ALJ that the manufacturer did not intend for nails to be exposed as they were in Mr. Day's courtroom demonstration regarding the Guadalajara reroof."

This is clearly a prime example of why ALJs should not be presiding over hearings of professional engineers. The TBPE heard the same complaint and were copied with all the correspondence, yet they exonerated me. Cloninger made no reference of this fact in her fifteen pages of faulty reasoning.

The evidence was very clear from my testimony that the manufacturer, Atlas, was contacted and told exactly what had occurred at Guadalajara, and they issued the bulletin in response to my inquiry. Therefore, they did intend for the bulletin to apply to Guadalajara. How Cloninger could get this so wrong is unfathomable. This incorrect statement on page 51 of "Cloninger Proposal for Decision" was as wrong as the judge who rejected the roof in Port Isabel by saying the damage was old when TWIA's own expert had stated the damage occurred during Hurricane Dolly. Both judges were wrong, and both should be held accountable.

SHADOWBROOK

Cloninger made the most insidious statement in the whole 110-page decision. After agreeing that I did nothing wrong in certifying the roof at Shadowbrook, she found that I was guilty of violating the ten-day-response rule, the infamous ten-day-response rule that legally does not apply to engineers. On Page 73, Cloninger writes the following:

> Staff proved its allegation that Mr. Day did
> not respond to Mr. Nelson's 11-7-2008 letter
> within 10 days as required by Texas Insurance
> Code 38.001. The evidence shows that Mr.
> Day responded 12 days after receiving the letter,
> but the ALJ notes the tenth day was Saturday,
> 11-22-08. Mr. Day responded on Monday,
> 11-24-08, the first business day after the tenth
> day. The commissioner is authorized to discipline
> Qualified Inspectors who do not timely reply to
> a "reasonable" inquiry from TDI. Therefore, Mr.
> Day is subject to sanctions for violating 38.001.

TDI is a state office and is not open on Saturday. The above statement is a reach even for Cloninger and TDI. Once again, the commissioner cannot discipline a professional engineer. And whether TDI and Cloninger wants to play word games and call engineers qualified inspectors, they are still professional engineers and are required to apply their engineers' seal to the WPI-2 state windstorm form. Notice that once again Cloninger capitalizes *Qualified Inspector* but never does *professional engineer*.

Were Nelson's inquiries of me reasonable inquiries? Quite the contrary; Nelson was asking me to provide verification that deficiencies had been corrected. And then Nelson demanded that I ensure the roof was corrected. The only thing Nelson could legally do was evaluate the same information that I used to certify the roof. There being no evidence that CASA reports contained any errors as proved by Cloninger, there should have been no further inquiries of me. Cloninger even stated on page 93, find 50, "No evidence was presented to support a finding that Mr. Day had a responsibility to develop a corrective action plan for a roof that was completed prior to his inspection and certification." Although this was written for Greenbriar, it would apply to all after the fact inspections.

For Greenbriar, North Shore, and East Levee, none of TDI's inquiries were reasonable. None of these addresses had TWIA policies and therefore were not subject to TDI oversight. All three of these addresses were the result of an illegal request for audits especially since the three jobs, Plumosa, Shadowbrook, and Suntide III, that resulted in me being put under audit were proven and accepted by Cloninger that I had done nothing wrong.

Each side got to respond to the decision, and each side responded to each other's responses. Powell, on my behalf, correctly rebutted the decision, pointing out above all things that there was no mention of the board decision exonerating me and that the ten-day response had not even been discussed at the hearing. TDI did, as they always do, ignored any evidence proving they are wrong, and they just stuck to their story.

It was obvious that Cloninger was not going to be swayed and overturn her decision. As George Basham had stated, "In their response they were writing for the record." As predicted, Cloninger, like TDI, clung to her opinion no matter how flawed and issued her final ruling in the spring of 2013, standing by her ruling.

The Commissioner's Decision

In the time that I was appointed to the windstorm inspection program in 2000, there would be four commissioners heading TDI and three in the period from 2010 to 2014. Though all of my persecution from October 28, 2010, through the hearing had occurred under commissioners Mike Geeslin and Elanor Kitzman, a new commissioner, Julia Ratheberger, was appointed after Cloninger's decision was final. Whether it was by design or bad luck, the decision to revoke my appointment was made by Ratheberger on the first week that she took office. There is no way that she could have been fully briefed on a case with such constitutional issues and blatant abuse by TDI personnel, particularly Sam Nelson. There is no way that she was told about the treatment of Russell Sheffield and Wesley Clepper and the video. There is also no way she could have been fully briefed on the new legislation and the appointment process with the new list that I was currently on and how that differed from the list that ended January 1, 2013.

The odds are that Ratheberger was given the same old TDI song and dance that David Day was just a chronic malcontent just like all the other engineers who had been fined or taken off the list and that I had no case against TDI. So Ratheberger, in her first week in office, signed an order that may put a permanent stain on her career. What are the odds?

Sam Nelson was so ecstatic on the day that the ruling came out the he immediately issued an order to remove me from the appointment list, apparently without the advice of TDI attorneys. Nelson was apparently unaware that the commissioner's decision was appealable. Nelson was forced to put me back on the list.

The commissioner's decision was appealed, and as expected, she stood by her decision. This time Sam Nelson got his way and removed me with a letter requesting I inform my clients that I was removed from the list.

I was under no obligation to honor this request and did not. In reality, nothing changed for me other than that my name was not on the list for the occasional client who would call everyone on the list, price shopping. I had not certified a property in my name for three years. The last two jobs that I had certified after October 28, 2010, were Emerald by the Sea in Galveston and the North Shore residence that TDI accused me of not turning in the information that they had in their possession for over a year and refused to act on.

All other jobs, which were just as frequent as before October 28, 2010, were handled by other engineers to keep TDI from punishing innocent TWIA policy holders. Three of the projects were audited by TDI without any problems. In reality, I had all of my over five hundred jobs after October 2010 audited by my peers. My clients had the bonus of having their projects looked at by two professional engineers. With the outrageous abuse that I had gotten at Guadalajara, it is likely that the majority of the over five hundred would have been rejected. It was obvious that TDI had no intention of accepting anything with my name on it unless it absolutely met perfection. This was obvious from the statement that Welch Watt had said to Benito Garcia, "Go and find something wrong with Guadalajara."

At Guadalajara, TDI employees made up defects (scuff marks), ignored manufacturer's directives (the Atlas Pinnacle Technical Bulletin on covering nails with roof cement), and lied under oath in an SOAH hearing. I protected over four hundred clients from this same abuse and kept over four hundred properties in the TWIA risk pool.

The commissioner's decision was immediately appealed to district court in Austin; the appeal should be required reading for attorneys representing professionals. The most important word in the appeal was *shall*. The new list for appointed engineers was created by the 2011 legislative session and signed into law by Governor Rick Perry in September of 2011. It required the board to create a roster for appointed engineers. It then provided the language "Once an engineer is placed on the board roster, TDI *shall* place the engineer on the appointment list for qualified inspectors." In legal terms, the word *shall* means it has to happen, as distinguished from *may*, which means it is at their discretion. I was placed on the board's list in September of 2012 and immediately appointed to the qualified inspectors list by TDI as the law required. Only the board could remove me from the roster, and under the new law, TDI could take no action against an engineer without cooperation and input from the board.

What TDI did to me was totally outside the law, and not even Cloninger made any mention of the new list in her 110-page decision. She foolishly clung to her decision long after the list in question in her court had gone away. As stated earlier, when the old list was discontinued by the Texas legislature, the SOAH hearing and complaint against me should have ended. It would be the equivalent of a murder trial continuing when the murdered victim is found alive. Why TDI and Cloninger would continue with the hearing when their purpose to remove me from the old list was no longer available can only be and should be answered by them.

My future and basically TDI's future now rested in the hands of a district court judge. Would justice finally be served? What would be the odds?

The Appeal

The appeal was filed, and TDI was now represented by the attorney general's office. The young attorney assigned to the case parroted the SOAH judge's findings as if they were infallible and offered no legal basis for his arguments other than TDI had the power and discretion to do whatever they wanted.

The appeal is a matter of public record and should be required reading for law school students. I was up against the unbridled power of the state but knew in my heart that truth and justice would eventually have to prevail.

While waiting for a court date, I came upon a movie at the Redbox movie-rental kiosks that are found throughout many cities. The title of the movie *Still Mine* caught my eye. The cover of the movie pictured the actor James Cromwell, whom I was a fan of, and I fondly recalled one of my favorite lines from the movie *Babe*, in which Cromwell's character told the sheepherding talking pig, Babe, "That'll do pig." He said this after Babe had won the sheepherding contest and was basking in his victory at the feet of his caretaker.

I rented the movie *Still Mine* for $1 and watched it that afternoon with Paz. The movie was based on the true life experience of Craig Morrison, an eighty-seven-year-old farmer and rancher in New

Brunswick, Canada. Morrison's wife, Irene, was in the beginning stage of Alzheimer's, and their large family home was becoming too much for him and Irene, who was played by the actress Geneviève Bujold, to handle. Morrison, who had been a home builder in the sixties, decides to build a smaller, more manageable home. On Morrison's property of two thousand acres was a sawmill, where Morrison milled his own lumber from the heart of the spruce trees that he had hand selected from his own property. Morrison's father had been a shipbuilder and had taught him the art of framing.

When Morrison starts building his home, his cantankerous neighbor comes over and informs him that he needed to get a permit. The laws had changed since the sixties, and New Brunswick had adopted the same international codes that Texas and most states had adopted. So the neighbor was correct. When Morrison goes to get a permit, he is asked to provide plans before he can start. This is still the correct process. One of Morrison's grandsons was a mechanical engineer, so he enlists his aid to produce a set of plans.

With the plans submitted, Morrison proceeds to start building at eighty-seven years of age with the help of his family. He does most of the framing himself. The trouble starts when the building official red-tags his home with a stop-work order. Morrison keeps building because all of the framing is exposed, and he feels he can address the red tag when the building official comes to visit.

The building official explains that the home was red-tagged because there was no stamp-graded lumber. Morrison explains that he milled the lumber himself and that there is not one knot on any of the lumber. The building official doesn't budge and orders him to remove it or get it graded. The building official points out that since Morrison built his own roof trusses, he will have to have a structural engineer evaluate the frames and provide signed, sealed drawings.

Morrison, with the help of his family attorney, gets a stamp grader, who states that the lumber is the highest quality. He then gets sealed calculations on his trusses. He then gets a neighboring building official to inspect the home, and the neighboring building official states in writing that the home exceeds all code requirements. The problem is that the Brunswick building official never approved the framing before it was covered up and refuses to give a condition of occupancy and even threatens to bulldoze the home if Morrison moves in.

The movie begins and ends with Morrison in the courtroom, defending his home. He matter-of-factly tells the judge that his home is sound, and he will either move in or go to jail, but either way, he will have a clear conscience. The judge forces the city to allow Craig and Irene to move in.

The movie was an excellent tale of the struggle with Alzheimer's and the struggle of a citizen with an unaccountable bully agency. In the end, Morrison defied the odds, and justice finally prevailed. I could not help but compare my plight with that of Morrison, the only difference being that I never violated any code or law, but I was still bullied by an unaccountable state agency, TDI.

Still Mine should be required viewing for all building officials and even all state agencies.

I finally got notice that I would have a hearing in Travis County Civil Court, State District Court 53, the Honorable Judge Scott Jenkins presiding. The hearing was set for October and then delayed until November 4.

After I got notice of the trial date, on the advice of my attorney, I reapplied to TDI to be a qualified inspector. The purpose of this was very clear. The 2011 legislation had changed the process to become a qualified inspector. The board would create a roster of engineers qualified to do windstorm design and inspection, and TDI *shall* appoint the engineer as a qualified inspector. I was already on the board's list and had not been removed from it after the commissioner's decision.

Cloninger and the SOAH court had only ruled on the old list, which went away on December 31, 2012. On January 1, 2013, the new list went into effect. The commissioner had taken me off the new list based on the decision of the SOAH court. This was improper. I reapplied to see what TDI would allow and more so to get them on record on the new list.

After fifteen days, I received the one-page reply from Steve Thompson, PE, the new director of engineering for TDI, as Nelson was now in Alexis Dick's former position as director of windstorm inspection. My application was denied, and the below letter expressly states that the reason for denial was the SOAH court decision.

Texas Department of Insurance
Property and Casualty Section – Engineering Services Program
Mail Code 103-3A, 333 Guadalupe • P. O. Box 149104, Austin, Texas 78714-9104
512-322-2212 telephone • 512-463-6693 fax • www.tdi.texas.gov

October 29, 2014

Mr. David Day, P.E.
CASA Engineering
1117 North Stuart Place Road
Harlingen, Texas 78552

RE: Application for Appointment of Engineer as a Qualified Inspector;
Disapproval Letter

CERTIFIED MAIL NO.: 7013 3020 0000 9493 7204
RETURN RECEIPT REQUESTED

Dear Mr. Day:

This letter acknowledges the receipt, filing, and review of your application for appointment as a qualified inspector by the Commissioner of Insurance pursuant to TEX. INS. CODE ch. 2210 and 28 TEX. ADMIN. CODE § 5.4604.

Pursuant to 28 TEX. ADMIN. CODE § 5.4604(e), the Texas Department of Insurance disapproves your application for appointment as a qualified inspector because the commissioner revoked your appointment and ordered your name removed from the list of qualified inspectors in Commissioner's Order No. 2743, issued on September 12, 2013. TDI is denying your application for appointment for the same reasons the administrative law judge (ALJ) cited when she recommended your revocation in her proposal for decision (PFD), which the commissioner substantively adopted in the final order revoking your appointment. The Commissioner's Order No. 2743 incorporated the PFD from SOAH Docket No. 454-11-3764.C and the resulting final order in their entirety as the basis for TDI's denial of your application.

Under 28 TEX. ADMIN. CODE § 5.4604(c), TEX. INS. CODE § 40.001 *et seq.*, and TEX. GOV'T CODE ch. 2001, you are entitled to a hearing to be conducted by the State Office of Administrative Hearings to determine whether the commissioner should approve the appointment. You have the right to be represented by an attorney, and you will have the responsibility to produce and present evidence to support the approval of your appointment.

It is important to note that the facts, issues, and causes of action pertaining to SOAH Docket No. 454-11-3764.C and Commissioner's Order No. 2743 have been finally adjudicated and cannot be re-litigated in any subsequent hearing you may request.

Mr. David Day, P.E.
October 29, 2014
Page 2 of 2

Pursuant to 28 TEX. ADMIN. CODE § 5.4604(e)(3), you have 30 days from the date of this letter to make a written request for a hearing. Send such written request to:

> **Steven Thompson, P.E.**
> **Chief Engineer**
> **Texas Department of Insurance**
> **MC 103-3A**
> **P.O. Box 149104**
> **Austin, TX 78714-9104**

TDI will send no additional notices regarding this matter. IF YOU DO NOT FILE A WRITTEN REQUEST FOR A HEARING WITHIN 30 DAYS FROM THE DATE OF THIS LETTER, YOUR PENDING APPLICATION FOR APPOINTMENT WILL BE DISAPPROVED.

If we receive a written request for hearing, a staff attorney will contact you with additional information regarding the hearing.

Sincerely,

Steven Thompson, P.E.
Chief Engineer
Engineering Services Program
Inspections Office
Texas Department of Insurance

cc: Sam Nelson, Director, Inspections Office
 Matt Sist, Manager, Windstorm Inspections Program
 Ginger Loeffler, Staff Attorney, Compliance Division, Enforcement Section

This denial begs the question, would I ever be eligible to receive an appointment from TDI? Even an engineer who loses his license can get reinstated. Does the commissioner have the power to give lifetime bans to an engineer or insurance agent? Not likely. At some point the legislation or the courts will have to deal with the improper, unethical, and illegal decisions from TDI and the SOAH courts.

The appeal hearing finally occurred on November 4 at three in the afternoon. I attended the hearing with Powell, Basham, and Dennis. The judge was in the middle of a child-custody hearing and had dismissed the jury for deliberations while he heard the oral arguments. Each side would be given thirty minutes to present their case.

Jenkins, who appeared younger than his fifty-three years of age, entered the courtroom and immediately addressed the parties. He was very curt and informed the parties that he had read the appeal and all the case law including the Occupations Act. He stated that he had read it over the weekend. He stated that he normally asks a lot of questions, but in this case "the law is clear" and that basically his mind was made up. He then stated that each party would be given thirty minutes. He stated, "You wanted your day in court, so you will be given thirty minutes."

Powell went first and reiterated all of the legal issues. First and foremost, the law was clear, the new legislation allowed for the board to create a new list, and that TDI *shall* appoint the engineer. The law was equally clear that TDI could only act to remove an engineer with the consent of the board.

Powell also reiterated that TDI did not have the jurisdiction to be deciding matters of engineering and that all TDI parties in the SOAH hearing had agreed that there was a difference of opinion between David Day and TDI.

The attorney for the attorney general's office representing TDI, Eric Hudson, was another young attorney who did not let facts get in the way of an enforcement action. His whole argument lasted ten minutes, and he basically said that I was found guilty of thirteen offenses, and TDI had standing to remove me from the appointment list. He also brought up a declaration action that Powell and Basham, on my behalf, had brought in district court in 2012. In this action, Powell had attempted to get the state courts to rule on whether the act that appointed engineers as windstorm inspectors was in conflict with the Occupations Code, which clearly stated that no entity including state agencies could require anything of an engineer but his seal.

A visiting judge from El Paso incorrectly sided from the bench with TDI and stated that "the practice of engineering is a privilege and not a right." No one was asking whether I had a right to be an engineer. The declaration action was to determine who had the right to control engineers, and the judge did not answer that question. I could not afford to appeal the decision and was in the middle of the SOAH hearing, so the declaration action was dropped.

Hudson was arguing that jurisdiction had been decided in that case, and Jenkins basically cut him off and stated that the declaration action had not been appealed.

The only other statement that Jenkins made during the arguments was also to Hudson. When Hudson was summing up his argument, he attempted to draw the distinction between an engineer and an appointed inspector. He made the comment that David Day may be a good engineer, but that does not make him automatically eligible to be an appointed inspector. At this point, Jenkins interjected about me, "And a metallurgist." Why he made that comment may never be known. Was he just being facetious? I was by far more qualified than anyone in TDI, who passed judgment on me, and I was definitely the only one who had any knowledge of metallurgy.

Powell had ten minutes for rebuttal and quickly seized on the distinction that Hudson was trying to make. An appointed engineer as a TDI qualified inspector was required to seal his WPI-2, and a state employee such as Doug Klopfenstein was not even required to submit a WPI-2 let alone seal it.

Jenkins then ordered the case closed and stated he would rule by the end of the week. He then informed each party that they had been requested prior to the hearing to submit an order for him to sign. An order is basically a demand letter for each party asking the judge to rule in their favor. TDI had received their request by e-mail and had produced a one-page, three-paragraph order asking the judge to rule in their favor.

Basham and Powell, on the other hand, had not received any instruction before the hearing. They quickly had to run to Basham's office in Austin and had less than an hour to produce an order. The request for the order eventually arrived by mail at Powell's office a week after he returned to McAllen. This was an inexcusable mishap on the part of Jenkins's clerk that put my appeal in jeopardy. It turned out, at least in my case, to be business as usual for Jenkins's staff.

I now had to go into the waiting mode while the decision was being made and filed. I would get called on a daily basis by the engineers who were following my case. I finally got word that the decision had been mailed on November 19, 2014. Mail from Austin should take three to four days, but I had still not received word by December 1, twelve days later. I had to spend the Thanksgiving holidays with my family in Houston without knowing the answer.

Basham was finally able to go to the clerk's office and obtain the order December 2, 2014. I was on a flight to Houston on my eventual way to Amarillo, where I would be assessing hail-damage claims (a subject for another book) when Basham sent the reply by e-mail.

Basham simply stated, "I was finally able to obtain the order. They ruled in TDI's favor. Sorry!" My employees were distraught and didn't know how to tell me. They eventually called my senior partner to break the news to me. I got the call at four thirty-five while waiting in line to get a boarding pass. I actually thought it might have been a mistake until I was able to sit down and go through my smartphone to obtain the e-mail. Months of waiting on the appeal process had boiled down to a single signature on TDI's "order." Jenkins had signed TDI's order. There was no other supporting document.

Remembering Jenkins's words, "The law is clear," I couldn't help but wonder what Jenkins found clear about the convoluted mess that is the TDI appointment list for engineers. It is a process that flies in the face of the Occupations Act and, if enacted against all engineers or any other profession, would have made its way to the wastebasket long ago. A conclusion of law would be asked for, and Jenkins will have to explain himself. Perhaps this book can enlighten him a little bit about the consequences of poor decisions by executors of the law. How could my attorneys, who had gone to the same law school as Jenkins and received the same degree as Jenkins and one of them,

Basham, had been an SOAH judge, have a completely different opinion from Jenkins. To them and the readers of this book, the law should have been on my side. Did Jenkins just feel that TDI and the SOAH court had a right to be wrong? If Jenkins is correct that the law is clear, then no engineer, let alone any professional or individual, is safe from abuse by the state because I am totally innocent. And by the way, Judge Jenkins, your decision never did arrive at Powell's' office. Not very professional! If district court judges spend only a Saturday afternoon studying an appeal that had over one thousand pages of testimony and their staff cannot properly relay orders or file the opinion, then truly innocent victims of witch hunts have no recourse other than the court of public opinion.

I actually felt more disappointed for all the people who were following my case and pulling for me. It was as if I had let them down. But it is just the beginning of a new battle, a further appeals process until someone will eventually follow the law as I, Powell, Basham, and numerous other engineers, attorneys, and even state legislators see it.

My story, just like Craig Morrison's story, needed to be told. A new Texas legislative session was just around the corner, and it was now round 2 for an individual who always defied the odds. The TDI Goliath still needs to be taken down. What are the odds?

Update; on 6-18-15, the law appointing windstorm engineers changed. See post script at the end of Epilogue.

Epilogue

What can be done to stop the TDI abuse and prevent further abuse? As Don Lee said in his letter to the commissioner, Eleanor Kitzman, "With the public sector now turning to engineers and design required on all homes in coastal regions, there is no longer a need for the windstorm appointment process, and the TDI inspection department needs to go away."

Don Lee sponsored the legislation that created the windstorm inspection program, and no one better than he would know if the current program was still needed. Don Lee had left TDI because he did not like where it was heading, and when he heard about David Day's plight from his son, Delton Lee, he vowed to do what he could to end the program. Unfortunately, Don Lee passed away shortly after he sent his letter to Commissioner Kitzman.

It is time for the twenty-six-year-old experiment to end. If this program affected the entire state and all counties, it would have ended the year it began. There is no other state that has a similar program, and for good reason; as my four-year odyssey showed, it is subject to widespread abuse.

No professionals should ever have to answer to any authority other than the legislatively created board that governs them. And in no other state or any county in Texas outside the fourteen coastal counties does a professional answer to any other entity.

No public official should be able to use their office to harass an individual as was done to me and other engineers by Sam Nelson, Alexis Dick, and Welch Watt. These three should be criminally investigated and prosecuted. Whoever was responsible for putting Russell Sheffield and Wesley Clepper on probation and firing them should be criminally investigated and prosecuted.

The improper rejection of roofs by TDI inspectors cost roofers, contractors, homeowners, and engineers, millions of dollars in damage. All inspectors and engineers in the TDI inspection program should be fired for cause. Only one of the TDI employees in the Wesley Clepper video was terminated, and that was for making racists comments. The rest who exhibited severe abuse of the public are still employed, and the two employees who exposed the abuse, Sheffield and Clepper, were fired.

The entire TDI system needs to be investigated from top to bottom; and the public should demand answers. Why are TDI inspectors and engineers treated as if they are infallible? Alexis Dick was obviously unqualified and incompetent to be in charge of code enforcement. But why were the TDI attorneys so eager to persecute professional engineers? Yes, there were some bad apples in the program, but those are matters for the board to handle and not TDI attorneys and SOAH courts.

The seven-day attack on me in an SOAH court was a public embarrassment that should have never been allowed to happen. The Texas legislature should immediately repair and rectify the monstrosity created in 1988 called the TDI Windstorm Certification Program. The TDI attorneys responsible for the mistreatment of me, Henry Segura, Vera Green, and hundreds of other engineers should be reprimanded at least. Certainly some pink slips should be handed out and disciplinary action taken by the Texas bar.

What about TWIA? Was it ever necessary? In the decade from 2004 to 2014, which included three hurricanes in Texas, Rita, Dolly, and Ike, there were more homes damaged by hail and fires than by the three hurricanes. The international codes have greatly improved building practices and products. Homes in Florida and Texas that were built under the new codes fared much better than older homes during recent hurricanes. If TWIA remains, it needs to be out from under TDI and allowed more discretion to accept homes into the program to make it more solvent, including homes outside of the fourteen coastal counties.

Texas Board of Professional Engineers has been nothing short of abysmal in their handling of the TDI Windstorm Certification Program. Not only have they done nothing to prevent unconstitutional appointment of engineers from happening, they have done nothing to stop false accusations against engineers and, in fact, have aided and abetted TDI in their efforts to punish engineers who dared to disagree with TDI. From my own experience, the board inspectors do a terrible job of investigating complaints against engineers. The board incorrectly found me guilty of improperly certifying roofs, and I had to appeal their decision before I was exonerated. Most engineers in my position just take the minimal fine and probation and leave the windstorm program. The board also refused to take action against Nelson and Harp in complaints I filed against them in which there was overwhelming evidence of incompetence on Harp's part and illegal conduct from Nelson. The board did not contact any of the witnesses that I provided. The board needs to be completely overhauled and given proper direction and legal counsel. They have failed horrendously in doing their duty to protect engineers and the public. The cases against Vera Green and multiple engineers who were wrongly accused by TDI should be given a second look and the disciplinary actions erased and expunged from their record. The board publishes a quarterly newsletter and within publishes disciplinary action against engineers. Since the board stopped TDI from fining engineers, the majority of the disciplinary actions have been against windstorm appointed engineers, and the complaints were not brought by the public but solely by TDI. What are the odds that less than 1 percent of engineers would receive the majority of complaints against all eighty-eight thousand engineers and all of those complaints would be brought by one entity, TDI? This fact is embarrassing! What are the odds?

Postscript

As a result of years of abuse of windstorm appointed engineers detailed in this book, the 2015 Texas legislative session adopted and passed House Bill 2439 which repeals the windstorm appointment program and includes the language "The commissioner may not adopt or enforce a rule that requires an engineer to affix the engineer's seal to an inspection form." It passed the House 146-1 and the Senate 31-0 and was signed by Governor Greg Abbott on 6-18-15 and will go into effect September 1, 2015.

What are the odds!!

Texas Department of Insurance
Property and Casualty Section – Windstorm Inspections Program
Mail Code 103-1E, 333 Guadalupe Street • P.O. Box 149104, Austin, Texas 78714-9104
512-322-2203 or toll free 1-800-248-6032 • 512-322-2273 fax • www.tdi.texas.gov

Inspection Verification
Form WPI-2-BC-5
For projects that commenced construction on or after January 1, 2008

I, the undersigned, do hereby ACKNOWLEDGE that I am a professional engineer licensed to practice in the State of Texas and that I am a qualified inspector appointed by the Commissioner of the Texas Department of Insurance to perform inspections in accordance with Article 21.49 §6A of the Texas Insurance Code and with 28 Texas Administrative Code §5.4604. I do state that I am personally responsible as the engineer-of-record for the windstorm inspection of this project and I have provided standard and customary construction review services including an inspection or inspections by myself or an employee under my direct supervision for:

- [ ] Entire Building (Type): _____
- [ ] Entire Re-Roof (Type): _____
  - [ ] Re-decking: _____
- [ ] Partial Re-Roof (Type and Area): _____
  - [ ] Re-decking _____
- [ ] Alteration (Type): _____

- [ ] Repair (Type): _____
- [ ] Mechanical Only (Type): _____
- [ ] *Foundation Only (Type): _____
- [ ] Addition (Type): _____
- [ ] **Retrofit of ALL Exterior Openings: _____
- [ ] Other (Description): _____

Comments: _____

*The foundation has been designed in accordance with the wind load provisions indicated below and the entire structure was considered in the design of the foundation.

** For windborne debris protection only (impact resistant exterior opening products or shutters). All exterior openings shall include windows, doors, garage doors, and skylights.

The building is located at: (Complete 9-1-1 Street address including house/building number):

Street Address: _____ City: _____ County: _____

- [ ] This does not meet the applicable Building Code standards as evidenced by the signature, date, and seal below.

I certify that the project was designed and inspected in compliance with the wind load provisions of:

- [ ] International Residential Code, 2006 Edition   or   [ ] International Building Code, 2006 Edition
  (Amended with 2006 Texas Revisions)   (Amended with 2006 Texas Revisions)

The design conditions used were:
Wind Speed (3-second gust):
- [ ] 110 mph (Required for Inland II)[1]   [ ] 120 mph (Required for Inland I)[1]   [ ] 130 mph (Required for Seaward)[1]

Exposure Category: [ ] B [ ] C [ ] D

Note: [1] All exterior openings (exterior doors, windows, garage doors, and skylights) contain products that have been designed and inspected for compliance with uniform static wind pressure requirements (Applicable only to those projects which include the installation of exterior opening products.)

Protection of Exterior Openings:
- [ ] Provided for as specified in the Texas Revisions (required for projects located in the Inland I and Seaward areas).
- [ ] Not provided for as specified in the Texas Revisions (applicable to projects located in the Inland I area).

Date(s) of Inspection(s): _____

I understand and intend that the Texas Department of Insurance will rely upon this statement of compliance in determining whether to issue a Certificate of Compliance for the building/structure and to notify the Texas Windstorm Insurance Association that the building/structure is eligible for a windstorm and hail insurance policy.

Seal (Stamp or Ink)	Print or Type Name
	Signature
	Address
	City, State, Zip ___ Business Telephone

Texas Registration Number _____   Date _____

As per Article 21.47, Texas Insurance Code, a person commits an offense if the person knowingly or intentionally makes, files, or uses any instrument in writing required to be made to or filed with the Texas Department of Insurance or the Insurance Commissioner, either by the Insurance Code or by rule or regulation of the Texas Department of Insurance, when the instrument in writing contains any false, fictitious, or fraudulent statement or entry with regard to any material fact. In this context, "Texas Department of Insurance" includes any association, corporation, or person created by the Insurance Code. An offense under this article is a felony of the third degree.

PC382 Rev. 01/08   Page 1 of 2

Texas Department of Insurance
P. O. Box 149104
Austin, TX 78714-9104

January 3, 2012

Commissioner Elenor Kitzman,

My name is Don Lee. I served in the Texas House of Representatives from 1981 to 1987 for District 38 and 51. In 1987 I was a supporter of the legislation that created the Windstorm Certification Program for Texas Department of Insurance (TDI). The intent of the legislation was to provide an affordable program for the residences of the 14 coastal counties that insured homes were built to resist the higher winds from hurricanes.

In 1988 I joined TDI as the manager of Wind Pool Operation. I served in this capacity until 1992. From 1992 to 1995 I served in the position of liaison between TDI and Texas Windstorm Insurance Association (TWIA).

During my 1988 – 1995 tenure as TDI Manager, I visited state agencies in Florida, South Carolina and New York to research effective affordable windstorm insurance. At TDI we were attempting to pattern our risk pool management similar to that of Florida. We wanted local control of building practices and established local offices to provide timely affordable inspections to these builders and homeowners that wanted insurance through TWIA.

In our seven regional offices there was a good working relationship with the builders and homeowners. The exception was the Angleton office that was managed by Welch Watt. There were constant complaints from this area due to Mr. Watt's excessive rejection of new construction and reroofs.

As personnel in Austin changed in the Windtake Division, the focus and intent of the program changed completely. Instead of enforcing standard codes, TDI began to dictate design and construction procedures through prescriptive guides that were treated as code. They also used their power to control local Engineers. Under the leadership of Mr. Watt, the majority of local TDI inspectors left the program and the majority of windstorm inspection was transferred to private Engineers and inspectors. This was never the intent of the original legislation.

The process in affect today is expensive, harmful to homeowners and subject to wide spread abuse. TDI Engineering Department under the supervision of Sam Nelson, P. E., has completely destroyed the original intent of the program to help homeowners. Mr. Nelson is abusing his power and using the

Administrative Law Court (ALC) to accuse Engineers with fraud who disagrees with him on matters of Engineering.

I have become familiar with the case of TDI vs. David Day, P. E. of Harlingen, TX. I have read the complaints against Mr. Day and the replies from Mr. Day. Mr. Day's case and all others like them are an abuse of the ALC system. If Mr. Nelson has a problem with Mr. Day's or other Engineers engineering decisions, he should get an opinion from the Texas Board of Professional Engineers (TBPE).

At present Mr. Nelson has no adequate supervision or oversight. When I was manager of Wind Pool Operations, I would never have supported Mr. Nelson to take the actions that he is taking.

The TDI is allowing Mr. Nelson to illegally prosecute Engineers. This action will lead to class action suits against TDI. It is my understanding that Mr. Nelson currently has two formal complaints against him being investigated by the TBPE with more likely to come.

TDI needs to stop the abusive practice of using ALC's to take actions against Engineers. Mr. Nelson should be relieved of his duties until the TBPE evaluates the complaints against him. All ALC actions against Engineers should cease until the TBPE has evaluated the Engineers for any alleged wrong doing.

I am willing to attend any meetings or hearings to discuss the TDI Windstorm practices, past, present or future.

Respectfully submitted,

Don Lee

May 5, 2011

Dick Roland
3129 Boar Thicket Dr.
Corpus Christi, TX 78414

Attn: To Whom It May Concern

My name is Richard Roland Jr. For five years I served as Windstorm Manager for Texas
Department of Insurance (TDI). I served in this capacity from September of 1992 until the end of
1997. At that time there were seven field offices.

Each year there would be area supervisory meetings with the field office managers in attendance.
At that time the performance of each field office was evaluated. The average acceptance rates of
the field offices were over 80% for new construction and re-roofs. The exception was the
Angleton field office where Welch Watt was manager. This office had over 90% rejection rate.

The contractors and roofers were not given a chance by Mr. Watt to correct their work and
therefore had to get local appointed engineers to inspect their work.

After 1998 I retired from TDI and worked with Private Engineering Firms as an inspector. All of
the engineers I have worked with have been professional and competent and fully capable of
handling the work that they took on. From 2002 until 2006, I worked for David V. Day, P.E. as
a field inspector.

Mr. Day was a very conscientious engineer and would often take on difficult projects that other
engineers turned down. I can personally vouch for his integrity and professionalism.

With the contractors and roofers unanimously employing Engineers to certify their work, I fully
expected the field offices to be eliminated. I have worked for TDI as an inspector, a field office
manager, the windstorm manager, the position currently held by Welch Watt, and as inspector
for private engineers.

The TDI inspection and oversight program was established to assist homeowners in Coastal
Counties to get windstorm insurance. With that function now being served by private
engineering firms, the need for oversight is no longer necessary. Engineers are governed by the
Texas Board of Professional Engineers and having an oversight group within TDI is not
necessary and is redundant.

Sincerely,

Richard C. Roland Jr.

Richard Roland Jr.

2

Before me, the undersigned authority, on this day personally appeared
Richard C. Roland Jr known to me to be the person whose name is subscribed to the foregoing
instrument in the capacity therein stated, who being first duly sworn, stated upon his/her oath
that this statement is true and correct. I further certify that the records attached are exact
duplicates of the original works.

SWORN TO AND SUBSCRIBED before me this _12_ day of _May_ , 20_11_

SHERRY S. DURST
Notary Public, State of Texas
My Commission Expires
FEBRUARY 19, 2015

Sherry S Durst
NOTARY PUBLIC

My commission Expires: _2-19-15_

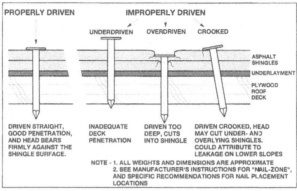

Figure 13 Example of fastener set for shingle nails.

C. Re-cover roofing (the application of new asphalt roofing materials over existing asphalt roofing materials), requires the use of longer nails that will extend through all layers of roofing and penetrate the substrate, providing sufficient attachment to the roof deck.

D. Generally, the nailing of hips, ridges and some roof accessories (e.g., some roof ventilators) requires the use of longer nails, as the fastener must penetrate through more layers of roofing and/or material. However, if more than sufficient length nails are used in the field of the roof, then the same length nail may be adequate for attachment of hip and ridge shingles, providing the nails penetrate the deck per the requirements as noted above, and as set forth by the shingle manufacturer.

Note: If properly applied, either hand-nailed or pneumatically (power) actuated nail applications are acceptable.

E. For individual full-width three-tab shingles, a minimum of four nails are required. For some areas and climatic regions (i.e., areas where building codes dictate or where high wind regions require), six nails per full-width three-tab shingle are required. (See Figures 14 and 15.)

ROOFING CORPORATION

Technical Bulletin

Re: Fastening of Atlas Shingles

Atlas requires the use of roofing nails, to comply with the following installation criteria to install shingles onto a clean roof deck and underlayment. Re-roofing over a single layer of a flat, smooth surfaced 3-Tab roof covering is permitted, but the fastener lengths must be increased by at least ¼".

- The galvanized shingle nails need to be a minimum of 1 ¼" long with nominal 3/8" dia. flat heads for the fastening of the Pinnacle and StormMaster Shake laminated type shingles.
- The nails need to be a minimum of 1" long for the fastening of the GlassMaster 25 shingles.
- The nail head must not cut through the top surface of the shingle when driven.
- All nails must be driven through the double thickness, overlapping laminated area of the shingles.
- The shingle nails may penetrate and/or overlay the sealant strip material to assure that the nail shaft penetrates the double thick area of the shingles.
- ✳ Any inadvertent exposure of nail heads may be corrected by applying a minimal amount of caulking gun grade asphalt adhesive to coat the exposed portion of the nail heads.
- The points of the nails must penetrate into the Building Code approved decking materials at least ¾". If the decking is less than ¾" thick, the points of the nails must penetrate and protrude at least 1/8" through the bottom of the decking material.
- The fastener placement and all fastener criteria stated herein, as well as those on the bundle wrappers, must be adhered to in order to receive coverage under the Atlas Limited shingle Warranty. Incorrect or incorrectly placed fasteners will void the Limited Shingle Warranty.
- The use of staples is specifically not recognized as proper shingle fasteners due to the staple's inherent inconsistency in controlling the driven depth and difficulty to consistently drive them parallel to the length of the shingle.
- Following these guidelines will maintain the Atlas Shingle Limited Warranty in effect at the time of the installation.

Atlas Roofing Corporation

2000 RIVEREDGE PARKWAY · SUITE 800 · ATLANTA, GEORGIA 30328

Guadalajara two years after TDI said it needed to be removed because it was marred with scuff marks and unacceptable.

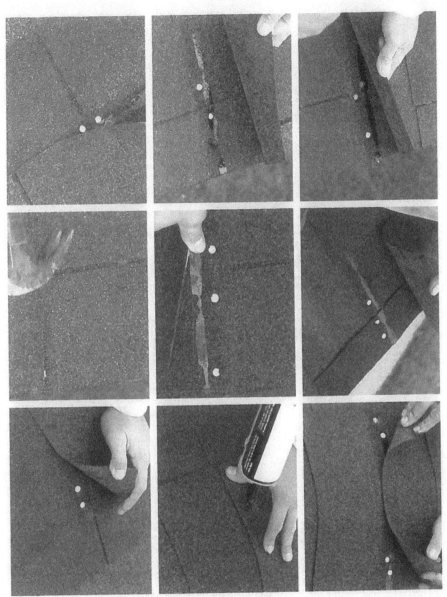

Nails at Fannin that TDI said were 66% overdriven

Editorial:

Texas Legislature needs to un-act some regulation pronto
By Editorial Board

Posted February 19, 2013 at 3:01 a.m.

CORPUS CHRISTI — The state's windstorm insurance certification program brings to mind the children's song, "There was an old lady who swallowed a fly." For those who don't recall: She swallows a spider to catch the fly, a bird to catch the spider, and so on until she dies from swallowing a horse. Her deadly cure, like windstorm certification, was administered with the best intentions.

New requirements on the engineers who certify the windstorm resistance of structures have caused problems that, without emergency revision, will kill the Texas coastal real estate market. Strangely for a state that prides itself for nonrestrictive government, way too much of it is causing the fatal condition and a lot less of it is the only cure.

A story in Sunday's Caller-Times by Rick Spruill describes a nightmarish regulatory double whammy. The engineers face a new certification requirement that they say their engineering licenses more than trump as a measure of competency. They also face audits by the Texas Department of Insurance that are both expensive and frequent enough to make their participation no longer financially sustainable.

The predictable result is that Atlas is shrugging just like the late Ayn Rand warned. Engineers are taking their rigorously licensed know-how elsewhere rather than have it second-guessed by auditors whose background is insurance rather than engineering. The number of engineers in the program shrank from 900 last year to 201 as of Feb. 15. In Corpus Christi alone, the number shrank from 41 on Dec. 31 to 23 as of this month. Those who remain probably are doing so only until they must recertify or are audited.

Who can blame them? They deserve applause from the many Ayn Rand fans in the Legislature that is the source of this mess.

The intent of the legislation was to raise standards in a beneficial way. But at the rate that engineers are leaving, the coastal real estate market will be in real peril soon. If no one certifies buildings or new roofs as windstorm-compliant, they're virtually uninsurable. No insurance means no lending, which means no buying, at which point there's no reason to build or renovate.

Spruill described how one audit situation led to the ruination of builder Bill Underbrink. The engineer who had designed three houses built by Underbrink dropped out of the certification program, which meant that Underbrink had to find another engineer to certify them. The second engineer wanted Underbrink to remove brick and roofs and tear out walls for re-inspection. Underbrink couldn't afford it.

A Texas Department of Insurance spokesman told Spruill that a builder in Underbrink's situation should contact the department "so that we can assist him with finding other engineers who may be able to conduct a post-construction inspection that incorporates existing documentation to" — pay attention

246

— "POSSIBLY MINIMIZE (emphasis ours) having to open walls."

That's the over-regulatory state of mind speaking itself. As if possibly minimizing were enough of a remedy. Why should engineer-certified walls built to much more stringent standards than those of the countless buildings that survived Hurricane Celia (circa 1970) be opened at all?

The coastal economy is resilient, as apparently was the old lady in the song, who inexplicably survived swallowing a cow. But it is in peril until the Legislature remedies the situation with less regulation.

Whether the governor declares it or not, this is an emergency.

Van at bottom of embankment

Driver's side

Ice chest that had been sitting next to Christina

Original Proposed Book Cover by Dennis Day

About the Author

David V. Day, P.E. is a registered professional engineer, licensed to practice in Texas and Louisiana. His general practice is civil structural and forensics. He has served as an expert witness for storm related insurance claims on numerous occasions.

He was born and raised in Baton Rouge, LA and graduated in 1980 from Louisiana State University with a degree in construction. He has lived in Texas since 1987, and currently resides in Harlingen, TX. David V. Day has done over 1000 forensic inspections and has over 3000 windstorm design and certifications to his credit. He teaches codes and metallurgy at Texas State Technical College.

In addition to working full time, David Day is active in church and civic groups and is an active participant in Senior Olympic throwing events.

CPSIA information can be obtained
at www.ICGtesting.com
Printed in the USA
BVHW071924091019
560658BV00001B/99/P

9 781681 394848